How proud I am to be associated with a WarBird. Thanks for all you did for America.

My best,

Rachel Roberts

2003

ART SMITH

Pioneer Aviator

Rachel S. Roberts

McFarland & Company, Inc., Publishers
Jefferson, North Carolina, and London

LIBRARY OF CONGRESS ONLINE CATALOG PUBLICATION DATA

Roberts, Rachel S., 1940–
Art Smith : pioneer aviator / Rachel S. Roberts
p.   cm.
Includes bibliographical references and index.

ISBN 0-7864-1646-7 (softcover : 50# alkaline paper)

1. Smith, Art, 1890–1926.
2. Air pilots—United States—Biography.
I. Title
TL540.S6R63   2003   629.13'092 B—dc21   2003009926

British Library cataloguing data are available

On the cover: Publicity photograph of Art Smith;
postcard photograph of his airplane
(courtesy of Wertman-Stackhouse);
background image © 2003 PhotoSpin

Manufactured in the United States of America

*McFarland & Company, Inc., Publishers
Box 611, Jefferson, North Carolina 28640
www.mcfarlandpub.com*

For James Alfred Roberts
and a tip of the wing to
the Hoosier Warbirds

Contents

Preface

Art Smith wasn't shy. Wasn't shy or backward about anything, especially his dream of flying. He was daring and a consummate showman, and he had the gift of inventiveness. He not only glamorized and popularized aviation, but tested the very boundaries of aeronautical principles. Anyone interested in flight or history will enjoy the story of pioneer aviator Art Smith, whose daredevil stunts, barnstorming, skywriting, and aeronautical innovations led to important developments in early aviation. Had he not died at a young age in 1926, his name probably would be familiar to most Americans.

The story of American aviation is one of fact and legend, and Art Smith contributed to its romance and mystique. Credit must go to Glenn Curtiss and the Wright brothers, of course, but Art Smith probably did more to kick-start the aviation industry than anyone during his time, and he boosted the state of the art of flying performance just in time for World War I when it was most needed.

Art Smith's name or place in American aviation history didn't register with me until the mid–1980s, when I read some articles by Hubert L. Stackhouse about some of the people who figured in various historic happenings in Northeastern Indiana during the early part of the century. His accounts led me to become interested in learning more about the young man who became known as Fort Wayne's "Birdboy."

As I researched Smith's life, I found him to be an intriguing character and an adventurer of the grandest sort. As a young man, he longed to fly, yet he had little training in mechanics and had never seen an airplane. He was, however, curious and highly motivated, and he knew he could learn to fly. His parents believed in him, and he was fortunate to have a best friend, Al Wertman, who helped him build an airplane. Smith's goal was to fly, and fly he did.

Art was outgoing, enthusiastic, and courageous. He perpetrated the image of a

1

boy wonder and became a showman, whose stunt flying thrilled the world. He used his fame to become an effective spokesman for military preparedness.

At the pinnacle of his success in 1915, Art spoke about the view from his airplane. He said, "The seacoast is only a green, wavering line thousands of feet below it [the airplane]. Mountains are just heaps of earth — it skims over them. There are no boundaries between states or countries when you look down upon them from three thousand feet in the air."[1]

Art Smith seems to have been well selected for the role in life assigned by fate, wrote Hubert L. Stackhouse in *A Brief Candle* (1998), a forty-four page sketch of Smith's life. "He was neither intellectually nor mechanically gifted, but 'adventurous' might well have been his middle name. Accordingly, the mechanical genius he lacked would then, for the most of his building efforts in years to come, be supplied by Al Wertman. They were of similar age and both had sprung from carpenter fathers who were fast friends."[2]

Art relied on Al Wertman for improvements to his craft and depended on his uncle, Edgar E. Johnson, to help him dismantle, ship, and reassemble his airplane during his barnstorming days. As Art's career went farther afield, he was supported in keeping a well-maintained aircraft by the Mills Aviators and later the Lincoln Beachey organization.[3]

Few sources of information are available about the pioneer aviator; no hardbound works exist at Allen County Public Library in Fort Wayne, Indiana; Eckhart Public Library in Auburn, Indiana; or the Auburn Cord Duesenberg Museum — all logical sources. Mrs. Allegra Wertman Stackhouse, of Marietta, Georgia, and her brother, Mr. Herbert Wertman of Portage, Michigan, however, had numerous news clippings and other memorabilia, which Stackhouse was able to use for his brief biography of Smith.[4]

Stackhouse's cousin Robert was married to Allegra Wertman, whose father, Al, was Art Smith's best friend. Through his Wertman connections, Stackhouse acquired Art Smith's autobiographical booklet published in 1915 by the San Francisco *Bulletin*, and most impressive of all, postcards in Art Smith's own hand mailed to Al Wertman of Auburn, Indiana.

Stackhouse shared his trove of memorabilia with me and later gave them to me for safekeeping. Because of his generosity and his memory of facts, I have been able to document how Art Smith achieved his lifelong dream of flying. Additionally, I was privileged to have a number of conversations with people knowledgeable about Art Smith. Even so, other facts and tales are yet to be told.

I am indebted to Roger K. Myers, founder and curator of the Greater Fort Wayne Aviation Museum, for the use of scrapbooks and historical materials about Art Smith. The aviation museum is located on the second floor of the Fort Wayne International Airport, near which hangs a replica of Art Smith's first successful airplane.

The fall 1998 issue of *TRACES of Indiana & Midwestern History* featured an article I wrote about Art Smith, and in January 1999, *Across Indiana*, an Indianapolis public television program, produced a special on Smith's life based on the *TRACES* article. After doing additional research about Art Smith, however, I discovered inconsistencies regarding the dates of his first flying attempts, exhibitions, and the year he entered the U.S. Mail Service. In this biography, I use the dates most frequently cited and documented. I wish to thank George R. Hanlin for his advice about these matters and also for providing me with photographs from the *TRACES* archives. I wish also to thank Don Goss for his help and photographic skills.

Most of all, it gives me pleasure to thank Ann Perry Wintrode for her friendship and generosity, especially for reading my manuscript numerous times, making suggestions, and encouraging me to record Art Smith's place in the history of aviation.

Many clippings and photographs in the Wertman scrapbook and the two 1915 scrapbooks, which are located in the Greater Fort Wayne Aviation Museum, are without dates or sources. In these instances I make reference to the specific scrapbook in which the clipping was pasted, either Scrapbook No. 1, which is comprised mostly of newspaper accounts, or Scrapbook No. 2, which is primarily a collection of photographs. Both 1915 scrapbooks are oversized and extremely heavy. The Wertman scrapbook is much smaller and belongs with the Stackhouse memorabilia. Sometimes the same clipping appears in all three scrapbooks.

Wherever possible in this biography, I use Smith's own words, recollections, spellings, and descriptions from his autobiography and from newspaper articles in order to capture his personality and observations. Although Smith explained theories of aviation, his dialogue was natural, informal, and conversational. Readers can almost hear his enthusiasm for flying.

In *The Autobiography of the Boy Aviator*, which first appeared in serial form in the San Francisco *Bulletin*, Smith explained how he became interested in aviation. Much of it reads like fiction. Art's early writings reveal a lack of application of those rules of spelling and grammar he had been exposed to before leaving school when he was sixteen or seventeen. The letters he wrote when he was in his thirties, however, show a fine command of the language.

Art was ideal for what he chose to do. With Fred Hoover and Nels J. Nelson, he flew exhibitions for Ivan Gates that led to the beginning of the legendary Gates Flying Circus. He was known variously as "Smash-up Smith," "The Human Comet," and the "Boy Aviator." His repertoire included night flying with Roman candles attached to the wing struts of his Curtiss biplane while he flew loops.[5]

Art Smith's life falls into three stages—his early flying attempts, the sixteen-year period when he was a celebrity and as famous as anyone in America, and his last ten years when his life changed because of world events.

1

Blue Skies—1909

In Fort Wayne, Indiana, the morning edition of *The Journal Gazette*, August 16, 1928, carried the headline: "Homage Paid to Art Smith." The article featured photographs, descriptions, tributes, and details about Art Smith's life, flying career, and family. "The last scene of all will linger longest in the memory of those who were privileged to see it," penned the writer.

> It was after most of the crowd had turned away and Mr. and Mrs. James F. Smith, the father and mother, walked to the memorial. The mother took the hand of the now-blind father and directed it to the inscription upon the column that he might feel it with the tips of his fingers. These were the parents who had been held up to public ridicule eighteen years ago because they placed a mortgage upon their home that Art might have money to build a winged buggy, the then-derided airplane.[1]

The monument dedicated that day was built by money donated by the citizens of Fort Wayne and the people who had followed the fight that Art made against great odds to become one of the most famous aviators of his time. It honored Art as a pioneer aviator whose daredevil flying had thrilled the world and brought distinction to his hometown. It was a monument that Art would have liked, one that was purported to be the tallest in the state of Indiana in honor of a single individual. The year was 1928, but Art's story begins in the fall of 1909.

At that time, American aviation was mostly a matter of experimentation by single individuals in backyard sheds and barns. It had been only about six and a half years since Orville and Wilbur Wright first flew their machine, and no one knew about airports, control towers, or radar. There was no such service as airmail. The story of how Art Smith learned to fly and how he became an international celebrity is told in his autobiography.

For two weeks, during the summer of 1909, Art Smith, his mother, and some friends had pitched two tents by Lake James in Steuben County, forty miles north of their home in Fort Wayne, Indiana. Art and his best friend, Al Wertman, bunked in one tent while his mother, Al's girlfriend, and Art's girlfriend, Aimee Cour, used the other one. Al's father, Samuel Wertman, was a carpenter who worked with James Smith, and the two families got along well. It was no wonder that the boys became lifelong friends. Their vacation was lazy and relaxing. Camping was great, especially the fishing and swimming. In the evenings, over coffee made on a campfire, they talked about school, roller skating, and the circus.[2]

According to Art's autobiography, his quest began shortly before sunset on a glorious evening. Aimee sat in the stern of the boat with a big bow in her hair, while Art lay on his back in the bottom of the boat watching a turkey buzzard soar around in big circles without moving his wings. "I got to puzzling how he did it," Art said.[3] The buzzard reminded him of an article he had read about aeronautics and the Wright brothers. Thinking about their invention, Art wondered about the buzzard's wings, airplanes, how a heavier-than-air machine could stay off the ground, the principle that kept flying machines in the air, and what that principle or force was. He related the following exchange.

"If that's all the attention you are going to pay to what I'm saying, you can go rowing by yourself," fourteen-year-old Aimee Cour said, tossing her head.

"Uh — what?" Art Smith answered. He hadn't been listening. Art jerked to attention. Aimee was enjoying the scenery, but she was annoyed with him for not listening.

"I was figuring out how to fly," Art said pointing to the big turkey buzzard. "Look at that bird. It's flying on air currents." Aimee didn't answer.

"I'm going to make a machine and fly in it," Art said, even though he was aware that he didn't know a single thing about "the treacherous whirlpools in the air or about swift, rushing torrents and dangerous air rapids."

"How?" Aimee asked.

"I don't know just how I'll do it, but I will. You'll see," Art answered, looking up at the clear blue sky.

After a moment, Aimee said, "Well, of course, if you say you will, you will."[4]

Art lay in the bottom of the boat thinking how Aimee was the only girl who had ever appealed to him as much as roller skates or a circus billboard.

Art said he never cared much for girls until he met Aimee. She was adventurous and a good swimmer, and she had been a great pal since childhood. He liked her hair in braids. Even when she was "a chunky little girl with red cheeks and the jolliest laugh I've ever heard," he said, "she was fun to be with." He remembered how she'd come over to play, wearing a red sweater and a cap with a tassel on it.[5]

His interests were skating, Buffalo Bill, and mechanics, especially mechanics. He

Opposite: Dedicated in 1928, this 40-foot monument to aviator Art Smith stands in Memorial Park, Fort Wayne, Indiana. Courtesy: Allen County–Fort Wayne Historical Society & Museum.

liked to think things out. He liked to make things that would go. Art said that he made the first little wagon in town that would run with pedals, long before such things were on the market. He had a barn full of kites of all sorts, rigged up to drop little parachutes or whirl in the air. He experimented with electricity too, one time shocking his solemn old house cat by giving her a saucer of milk attached to a dry-battery circuit.[6] Art was the first in his group to get to the railroad tracks in the middle of the night to watch the circus train unload the elephants. Every stunt the circus performers did, he tried to imitate.

Most girls weren't interested in such things and so he wasn't interested in girls, but Aimee was different. She was game to the core. She understood his efforts to "leap the gap on the bicycle," a stunt done in Buffalo Bill's big show on the circus grounds at the edge of Fort Wayne. After seeing that stunt, even though Art didn't own a bicycle, the next morning he got up before daylight and with a hammer tried to rig up the same sort of springboards in his back yard. By the afternoon, he was leaping the gap on roller skates before his mother's horrified eyes. He could leap a gap ten feet before the boards fell to pieces.[7]

Art felt lucky to have a friend like Aimee. He sat up in the boat and began to talk. He asked, did she remember how he was able to leap the gap ten feet with his roller skates? Art then told her that when he got back to Fort Wayne, he was going to get all the magazine articles on aeronautics he could find and study them.

Aimee knew he would.

Art's father, James F. Smith, was a carpenter-contractor, "a slow, quiet man, with a kind of silent strength."[8] For seventeen years, his father had worked to establish his own business, but just as things he wanted to do were almost within his reach, he began to go blind. Art wrote that his father's blindness was the effect of sunstroke, brought on by working too hard when he was a carpenter's helper. Even though his father fought his blindness every inch of the way, good contracts went to other carpenters. Art said that his father never spoke about it, but little by little, he lost his grip on the business. It was a heartbreaking situation, a tragedy that made Art determined to succeed. Not only would he provide and care for his parents, but he would also make them proud. It was a promise and commitment that guided him throughout his life.

The year before the Lake James vacation, Art dropped out of school to work in an architect's office. "All Dad had was the little cottage we lived in," Art said, "and the income from his work was getting smaller every month."[9] At Mr. Weatherhogg's architectural firm, Art studied drafting. In the evenings after supper, he helped his father figure contracts. Once Art said that "the man of few words," a character in John Greenleaf Whittier's long poem "Snowbound," reminded him of his father. "He never had much to say, but you always knew he was there."[10]

After the camping trip, Art collected all the books and magazine articles on aeronautics that he could find, which at that time were very few. Two that were helpful were *Practical Aeronautics* by Hayward and *Vehicles of the Air* by Victor Lougheed.[11] Instead of visiting Aimee, he spent evenings poring over his books, studying aircraft construction, designs, and patents. He believed he could build a plane that would fly better than the Wright brothers' airplane because he had an idea about using a large stabilizer that would make his airplane fly better than other airplanes. He planned to get his stabilizer invention patented.

But Art was driven by more than a personal desire for adventure. He was determined to find a way to help his father. While reading articles about aeronautics, he found that thousands of dollars were being offered in prizes, such as the *Scientific American* and the Schebler prizes, in all, nearly $100,000 "for good work in the air."[12] Winning some of those prizes would make him financially secure for life. A few hundred dollars might save his father's eyes.

Neither his father nor mother said much about Art's dropping out of school to help with living expenses, but they knew it was necessary. Art's mother was wiry and energetic; she kept the house clean, had a big garden, and did a great deal of church work, but she had no way to make a living. She was president of the Ladies Aid Society, and if she started to get a new church carpet or pay up the minister's salary, Art said it was as good as done. She always had time, however, to help Art build a kite or a boat.

One evening a month or so after Art began studying articles about flying, his father reached for something at the supper table and upset his glass of water. His mother caught the glass as it splashed over. No one said anything, but Art cringed. After a few minutes, his father suggested they work on a contract.

"I was sitting on the other side of the table, with my elbows on it, and my chin in my hands, thinking," Art wrote. Then he said, "Dad, I want to be an aviator."[13]

Art said his statement must have sounded like a bombshell to his father, who was silent for a few minutes then finally asked why. Art said the reasons he wanted to be an aviator were "tangled in my head," but he tried to explain about the Wright brothers. He then read from some articles to his father. His mother came in with some mending, and his father announced, "Art wants to be an aviator." She was thunderstruck at the notion. When she asked about the dangers of flying, Art answered, "There is no danger if the aviator keeps his head, and the air currents hold steady, and nothing is wrong with the machine."

His father asked, "How much would a machine cost?"

Art was ready. "About eighteen hundred dollars."[14] He then went on to explain that nearly one hundred thousand dollars was available in prizes for aviators.

His father, the man of few words, said they would talk again when Art had figures.

A week later, Art had his numbers.

"An airplane will cost $1,756.60, if I do all the work on it myself," he said.

His father nodded, but that was all. Then, according to Art's writings, he told his father, "You can get that much by mortgaging the house." At that, his father's jaws tightened and set. "He was pale," Art wrote. "The house was clear; it was all we had."[15] It was, however, something Art wanted his parents to consider.

Meanwhile, Art spent most of his spare time in his barn workshop building a model airplane. It was about twelve inches long and made of tiny pieces of wood. Even the wings were wood. He used some sheets of veneer from a furniture factory for the wings because he couldn't find cloth that was light and strong enough. He sandpapered the veneered wings until "they were thin as tissue paper, and transparent."[16] The engine was made of wooden wheels and rubber bands. It took three or four months, but one evening after supper, he brought it out to show his parents.

"It ran along the floor," Art said. "We stood there hardly breathing, watching. Then suddenly the little plane caught the air. Up it went. Three feet in the air, the little machine sailed down the room." He and his parents took the little plane, which Art termed "a beauty," outside. It was a still evening, and when he wound up the tiny engine, he let it run down the garden path between the tomato vines. "Ten feet away it rose again, flying beautifully — rose and rose, steadily."[17]

It hit the clothesline and fell to the ground, smashing into bits.

His father asked him about the plane's construction. Art explained how he'd built it after studying every drawing of an airplane he could find for ideas. His father went into the house, and Art told his mother, "If I could make a real machine and fly in it, I could make money, lots of money. Dad could go up to Chicago and see the doctors there."[18]

Art believed that if he could get a machine, the rest would be easy. Later he said, "That was because I knew nothing whatever about flying." To him, the air was only something to breathe. He did not know that air has "the fluid, swirling force of a roaring waterfall and the crushing weight of an avalanche."[19]

Art turned over in his mind every possible way to earn or get eighteen hundred dollars. He tried to think about people he could approach for loans. He studied the aviation magazines and began to build another little model. Sometimes his father helped sandpaper some of the parts. As they worked together, Art explained the principles of flying — how planes rest on cushions of air, compressed by the speed of the machine. Although his father said little or nothing, Art had the feeling that his parents were considering the notion.

One evening in the fall, Art said his parents seemed awkward and nervous at supper. He wondered what was wrong, and he worried that perhaps the doctors had determined that his father's eyes were worse than they thought. After he finished his pudding and pushed back his plate, his mother got up suddenly and stood by her husband, her hand on his shoulder.

"'Art,' his dad said, 'we think you can be depended on. We mortgaged the house today. You can have the money for your airplane.'"[20]

With his eyes failing, his income almost nothing, perhaps his father felt he had nothing to lose, Art said. It was the beginning of Art's dream, but that is all it was at the time — a dream.

According to the best of records, Art was born on February 27, 1890. Newspapers erroneously published his birthdate as 1894, which would suggest that Art was something of a prodigy. It was a presentation of himself that Art did not deny but instead cultivated. Such a date would have made Art precocious indeed. One historian observed that it is hard to imagine a fifteen-year-old boy convincing his parents to mortgage their home to underwrite buying a flying machine, especially before he knew anything about flying.

On March 18, 1933, a newspaper article announcing the 50th anniversary of Mr. and Mrs. James F. Smith, parents "of Fort Wayne's Birdboy Art Smith," said "the Smiths moved to Fort Wayne in 1890, the same year Art was born."[21]

It was in Art's interest to perpetuate the myth that he was a prodigy. His later successes, press releases, and interviews seemed all the more fantastic to the public, and they flocked to see "The Beardless Aviator," "The Birdboy," "The Smash-up Kid," or whatever he was billed as at the time. The idea that he was so young made these exhibitions even more thrilling.

By that time, of course, Art Smith had proved himself, but in his earlier days when he first announced he was going to be an aviator, he was laughed at. He wrote that people said, "He's just a fool kid with a crazy notion." They acknowledged, however, that he had "bulldog grit."[22]

Art did have grit. "It was all I did have — but it was not the bulldog variety," Art wrote about himself. "A bulldog hangs on, but he does it with his teeth alone. I never noticed that a bulldog cared much about what he hung onto, just so he hangs on. I stuck to my idea, but I did it with all the brains I had."[23]

Art said that the libraries were full of books written by men with their feet on the ground — books about human life, human relations, why people change, and what will happen next, but he admitted that he had not read those books. "I am too busy flying," he said. "But I know that everything in the world today is built upon the idea of boundaries. I know that the airplane destroys them. I know that the changes which were made when the ocean was opened to travel, or when the railroads were built, meant nothing to mankind in comparison with the changes that will begin when the air lanes are open."[24]

Art said that when his father placed the check for $1,800 on the table before him that night in 1909, for the first time, he knew a man's courage and strength. "I knew I was going to fight and win."[25]

2

The Mortgage — 1910

On St. Patrick's Day, March 17, 1883, at the Presbyterian Parsonage in Decatur, Indiana, Ida Krick married James F. Smith. Never would she have guessed even in her wildest imagination that someday she and her husband would mortgage their house to buy a flying machine. Nor would she have entertained any thoughts about being famous or well traveled, but both circumstances occurred. "We were just kids," Mrs. Smith said fifty years later. "I was seventeen and James was twenty-two."[1]

After their wedding, the young couple went to Geneva, Indiana, to spend several days with James' brother. James worked as a carpenter until his eyesight failed. According to Ida's niece, Mrs. Harold Moore, "Art was the fourth child and the only one to live to maturity." The oldest child was a girl who died before she reached school age. Boy and girl twins were born next. The girl was dead at birth, and the boy lived until he was eleven years old.[2]

Art, named Arthur Roy Smith, was a high-spirited and curious child "with a lot of nervous energy." He attended the McCulloch and Clay grade schools in Fort Wayne, Indiana, and later Central High School.[3] Art recalled that his mother always had time to help him with his kite projects, went camping with him, and took time to visit and get to know his friends. She not only encouraged him to follow his dreams, but helped him every way she could.

Physically, Art was short, wiry, and healthy (if the speed and frequency of his healings can be used to judge). His salient feature was his glowing smile, which, coupled with his stature, contributed to his boyishness.[4]

When Art dropped out of high school, his mother understood. With her husband's deteriorating eyesight, Art needed to help support the family. He also may have been following the path of many young men of his time, where college was neither an option nor an interest.

It is an understatement that his mother was devoted to Art and he to her. Seemingly she supported his every project. When he decided he should visit some aviation centers in Chicago, he first talked it over with his mother. "Mother was cheerful, as ever, but when I told them my idea of going to Chicago, she looked troubled. She said she did not like my going so far away from home. Mother was never meddlesome, but she always had a great influence over me."[5]

Art also gave his mother credit for his good habits. When people asked him why he didn't smoke or drink, he said: "They think it is because I must keep my nerves steady. It is partly that, of course, but the reason I never began those habits when I was a boy was because of Mother. She wanted me to keep away from things that were not clean and fine. I suppose all mothers feel the same; but when my mother wanted anything done, she saw that it was done."[6]

Art never forgot that his parents mortgaged their house so he could fly. He said that everything he did after the evening his father placed the check for $1,800 on the table was to repay and honor them.

The next morning Art was so excited, he could hardly work at Mr. Weatherhogg's. Owner and manager of the business, Mr. Weatherhogg was beginning to be known as a successful architect, and Art was doing well in the office, learning drafting and construction design. Art wrote that "as every boy has a hero, Mr. Weatherhogg was mine." That Art respected him is even more apparent when he said, "I knew he would have a better opinion of me if I did not drink, and become friends with the boys who hung around the saloons."[7]

On the momentous day when Art announced to Mr. Weatherhogg that he was quitting his job, his boss asked, "Is it a matter of salary?"

Art answered, "No, sir. I'm going to build an airplane."

Mr. Weatherhogg's reaction was predictable. "Build a WHAT?"

Art's answer couldn't have surprised him more. "An airplane, sir. I'm going to be an aviator."

Incredulous, Mr. Weatherhogg pressed, "Do you mean to say you can build an airplane, and make it fly?"

Art explained that he not only planned to build an airplane in about six weeks' time but that he had already ordered the engine. Art didn't say anything to Mr. Weatherhogg about his father's blindness, but his father's situation was worsening. Art was desperate to fly profitably in order to help his father.

Later when Art recalled those days, he said he could tell that Mr. Weatherhogg did not believe he would succeed. He "very cordially" offered him his job back at any time. Mr. Weatherhogg repeated his offer a second time that day, and a second time, Art declined. He left the office with his five-dollar check in his hand, "the last of the family income."[8] His father was still doing all the work he could, but there was nothing regular about his earnings.

In order to accomplish his goal, Art cleared out the workshop in his barn, and he and Al soaped the windows so curious neighbors could not see what was going on, the main reason being that Art was incorporating his own design into his front stabilizer. "I had a great idea for a stabilizer," he said. "When that stabilizer appeared, all danger in flying was to be over. I would be not only rich, but famous." He believed his invention would make his airplane fly better than the Wright brothers' plane and that it would be worthy of a patent.[9]

When Art began work on his airplane, he knew nothing of the engineering problems involved, the stresses, the shifting of the center of gravity, or the balancing. He began by carefully drawing and outlining his plans on paper, basing his idea on pictures from his magazines and books. Suddenly he realized that he did not know how to proceed.

Hearing that the Wright brothers were scheduled to give an exhibition in Indianapolis that fall, Art felt it would be a good idea to go and see their machines, and, if possible, to study them firsthand. He hated to spare the money because he needed every penny for parts.

At the exhibition, Art had no chance to examine the planes. He said, "I saw them. I sat in the bleachers and saw those machines rise from the ground and fly."[10] The Wright brothers flew their planes about two hundred feet high, landed, then rose again for another short flight. Watching them, Art believed his machine would outperform theirs because of his idea about the stabilizer. Inspired, he returned home to his workshop, more confident than ever.

The six weeks predicted for the construction of his plane lengthened to three months. Every piece of wood used had to be air-dried, absolutely flawless, and tested in every possible way for strength. Even the wire had to be tested. "I used several hundred feet of wire — piano wire — on my first machine," Art wrote.[11]

Every day that fall was dedicated to the building of the airplane. Sometimes his best friend, Al Wertman, helped. His mother, as always championing her son, helped by sewing the cloth for the wings on her sewing machine. The rest Art did himself except for some sandpapering that his father helped with in the evenings.[12]

Art had seen Aimee every day during the summer, but in the fall after the engine arrived, he had no time for socializing. "I saw Aimee only on Sundays, and once in a while she came over, and she and Mother watched me at work." According to Art, Aimee didn't mind. "She was excited about it almost as much as I was."[13]

During the winter, Art continued his work. During the coldest part of the winter, he kept a small stove going in the barn, and his mother would bring out a hot lunch. He said he didn't waste time because "time was going fast, and Dad had not been able to get the mortgage for longer than a year."[14]

Sixty years later, an account by Paul Hobrock about the early days of Fort Wayne aviation began with his recollections that on Saturday mornings in 1909, he often would visit a friend on Bass Road, Fort Wayne, who lived close to Art Smith and his folks. "Since Art was building an airplane, we naturally went to his house to see what was going on," he wrote. He added, "Art was glad to have us do little chores such as sandpapering struts and other wooden members. I remember stirring a big pot of alcohol and sealing wax, which was used to paint the cloth instead of dope, as we later knew it, to shrink the fabric."[15]

Finally, on January 17, 1910, the plane was finished. It was a Curtiss-type biplane with a two-cycle, 40-horsepower, Elbridge engine. It had two wheels, and under the wings, Art had built wooden supports. On top and bottom, the parts of his stabilizer were visible. Art said, "To me it was the most beautiful thing in the world." He walked downtown, "enjoying the open air, and feeling more triumphant than I have ever felt since." The plane was finished, and all that remained was for him to fly in it.[16]

Only $23 was left of the money. Having read that at high altitude the air was said to be intensely cold, Art spent eight dollars of the twenty-three and bought a warm sweater to wear for his first flight.[17]

"In the middle of the night, so that no one should see the machine," Art ran the airplane out of the barn. With the help of his father and Al Wertman, they pushed it through the deserted streets of the city to the old ballpark. "I meant to astonish all Fort Wayne next morning with the sight of me

Front view of Art's first plane built in 1910. Note wheel in front and wheel aft. Courtesy: James Wigner.

flying high over the town," he said.[18] They put up a tent to protect the machine, and Al Wertman spent the night with the plane.

In the morning, Art was so excited, his fingers shook. He had planned everything: "I was going to have my stabilizer patented, win at least two of those aviation prizes, and send Dad to the best oculists in America. The mortgage was to be paid, Dad's eyes were to be saved, I was going to be rich and famous."[19]

His mother invited Aimee to breakfast, but as Art recalled, they were all too excited to eat much. His father "did not say a word," and his mother "could not sit still a minute."[20] Will Peters, another friend, joined the group at the ballpark. No one else was present. They intended the first flight to be kept secret for fear someone would see the stabilizer before Art got it patented.

Art's father's eyesight had worsened to the extent that he couldn't help much, so the boys fastened back the tent flaps and pushed the plane out. Art's mother and Aimee watched. It was a clear, sunny morning, and the machine looked beautiful. In the sunlight, it shone with its new wood and bright metal. Art inspected the plane carefully to see that everything was tight, especially the nuts and bolts.

Even before he took the plane up, his mother looked anxious, telling him not to go too high the first time. His father simply asked, "Is she all right, Art?"

As Al and Will held the machine steady, Art took out the supports from under the wings. He settled himself on the seat and gripped the wheel firmly. "Let'er go," he yelled.

Al gave the propeller a whirl; the engine started, and he was off on his first flight.[21]

In order to leave the ground, the plane had to be going nearly fifty miles per hour. There had been a light snow the previous night and it sparkled so that Art could barely see as the airplane raced down the ballpark, but he could feel the wind hard against his face. When he judged that he was going fast enough, he leaned back and pulled the wheel toward him.

The machine rose into the air.

It was an exhilarating feeling that stayed with him throughout his career. Years later, Art said, "To this day, I still feel like shouting for joy at the little lift of the wings as my machine left the ground. I was really flying, at last!"[22]

Then he realized he was driving straight up in the air, too straight and too fast. The speed was terrific. "I pushed the wheel forward," he said "and the machine turned over, and drove directly downward."

He pulled the wheel back. It was just in time. The machine grazed the snow, and up he went a second time. Straight up. Something was wrong. He had no time to think.

He pushed the wheel again, "just the least bit." The airplane was going fast, about twenty feet high. At his touch, the machine dived downward again, almost on end. He pulled the wheel back again. Up he went.

"I tried desperately to think what to do," he recalled. He was about forty feet in the air, driving upward with all the power of the machine. There was nothing ahead of him but blue sky. For the third time, he pushed the wheel over. The machine turned a half circle, at tremendous speed, and dropped. It crashed. Pieces of the plane scattered all around.[23]

Art said at the moment he crashed, he realized what was wrong with his controls. They were too sensitive. "I had an elevating plane [stabilizer] in front and flaps on the tail, both. Either one would have answered the wheel with an up or down slant to the flight. Both of them, on my light machine, were too much. They tipped the machine either straight upward or downward."[24]

He was thrown clear of the wreck onto the frozen ground.

Side view of Art's first plane. Courtesy: James Wigner.

His mother screamed. His father reached him first. He had been in the tent listening to the sound of the engine. When he heard the crash and heard his wife scream, he rushed toward the plane. "When I opened my eyes," Art said, "he was groping about the smashed machine, shaking terribly," calling Art's name over and over.[25]

"I'm all right," Art called to him. He said he would never forget the look of relief on his father's face. Then he added, "Daddy, I think the engine's all right, too."

With that, Art tried to get up but promptly fainted.[26]

According to popular accounts, Art spent the next six months lying in bed, although in his autobiography, he says he lay in bed for five weeks recovering from a badly wrenched back. In any case, while recuperating, he spent his time thinking through all the theories he knew and analyzing the problems he had with his machine. He decided the oversized stabilizer was too sensitive. He also decided there was nothing else to be done except build another plane. Time was his enemy. He had only fifteen dollars left and the mortgage was due in less than five months. He would have to hurry or there would be no hope of winning one of the aviation prizes.[27]

His mother and father had other ideas. "Don't worry about the plane," his mother told him. "You just get well and go back to work for Mr. Weatherhogg." She tried to tell him that they would manage. She repeated this each time she came into the room and found him working over a drawing of some part of the plane.[28]

But Art was undeterred, even though he knew his parents were worried. One night his father came into the room and asked how he was progressing. When Art told him he was going to start work on another plane the next day, his father sat quietly for a long time. Finally, his father suggested he go back to work for Mr. Weatherhogg.

"You know your mother and I don't want you to get hurt," his father said.

"What about the mortgage?" Art asked.

"That doesn't matter," his father said. "We don't want you hurt."

Art admitted he had to face reality. What if he fell not from forty feet in the air but from four hundred feet? What if he could never succeed? What if he couldn't pay the mortgage? What if he kept on trying and kept on having accidents?

Then he said, "But Dad, I *want* to be an aviator."

"I will help you all I can," his father said.[29]

The next day, the two began work again. Art knew it would take six months to rebuild the machine. Fortunately he had a few leftover materials from the supplies he had first ordered. His first job was to repair his engine. To do that, Art had to remove the elevating stabilizer in front of the machine, leaving only the tail flaps. It was tedious, hard work.

Art put in sixteen and eighteen hours a day on his plane. He didn't take time out to see any of his friends. He was too busy, and he also was aware that "they were all laughing at my idea of being an aviator," he said. Most were earning good wages, having a good time, and some were even taking Aimee out to picnics and parties. "I had no time to see her except Sundays," he said.[30]

Aimee kept her Sundays available for Art, and he took her to church on Sunday evenings. He talked incessantly about his machine. "She believed it would fly," Art said, and "told me a dozen times every Sunday. After I talked with her, I always hated to wait until Monday morning to get back to work on it."[31]

In the evenings, Art's father helped him by sandpapering some parts while Art worked on other parts. By this time, his father had given up his carpentering business altogether, but he kept the family bills paid with a few small deals he made in real estate. Art said his father didn't say anything about the mortgage. But his mother did. She worried. She managed. She saw to it that Art had good, substantial meals. She made bread pudding from stale bread. She helped wherever she could.[32]

Even his friend Al Wertman was skeptical. "Do you think she will fly this time?" he asked. When his own work was done, Al, a cigar maker, often came in the evenings to help work on the plane. It was at this time that Art ran into Mr. Weatherhogg on the street one day. His old boss asked about the plane project and told Art he would make a good architect, adding that it was foolish to waste so much time on the airplane. He offered Art his former job, saying, "Whenever you get over that idea, you come and see me."[33]

Time flew by so quickly that summer, Art could hardly keep track of the days. He said things were always going wrong, and he often had to redo his work—for instance, the connecting rods had been badly bent, and he had to repair and straighten them and make them fit. They had to be absolutely straight, and it was hard work and the barn was hot. Even so, he worked feverishly, anxious about the mortgage coming due.

Art's father managed to keep the interest paid but that was all. Art believed that if he could finish his plane, he could raise some money. Now all he could hope for was for his father to get the mortgage renewed. As their property had increased in value, Art and his parents thought that such a thing might be possible.

"One night, at supper, [my] mother was so determined to be cheerful, I knew Dad had not succeeded," Art wrote. When Art asked about the mortgage, his father said, "The bank will not mortgage again." He explained, however, that the bank had given them the chance to trade their equity [house] for a couple of lots out on the edge of town.[34] There was no house on the lots.

When his father said that, Art's mother got up and went into the kitchen. While she was out, his father said, "I got permission for you and me to live here in the barn for a couple of months. Mother can go visit her cousin Annie in Ossian, Indiana."

Art could not say a word. His mother had always been proud of her house, and the idea of losing it was almost unbearable. Art said his mother returned from the kitchen and started talking about how happy she was to have a chance to visit her cousin.[35]

"I got up from the table," Art said. He went out on the front porch, walked up and down, then went to see Aimee. Art found her on her porch, dressed up, visiting with three boys. She was popular and sociable, but he was dumbfounded to find her visiting with three boys all at once, sitting there, "innocent as you please," entertaining them all "while they did not know what to do!"[36]

He called to her from the steps. He had worn his best suit, and he could see the other boys looking at it. Aimee airily said, "We were going for a walk, weren't we?" She got up and came down the walk and joined Art, leaving the boys sitting there. When they reached the gate, she stopped. "You mustn't come here any more, Art," she said. "Papa says I can't go with you any more. He says you're no good, because you haven't any steady job."[37]

Aimee knew nothing about the mortgage situation or that that very day, his father and mother had lost their home on his account. She was nervous. Perhaps it was because the boys were waiting or because she was afraid her father would see her talking with him. Instead of making him more discouraged, however, Art said her words made him feel like fighting.

"Your father thinks I'm no good, does he? I'll show him!" Art said, and announced he would be back to see her the next night. "You want me to, don't you?" he asked.

She admitted she did.

Later as he walked home, he thought about his parents and how they would be turned out of their house, how his father, nearly blind, would have to live in a barn away from his wife. He thought about his mother, "how game she had always been, always doing so much and proud of doing it well. I knew just how she would feel, visiting around, with no money and no home of her own."[38]

He ran into Al, who said, "I heard about the mortgage." The two friends walked together. Al then suggested that if Art needed more help, he would quit his job and help. "I have some money saved," he said. "Almost fifty dollars. We could use that." Art repeated that he believed the machine was going to fly. Al agreed, saying, "You can pay me back when it does."[39] The two friends began working on the plane the following Monday.

It was a lasting friendship. Years later, long after Art succeeded and Al owned a cigar factory, Art said, "I care for him today as deeply as I do for anyone on earth.

Every ounce of manly affection I can feel belongs to Al Wertman, for the splendid, unselfish service he gave me in those days."[40]

When Art told Aimee about his situation and asked about her father, she told him not to worry. "Mama told him not to make such a bother. She said it was a boy-and-girl affair." The young couple then confided to each other that their relationship was much more serious than a boy-girl affair. "They don't know much about it, do they?" Art said. "It's lots more than that, isn't it?" Aimee agreed that it was. Art wrote, "I suppose if I ever really proposed to Aimee, in words, that was the time."[41]

Art and Al put up a big tent on the old Buffalo Bill circus grounds and moved the airplane out there. One stayed over every night to keep watch on the plane. Art and his father lived in the barn. Ida Smith went to visit her cousin.

Within two months, however, Art's father made another real estate deal and got enough money to rent a house. Art and Al moved from the barn to the tent. They set up a couple of cots and a camp stove.

In truth, the boys had fun living in the tent with the plane. After a long day of working, they would sleep well. They developed a routine, getting up early in the morning, cooking bacon and cornbread on the fire. Then "we put something on to stew for dinner and supper, and went to work again," Art said. The only thing that disturbed them was the wind that used to come up in the night and sweep across the open field so hard it would pull out the tent pegs.[42]

Every day Art's father came out to be with the boys. And just about every day, Art took the airplane out to test it. He was exceedingly cautious. It would rise like a bird, but Art kept the controls tied so that it could not go more than four or five feet high. He was determined to learn to fly it before risking the machine again.

Up and down and across the field he flew, he wrote, "just a few feet in the air, learning how to fight bad air currents, how to manage the aerilions [ailerons], and balance, and how to turn around."[43] Turning around was the hardest thing, he said.

> Suppose you are going at a rate of sixty miles an hour against a wind blowing at the same rate. The machine will stay in the air, but it will be standing still. Then you turn around — the velocity of the wind and your own speed added means that you will go at the rate of 120 miles an hour. To make the turn sharply, as you would in an automobile, the wind will catch you in such a whirl of air and at the same time give you such a tremendous increase of velocity that your machine will be blown to earth like a leaf. You have to tack carefully, like a ship in a terrific storm. When an aviator makes a beautiful, sweeping curve he may be making a desperate fight up there in the sky.[44]

Every time Art took the plane up and then landed, something broke. All that summer, he and Al repaired and fixed. Usually it was a wheel that broke, but it seemed that every time Art landed, the pneumatic tires blew out and a wheel would be smashed.

The boys had so little money left, they decided they had to improvise. The rims of the wheels were iron, so when one crushed out of shape, Al and Art hammered it back into something like a circle and wound the rim with good, stout rope in place

Art Smith getting ready to fly in 1910. Courtesy: James Wigner.

of a tire. "We fastened the rope in place with baling wire," Art said. "Then I took the machine out and smashed the wheel again." In something of an understatement, Art commented, "Sometimes it was discouraging."[45]

One day when his father came to see the boys, he told them about some Curtiss "string flyers" who were to give an exhibition at Driving Park the following week. It was almost too good to be true. After nearly eighteen months of work on his machine, Art finally was going to have the chance to examine another airplane. "I thought perhaps I could make arrangements to fly at the exhibition, too," he said.[46]

When he got to Driving Park on East State Street, he went to see the manager of one of the aviators. While he watched the machine being put up, Art was introduced to the aviator. Art said, "It was a proud moment, and he seemed very much interested in finding an airplane in Fort Wayne and listened in amazement when I told him how I had built it."[47]

Art took the aviator to see his machine. He and Al wheeled out their airplane, and the aviator looked it over carefully while the boys explained parts to him. "It was a great moment, showing it to a real aviator," Art said. After a time, the aviator stood back and shook his head. "That machine won't make a flight," he said. "Never in the world."[48]

3

The "Smash-up Kid"—1910

"The plane is built all wrong," the aviator insisted. Even though Art told him he'd gotten the plane off the ground several times that summer, the aviator was unconvinced. He told Art hair-raising stories about the upper currents of air in which Art had never been, and then he pointed out every way Art's plane differed from his own. He was absolutely positive it would not last through "a real flight."[1]

After the aviator left, Art said that he sat for a long time and thought. He was convinced his plane would fly, but he had to admit he'd never taken it up more than a few feet from the ground. The more he thought about it, the more he realized how ignorant he was about aviation. Even so, he was convinced his plane would fly. The next morning he told Al that he would make a high flight that day. He had to find out.

By that time, the people of Fort Wayne knew about Art's interest in flying, and during the summer, little groups had come out to watch him work on his machine. Some had seen Art's low flying trials, which they called "trimming the daisies."[2]

It wasn't long before the rumor spread that Art would attempt a high flight. A crowd gathered. His mother and father were there, full of anxiety. With his father, Art went over the machine several times, checking to see that every bolt was tight. He deliberately did not tell his parents what the aviator had said.

When he was ready, he untwisted the wires that held the controls in place, got in the seat, and told Al to start the engine. The machine ran down the field, picking up speed rapidly. When it was going about fifty miles an hour and he was ready to pull back the wheel, he felt a shock. The machine skidded, leaped over the rough ground in great, shaking jumps. When the airplane stopped, the rear wheel was crushed beyond repair. Some in the crowd cheered a few words of encouragement. Others laughed. Then the crowd began to disperse.

Al and Art surveyed the damaged wheel. A new one would cost $6.50, plus the shipping cost from New York. There was no way they would be able to repair the wheel, nor did they have any money to order a new one.

Then an idea occurred to Al, and it was a good one. He suggested that they take the airplane to Driving Park, put it in a tent, and charge admission to see it. Since most people in Fort Wayne had never seen an airplane, perhaps they would pay twenty-five cents to see one. The boys felt that twenty-five cents would be too much, so they charged a dime for admission. They took in $15.50.[3]

Every day the aviators from the Curtiss exhibition came to see the plane. Art wrote, "They laughed about the machine. None of them took it very seriously. They thought it was a great joke, all patched up as it was. One wheel was gone, and the other had been hammered into shape so often it was about as round as an egg."[4]

But the aviators liked Art and thought he was a good sport. They showed him their machine, and several encouraged him to go to aviation school. Others suggested that he build his airplane differently. They were generous with their comments and liked sharing information about their machines and about flying techniques. As Art said, "It was the first time I had ever seen another machine."[5] Actually he *had* seen another flying machine, but he never had the opportunity until then to study one up close. It was a tremendous help to him.

When their impromptu exhibition was over, Al and Art discussed what they should do with their money. Fifteen dollars and fifty cents was more money than either had seen for months. They could either buy another wheel and some food or they could use it to learn more about aviation.

Having heard about the aviation centers in Chicago and St. Louis, Al and Art decided they should avail themselves of the opportunity to learn more about flying. Art talked it over with his mother. Then he went to see Aimee. He promised Aimee that he would come back, win an aviation prize, and buy her a ring.[6]

To get to Chicago, Art and Al traveled in an empty boxcar. They decided to use the money for food. The trip gave Art and Al a glimpse of city life. When Art talked about the experience, he said that he had never seen such poverty as he saw on that trip. Life in Fort Wayne, no matter how difficult, seemed better. "I could always have a good bath at night," he wrote. "In a big city it costs money to be clean."[7]

In Chicago, the boys stayed at the Buck Hotel located on Congress Street. Rent for little rooms that reminded them of cells in a bathhouse cost fifteen cents. There were no windows, and the partitions did not reach the ceilings. Art said that not even the sheets were clean.

When they visited the Chicago School of Aviation, however, they were impressed. It was a medium-sized airplane factory located on the south side of the city, and it employed twenty men. Art envied them because they seemed to have all the materials, models, and drawings they needed. According to Art, they were turning out "complete machines, beauties."[8]

After they found the manager, they inquired about enrolling. They were stunned to learn that it would cost $350 to work in the factory and even more to take flying lessons. The boys left. They spent the afternoon looking at the airplanes that were parked at the Hawthorne Racetrack. Many had the same engine Art was using but their chassis were built differently. The boys then went to Cicero Field, where they found every sort of airplane, and "a mine of information." There, for the first time, Art saw a Hall-Scott motor — an eight-cylinder beauty, all nickel-plated, running like a watch. He also saw a machine that was built of gas pipe instead of steel tubing. He made notes. Every day, they returned to Cicero Field, asked questions, and examined the machines. The boys increasingly became convinced that Art would have to redesign his chassis.

Staying at the Buck Hotel was horrible. There was no chance to take a bath, and it was hot. They stood it for two weeks. Finally with only twenty cents remaining, they knew they should head home, but another plane had come in to Cicero Field and Art wanted to study it. That evening, Al paid for a room, and after dark, Art slipped in. The boys ate a bag of buns for supper. The room was hot and close for one person, almost unbearable for two.[9]

The next day, they studied the plane and decided their chassis indeed was wrong. Moreover, it had only two wheels and was built into the machine incorrectly. They estimated it would cost them $200 to make the changes. They then went to the Chicago Public Library and found a map that showed the location of the Wabash Railroad yards. From there, they decided to hitch a ride home.

Two hobos showed them how to "grab a blind on a rattler." Art explained that the expression meant "watching for a chance to hop on the front platform of a baggage car on a passenger train."[10]

A brakeman caught them trying to hitch a ride and drove them off the train. That night they slept in a straw stack. The next day, they "grabbed" a ride and slept in barns. It was better than the living conditions they had experienced at their cheap hotel. Their Chicago trip had lasted three weeks.[11]

By the time they got home, Art and Al looked like tramps. The Smiths, who at the time were living in a little rented house, were glad to see them. After a bath and over supper, Art told his parents everything that had happened, adding that it would take around $200 to fix his machine. He asked his father if he knew anyone from whom he could borrow the money.

All that week, he and his father approached different people and visited the banks. They were told that money was tight and airplanes risky. Although polite and interested, not a person was willing to lend them money. That night, Art's father suggested that he could get $200 on a personal note, secured by his lots. "The lots were all Dad had left in the world after he lost the house he had mortgaged to give me a start," Art said.[12]

They arranged to get the money from the bank for ninety days. Art promised he would pay back the money on time. The banker told Mr. Smith that he was making a foolish investment.

Art believed he could order parts and make his repairs in six weeks. Then he planned to try for the cross-country record and win the *Scientific American* prize.

He and Al worked from dawn until dusk. His parents often would come to watch or bring food or lemonade. Sometimes Aimee came. Al put in as much time as Art. Both knew that the $200 had to be paid before the first of November. Both were also aware that they had no guarantee that the machine would fly any better than it had before.

By October, the machine was ready for testing. Not wanting to risk an accident, Art refused to take it up for a high flight. His practice runs were only about four feet off the ground. On Friday, October 6, 1910, he flew across a ditch and sailed the whole length of an adjacent field.[13]

The next day, after making eleven perfect trips across the length of both fields, he announced he would fly to New Haven, Indiana, a town six miles away. It would be a cross-country test of the machine and of his ability as an aviator. If he could accomplish the flight with no mishaps, he believed he would be able to enter the *Scientific American* competition and win the prize in time to meet the note.

A big crowd gathered on the day of Smith's announced flight. The area newspapers had reporters present to witness either Art's success or a bad accident. One newspaper arranged to have an automobile follow the plane to New Haven and back.

Art waited around for Aimee, but she didn't arrive.

Art took his little kitten, which he had named "Punk," and put her in a birdcage, which he had fastened behind his seat. He checked the air currents. It was a beautiful day, and he felt lucky. He checked the machine a second time, then realized there was no gasoline in the tank. He didn't have any money to buy gasoline.[14] Again Al had an idea. He took off his cap and explained the problem to the crowd. Passing around his cap, he collected $2.50. With the money, they bought gasoline.

With his mother watching and telling Art to be careful, Al gave the propeller a whirl. The engine began, and the airplane rose beautifully.

Little by little Art got the machine into the sky. He said, "At every lift I felt like shouting. There is no sensation in the world like that of driving an airplane up and up. The air beats against your face, things below get smaller; there is nothing around but air and light. There is no jar, no vibration, just smooth, swift going."

After reaching several hundred feet in the air, Art began his "straight-away flying." The crowd on the ground seemed like a black mass of people with white faces staring up. He swung the machine around and headed for New Haven.

Triumphantly he flew. It was real, and all his months of hard work seemed justified. Below him the flat farming land was beautiful. The wind was hard against his face, but he wanted to go higher. He lifted the machine upward to about five hundred feet. Suddenly, he heard a loud squall from the kitten in the cage behind his seat. At the same time, his engine stopped.[15]

His only chance to save the plane was to volplane back to earth. He had never done such a thing, but he knew the theory of volplaning. The only thing that keeps a heavy object in the air is momentum, and when the engine stops, momentum fails. He had to get the right angle for a forward glide. Fortunately, he found the exact angle. It seemed like an eternity, but Art slid the machine down to the earth. Recalling the incident, he said his wrists were aching and that he "felt quite shaky."[16]

Art's first successful airplane. Note the three wheels. Courtesy: James Wigner.

When he landed, he found "Punk" hanging to the top of the birdcage yowling because the bottom of the cage was full of boiling water. The connecting tube to the radiator had broken, splashing boiling water on the cat and on the magneto connections. The magneto had short-circuited and stopped the engine.[17]

By that time an automobile had raced up, and to Art's surprise, Aimee was with some newspaper reporters. While Aimee comforted the kitten, Art examined the magneto connections. All he needed was a soldering tool. Several other people had arrived, and a boy on a motorcycle volunteered to go to New Haven to buy one. Art was grateful.

When the boy returned, he asked for a dollar. Art didn't have a nickel. Aimee came to the rescue and offered the boy the dollar. The repair was made, the kitten placed back in the cage, and the trip finished. Art landed beautifully on the circus grounds in Fort Wayne. He said he landed so quietly the kitten was still sleeping in its cage.

Whether this was true is not certain, but what was certain was that Art's mother cried. She ran across the field, clutched her son in her arms "and went to pieces."[18] The crowd went wild. They gathered around the boy aviator and cheered. Somebody took a hat and started a collection. The crowd tossed in $28. It was the first money Art made in aviation. He was speechless. That evening, Art celebrated his success by taking Aimee to the moving pictures and buying her a soda.[19]

In two weeks, the $200 note was due so Art decided to give an exhibition at Driving Park, as the Curtiss flyers had done. He contacted the park managers, Mr. Streetor and Mr. Sprague. Although he had never negotiated with anyone about giving an exhibition, Art knew he would have to give the managers the larger portion of the receipts. He waited for them to make up their minds. He was shocked when he heard what they proposed.

"A boy like you is a credit to Fort Wayne. The whole town ought to do something for you. If the newspapers will give us space, and the printers will give the tickets, we'll give you the use of the park. You can have every cent that's taken in."[20]

The printing company did donate tickets, and the newspapers were enthusiastic. People stopped Art on the street to offer congratulations. The flying exhibition was scheduled for the twenty-first. The actual due date for the bank note was October 23rd.

On the day of Art's flying exhibition, the streetcar company put on extra cars to handle the rush. When Art went out to the park, he discovered that a large crowd had gathered. When the people saw him, they threw their hats in the air. Aimee was there, as were Art's parents. Several men put Art up on their shoulders and took him through the cheering crowd. For many, seeing an airplane in flight was a first.

The wind that day was choppy, and Art knew that he shouldn't take the plane up, but with the crowd cheering and urging him, he wanted to show them he could fly. Aimee was waving and clapping her hands. He didn't want to disappoint her either.

He got into his seat and took the wheel, and Al started the machine. The crowd cheered. The machine skimmed the field and rose. The minute he was up, Art knew he should not have gone up. Gusts of air caught the plane, tipping it. He had to fight to steady the machine. He couldn't make a curve and return to his starting place. He went higher and higher, hoping for a smoother current of air. Around two hundred feet, he found it. He turned the airplane around, but as he began to land, a gust of air buffeted the plane, turning it on edge.

He heard a tearing, crashing shock. The airplane dragged along the ground then stopped. The crowd cheered, but the left wing of the machine was smashed to smithereens.[21]

Art and Al had two days before the bank note was due. With the left wing hopelessly wrecked, they knew their only hope of paying back the note would be to fly again the next day.

That day, Art resolved he would never again make a risky flight because a crowd wanted him to. "The same foolish feeling I had that day has killed more aviators than I like to count," he said. "It is an aviator's business to know the air, to know his machine, and to take the risks which he must take with a cool head. I am glad I smashed only the machine the day I learned that lesson."[22]

4

The Birdboy—1910

Each day a crowd of interested people gathered around the tent to watch Al and Art work on their airplane, but meanwhile Art and Al were concerned. Their problem was serious because they had no materials for their repairs. The ribs of the plane were of wood, and every piece had to be air-dried, tested, and varnished again and again.

Mr. Streetor was doubtful about the scheduled benefit and urged the boys to postpone their exhibition. What Art didn't explain to Mr. Streetor was that he had to pay off a bank note the following Monday. Instead, he tried to convince Mr. Streetor that he would have the plane ready. He was successful because Mr. Streetor knew so little about aviation.

Art and Al worked all night getting the plane ready. The ribs wouldn't dry properly, but the boys decided they had to use them anyway. They searched for cloth but couldn't find any that would match. They experimented with different kinds of fabric. Nothing worked. Finally they found some linen that was light and strong enough, but there was no time to varnish it. They used shellac instead.[1]

They finished late Friday afternoon. That night it rained.

During the night, as Art listened to the rain on the tent he wondered what he would do if the rain didn't stop. By morning, however, the rain did stop but autumn was in the air. It turned out to be cloudy and cold with a gusty wind. Fortunately, the ground was still hard enough to allow the machine to be wheeled out. After a few practices, Art went to the bank to see if the note could be extended. "The banker said it would be impossible."[2]

Art returned to the park. By two o'clock a large crowd was on hand in spite of the disagreeable weather. Nearly three hundred tickets had been sold. Even though the plane looked odd with its two mismatched wings, the crowd was enthusiastic.

28

Art's parents waited in the tent. "We were never a demonstrative family," Art said, "but mother looked so worried that day I gave her a good hug before I started."[3]

With crowds cheering, clouds racing across the sky, the wind blowing in gusts, and the pressure of having to fly in such weather, Art flew low at first as he tried to get the plane under control. He also tried to remember all the things he had learned from the Curtiss flyers. He pulled back on the wheel and went upward. The air current was full of whirlpools. "They swirled around me as I flew upward, catching first one plane and then the other." He went higher, hoping for a chance to get the machine around and down. His hands became numb from the cold. A strong wind caught him about three hundred feet high and tipped the right wing upward. He swung to the right. The left plane rose. The machine righted itself, but the planes were rocking. Then the wind caught the left plane and flung it up. The machine stood on edge.

"I fell, sheer," Art said.[4]

Reflecting about the accident, Art said nothing saved him but his mother's prayer. "I know there are people who do not believe in God," he wrote. "They have never had a mother like mine, or they have never been aviators." He said, "I play a game with Death every day, up there in the sky—a game whose cards are God's own great, clean forces—gravitation, momentum, the keen, strong winds of the upper air—and I believe in Him."[5]

As the plane fell straight, giving no resistance to the air, carrying its half-ton weight of wood and metal, there was no time for thinking. Art threw every ounce of his weight against the controls and madly fought the planes [wings]. Twenty feet from the ground they gave way, fluttered, and straightened out. They caught the air. He landed two hundred feet farther down the field.

His mother ran across the field, grabbed him, then fainted. Al, Aimee, and Art's father raced out, too. They took Art's mother into the tent and revived her. The crowd shouted itself hoarse. Shaking his father's hand, Art said. "I guess that note's paid all right."[6]

Because of the weather, he refused to fly again that afternoon, but the next day, he made two short flights, both times coming down safely. Gate receipts totaled $589.50. Art and his father walked into the bank the following Monday morning feeling like millionaires. As his father paid the note, Art said, "I felt like playing leapfrog over that solemn banker's own desk."[7]

With the rest of his earnings, Art paid back some friends who had lent him money, gave his parents some cash, sent an order to New York for materials to rebuild the left wing properly, and ordered a new wheel. He tried to pay Al, but Al refused, saying he was going back to work now that the plane project was completed. Art didn't want to hear of it. He insisted on doing something nice for his friend. They went downtown, and Art bought Al a new pair of pants. "That was all he would take from me for the splendid, unselfish work of all those months," Art said. He recalled that he was never able to get Al to take anything for his work. "The only way I have persuaded him to take any help from me at all has been on the same basis I took his services in those days, because we are friends, and he needed help to realize his own ambition."[8]

Close-up of Art's first successful plane. Courtesy: Wertman-Stackhouse.

On the street, people walked up to Art and clapped him on the shoulders, saying they always knew he would fly. He was hailed as "Fort Wayne's birdboy" and "a credit to the city." Feeling so successful, Art thought his struggles were over. His plans were to win the aviation prizes, take his father to the finest oculist in Chicago, buy back the home place, and marry Aimee.[9]

As winter approached, the weather was too bad to risk additional flights, so Art stored his airplane in the barn. He decided he would work for Mr. Weatherhogg during the winter and spend his evenings and spare time making sure the machine would be ready to fly in the spring.

One week later, however, while having breakfast with his parents, a man came to the house and announced he was from Mills Aviators in Chicago. He told Art they had heard about his spectacular flying, and they wanted to book him for a series of flights in Texas during the winter.

"There's big money in it, big money!" the man said. Art said he couldn't help but notice that the man was fat, well-dressed, wore diamond rings and had a diamond in his tie. The man from Mills Aviators told him he already had bookings in Bay City and Bryan, Texas, both of which Art could fill immediately. He offered Art a year's contract and promised him he would make thousands of dollars. For the two arranged flights, Art would receive $2,500.[10]

Art was excited but cautious. He told the man he and his father would think it over and give him a reply that night. He then went to see Aimee. Aimee's parents were home, so all of them went into the sitting room by the fire. Mr. Cour was affiliated with a Chicago firm and was well-to-do. The Cours lived in a large, beautifully furnished home, and Aimee and her sisters always had pretty clothes and plenty of spending money. Mr. Cour was pleasant that day and talked with Art about his flights, congratulating him on his success. He told Art that the same amount of thought and effort would make him a very successful businessman. "He urged me to give it up and do something else."

Moreover, Mr. Cour explained that Art had a good personality, made friends easily, and could succeed as an architect. "You could make money, and have a nice little home after awhile, right here in Fort Wayne."[11] Art realized that Mr. Cour was telling him he would not object to Art's going with Aimee if he were to give up flying. Art then told Mr. Cour about his offer from Mills Aviators. Mr. Cour seemed disappointed and "did not say much more." Art had no chance to talk with Aimee alone that afternoon.[12]

After talking the contract over with his father, Art signed with Mills Aviators. He believed that if he came home in the spring with a big bank account, the Cours family would think differently about him. The next day, he began to take the machine down and prepare it for shipment. Three weeks later, he was scheduled to fly in Bay City.

"I had removed only a bolt or two when the whole machine collapsed," Art wrote. "All those small accidents while I was learning to fly had been too much for it. The whole framework went to pieces before my eyes."[13]

He spent the next three weeks splicing, patching, rebuilding, and strengthening piece by piece. Some parts had been rebuilt more than thirty times. The wingbars had been spliced at almost every strut connection. Three weeks later, he headed for Texas, the machine in as good condition as he could make it. The contract called for four flights for $1,350 in Bay City, Texas, and Art hoped to use the money for new parts.

Art's parents and Aimee went to the train station to say goodbye and wish him luck. He had not been able to see much of Aimee during the previous weeks, but he told her he would buy her an engagement ring with the Bay City money. She seemed pleased and told him she was confident that when he returned in the spring, her father would see things differently. Art set off with a light spirit.[14]

He reached Bay City on the morning of the day set for his first exhibition. The carnival had begun, and Bay City was in a flutter of excitement. Most of the people had never seen an airplane. Art discovered that no arrangements had been made for setting up the machine.

With his flight scheduled for 2:30 P.M., he did his best to set up the airplane, but it was difficult. The crowd kept crushing in on him; many tried to carry away parts as souvenirs. The weather was hot and the wind was blowing. He worked through lunch. He ran an hour late.

His exhibition flight lasted about two minutes.

He explained that the wind strained at the wings even before he left the ground, and the minute he was in the air, he knew a flight would be impossible. The extra weight of the spliced and patched parts made the machine slow. Forty feet off the ground, he felt the plane begin to sink. There was nothing he could do. The plane crashed, barely missing the park fence. The chassis broke. It was a wonder, but Art wasn't injured.

His contract guaranteed a payment of $350 in advance. The management paid it, extracting a promise from Art that he would fly again the next day. The rest of the afternoon and evening, he ransacked Bay City to find materials. He spent the entire night working on the chassis. At dawn, it began to rain.

It rained most of the day. At one point when the weather cleared, Art wheeled out his machine determined to give the crowd a show, but the wheels sank three or four inches in the mud. Conditions were impossible. The rain poured all day. There was nothing Art could do but ship his machine to the next stop.[15]

His contract for Bryan, Texas, stipulated that he would receive one-half of the gate receipts up to $1,200. He had assurances that aviators had given exhibitions in Bryan and that the country was a vast level prairie, which was a good place for flying. As the train neared Bryan, Art saw billboards advertising his show — "Birdboy Art Smith, the Indiana Wonder." In high spirits, he exulted in the fact that the weather was sunny and that his $1,200 was assured. "I guess I spent that $1200 a dozen times, in my mind," he said.[16]

But when he arrived at the aviation field, he was shocked. It was a half-mile track, and "the only twenty trees in the whole country were growing on it. If they had been set out to prevent an airplane flight, they could not have been arranged any better for the purpose."[17] On one side of the track was a small lake. On the other side, there was a high fence.

There was no alternative. Art decided he would have to start among the trees. He would have to zigzag around the trees and make a speed of fifty miles an hour to get off the ground. He posted large pieces of white paper at the curves to indicate where he should turn.

Two flights were scheduled, one on Saturday and one on Sunday. On Saturday, although it was clear, there was a steady wind. Art noticed that the crowd only half-cheered. He started the plane and got up to about two hundred and fifty feet. A strong downward current hit and the plane sank. About fifty feet in the air, the machine let go and dropped. It came down flat. Every part of it was smashed. The wings lay on the ground. Only the engine was left. The crowd jeered.

Art sent for a wagon and began to box up the engine. Alone, he surveyed the mess and decided to make a bonfire. A few small boys were standing around watching. As Art reached to strike a match, one came over and asked, "Mister, us boys — we're making gliders. I wish you'd leave us all that canvass and things." Art was happy to share. The boys gave a cheer, and Art said that was the brightest part of his visit.[18]

After dinner at the hotel, Art went to the freight office and shipped his engine to Fort Wayne. He barely had enough money for his fare home.

Going back to the hotel, one of the little boys met Art and warned that he "had better beat it quick before the crowd gets hold of you — they're going to rotten-egg you." The boy said the crowd thought Art was "another one of them fakes they've been having at the park."[19]

On the way to get his baggage, Art saw big new posters advertising that he would fly as scheduled the next day: "Everybody Come." When the clerk at the hotel looked at him in an odd way and asked if he were indeed going to fly the next day, Art knew the crowd was hostile. He didn't wait for the evening passenger train; he hopped on the first freight train that left the station.[20]

He had made no money in Bryan. All he made in Bay City had gone for repairs and expenses. He didn't have money to buy food on the train. He reached Fort Wayne without a cent. The Texas trip was a failure. Hurrying home, Art hoped he wouldn't meet anyone, especially Aimee or her folks.

5

Midwestern Flights—1911

Art's parents asked no questions. They were simply glad to have him home. His mother served him supper. Art said that over the meal, he told them about the smash-up. Instead of acting discouraged, Art said, they took the news in stride. "Mother kept hurrying around getting more for me to eat. She said the machine did not matter so long as I was well and safe."[1]

His father, who was almost totally blind by this time, sat across the table trying to see him. Finally, his father said, "You can raise money on those lots."[2] That investment risk was the last thing Art wanted to do. He decided that since everyone had been so enthusiastic about his Fort Wayne flights, perhaps he could get some financial backing.

During the next few days, he went to see several men who had praised him. None would lend him a dollar for another airplane. Art wrote in his autobiography that the men said they "were sorry about my machine, but money was very tight." Each one said airplanes were too risky and suggested that he give up flying.[3]

As always, his friend Al was supportive. He loaned Art enough to get the engine hauled out to the barn and offered to give Art a part of his salary for as long as he needed it. Art refused, saying, "It wouldn't be fair. Al needed his money, Al had a girlfriend, and Al wanted to get ahead in his own work."[4]

Art approached various businessmen in Fort Wayne and offered "to pay any amount of interest for a loan of two or three hundred dollars." Not one volunteered. He tried to get the Commercial Club to back him as an advertisement for Fort Wayne; he offered to sell stock and started a subscription list. Every plan he thought of failed.[5]

The only people in Fort Wayne who still believed in him were Aimee and his parents. Aimee encouraged him each time they talked. The idea of buying her an engagement ring now was merely a dream, and she insisted that she didn't care about a ring. The only thing she cared about was his flying. If that was what Art wanted, then that was what she wanted.

Finally, Art approached the bank about taking out a loan on the two lots his father owned. To his surprise, the banks turned him down, saying they didn't think it would be a safe loan. They remembered he had not paid off the other note until the last moment, and they too suggested he give up flying. Again he tried several businessmen, using every argument he could think of. They turned him down.

One day Art remembered that Steve Fleming, a senator from Fort Wayne, liked to race automobiles and kept a fleet of cars. An avid sportsman, Fleming was a millionaire many times over. As a last resort, Art decided to call on Senator Fleming and tell him his situation. As the senator listened, Art offered his father's lots as security and any interest the senator might want if only he would lend him enough money to rebuild the airplane.

"He listened to every word I said in silence. I remember just how he tapped his pencil on his desk," Art said. "At last he nodded."[6]

The senator suggested a longtime loan, a year or even two. He would do the paper work the next morning. Art said he almost broke down. "I cannot even think of him to this day," he said later, "without the deepest gratitude. He was a prince in the way he treated me."[7]

The next week Art headed for Chicago with his engine. The Mills Aviators had agreed to let him use their factory for the rebuilding process. By then, two years had passed since he first started building his flying machine. His hopes of becoming rich and famous had amounted to nothing. All he possessed were his old engine and a $600 debt. He decided that he would not return to Fort Wayne until he made enough money to take his father to an oculist and to make life easier for his mother.

Fortunately, Mills Aviators had booked Art for a flight in Stirling, Illinois, in three weeks. He promised them he would have his airplane ready. With the equipment at the factory, new tools, and new materials, Art worked hard all day and late into the nights. Every dollar he received from Senator Fleming went into the machine. Living expenses were small. He said he skipped breakfast and each day bought a ten-cent plate of beef stew for lunch and dinner. "There is a great deal of good food in a plate of beef stew when you are hungry," he remarked.[8]

Art rebuilt his machine. The day before leaving for his Stirling show, he counted his money. He had almost $30.00 left. Subtracting expenses to Stirling, he would have enough to buy a new suit.

Art needed a new suit. He had not bought clothes in over two years, and his one suit looked bad. He decided to splurge. He picked out a checked Norfolk that looked so good when he put it on that he spent an additional twenty-five cents to have a colored photograph made of himself in the suit to give to Aimee. [9]

Stirling beckoned. There he met Didier Masson, an aviator from California, who was booked for a series of flights under the management of Leon and Max Friedman of San Francisco. With a new suit and a new machine, Art was excited. He looked forward to his flight. A big crowd had assembled, and to Art it seemed that his percentage of the gate receipts, which he figured would be two hundred, at least, was within reach.

The engine worked fine. Every part of the machine was in splendid condition. The crowd cheered. He got into the seat and zipped down the track. He lifted the machine into the air. "It rose beautifully," he said. "The air was calm. I drove up to about sixty feet. Then I struck a smooth, strong current. The minute I felt it on the planes [wings], I knew what would happen; my engine would not carry me against it."[10]

The air current rolled the plane over slowly and easily. It dropped edgewise. The left wing caught the force of the fall "and smashed like an egg shell." Art described what happened. "I went through the front of the machine, taking the steering wheel with me. I landed in the next field."[11]

The crowd thought the young aviator had been killed. Half a dozen men pulled him out of a deep, soft mudhole. "When I recovered consciousness," Art said, "they were all standing around wanting to know if I was hurt."[12] He wasn't hurt, but he was muddy and disgusted. His new suit was ruined and the left wing was wrecked. There was nothing he could do but ship the plane back to Chicago. His stint at Stirling was over. He collected $52.70, barely enough for repairs.[13]

At the hotel, he studied his list of bookings. All but one paid on the basis of gate receipts. That booking was in Beresford, South Dakota, where he was offered $750 flat for a flight on the Fourth of July.[14] If he could manage that flight, he would be able to recoup his losses.

It was early March.

Back in Chicago, he rebuilt his wing. He hoped to make enough money in Mattoon, Illinois, his next booking, to make a down payment on a new engine because he had determined his little engine was too weak for the weight of his plane.

At Mattoon, there was an enormous crowd, and the managers were excited about the exhibition. Art looked over the infield, and his heart sank. It was too small and full of trees. The air was choppy with some gusting. Because he was down to his last cent and he needed a new engine, he decided he had to fly, no matter how impossible the situation.

He made a quick drive to get off the ground in the cramped space. He barely cleared a tree when the wind caught him. At about fifteen feet in the air, he turned his plane sharply in order to keep his balance. Right ahead of him "was a bunch of trees" and the fence. He pulled back on the wheel to lift the machine over the trees. His engine failed.[15] As he said, it was a choice between the trees and the fence. He took a chance on the fence and ploughed through it, wiping it out. He climbed out of the plane with a dislocated shoulder. He collected $27.00 as his share of the gate receipts.[16]

His friend Didier Masson flew for him at the next exhibition, while Art returned to Chicago to repair his plane. Mills Aviators advanced him the materials.

It seemed that every time Art flew, he had another accident. "I made barely enough money for repairs, but I kept on trying," he said.[17] It was a discouraging spring. He began to look forward to his Fourth-of-July booking in Beresford. The contract was for seven hundred and fifty dollars. To Art, that seemed like a fortune.

Before the Beresford exhibition, however, Art was booked to give an exhibition in Muncie, Indiana, on June 25, 1911. It was a trip he was anxious to make because it would give him the chance to stop by Fort Wayne and visit Aimee and his family.[18]

When he arrived at Muncie, however, he was not only disappointed but angry. The field where he was supposed to fly was full of trees. No aviator, according to the people he talked with, had ever succeeded in flying from the Muncie field. There was no place either to start or to land. Art hunted up the managers and complained. They insisted. He refused. They seemed unaware of the danger. Again, Art refused. They compromised.

If Art would set up his machine as an exhibit for the crowd, the managers would pay him his share of the gate receipts, and they would explain that he would not be able to give a flying exhibition.

On the scheduled day, huge crowds came out to the field. The grandstand was so crowded that people had to stand. The managers gave them automobile races, and the drivers raced the cars in every possible way, but the crowd kept calling for the airplane.

The managers then announced more automobile races. According to Art, "They had slow races, races on three cylinders, races against time, against other automobiles, against even more motorcycles. By this time," Art said, "the crowd was hooting and howling for the airplane."

When the managers announced yet another automobile race against time, "the crowd began to throw things."[19] The managers used every argument they could to convince Art to fly.

Art refused. Besides those trees, there was a strong wind blowing. Art would have to race with the wind and get up to a tremendous speed on the ground in order to lift the machine. There simply wasn't enough room. Moreover, Art had suffered too many smash-ups to take such a chance. Finally the managers announced that the airplane was out of order.

Their announcement made the crowd furious. They gave a howl and poured out of the grandstand "in one mad mob." The managers ran. Art stood on a box by his machine and tried to explain that it was impossible to fly in that field. "It would probably kill me to try it," he told them. They yelled that he was a coward, jammed around him and the machine, and shouted insults.

"Fly!" they shouted. "We'll make you fly!" Then someone shouted, "Let's wreck his old machine! It's a fake!" The crowd jumped at the airplane.

Seeing that the spectators were bent on destroying his airplane, Art said he had no choice. It was all he could do. The crowd stopped tearing at the plane. Jumping on the seat, he yelled back that he would fly, but that if he were killed he wanted them to know they had murdered him. Then he started his plane.[20]

With every bit of skill he had, he drove the machine, lifted it into the air just in time to clear a tree. The wheels tore at the branches as he went over it. He missed the fence by less than a foot. The engine was pulling hard. Outside the fence there was a hill with a sandpit in one side. He pulled back on the wheel. The machine headed straight for the sandpit. Art barely cleared the hill. Then his engine started missing fire. Flying low, he looked for a place to land. Finally he found a smooth meadow and came down. As the wheels touched the ground, the engine stopped.

There was no way to steer. The airplane raced across the meadow, jumped a ditch, and went head-on into a fence.

Art had not saved his airplane after all, and the Beresford exhibition was only a week away. He pulled himself out of the wreck, not only badly shaken up, but also feeling sorry for himself. He sat on the ground and tried to plan what he should do.

His first move was to find the Muncie managers and ask for some of the gate receipts. They gave him $50.00. That would pay for his trip to Beresford, but he would have to rely on Mills Aviators for materials to rebuild. Whatever it took, he was determined to have the plane ready for Beresford.[21]

He shipped the plane to Chicago and followed his machine, stopping off for a few hours in Fort Wayne to see Aimee. She was home. While other couples were out walking, Aimee was sitting on the porch alone. They only had a half hour, so they walked back and forth in front of her house and talked about his flying. She confided to him that if she couldn't be with him, she preferred not to go with anyone else. "It was a wonderful half hour," Art said.[22]

In Chicago, he convinced the Mills Aviators to advance him more materials—struts, wing beams, ribs, and linen for the planes. Working twenty hours and more a day, he feverishly rebuilt his airplane. Unfortunately he had to ship the plane to Beresford without some of the braces. Art barely had money for fare on a day coach, and he needed to get to Beresford in time to finish the machine and set it up for the flight on the Fourth.

The finance committee chairman, a tall, thin fellow "with a very dry manner," met him at the train and reviewed the contract.[23] Art was to give two flights of fifteen minutes each. Then the man took Art to the field.

Art was not only relieved when he saw the field, he was happy. It was a big, level grain field on the edge of town, surrounded by level country. The people had even cut the grain, so he could start more easily. They had also provided a tent for the airplane.

On the Fourth, a huge crowd gathered to see the Birdboy fly. Beresford's wide streets were jammed. The normal population was 7,000, but more than 25,000 people came to see the flying exhibition.[24]

The wind was strong, but Art noted that it was a steady wind. He was worried about his engine. Even though he had carefully gone over the magneto and carburetor, he couldn't seem to get it to run smoothly. It kept skipping. Art started his engine. The wind was blowing so great that the airplane lifted into the air while it was still going no faster than a boy would run. The machine rose perfectly; the wind was smooth. He made a low flight, testing the wind, and then went upward. At about two hundred feet, the wind buffed him. He curved carefully, edging into the wind again, then made a complete circle. The engine was missing so much he had to come down. He landed without an accident.

The chairman of the finance committee was standing near the tent, his watch in his hand. "Only three minutes in the air," he said, then added, "But it was a great flight, a great flight!" They shook hands warmly. Art worried about the fifteen-minute clause in the contract.[25]

All afternoon, Art worked on his motor. The wind wasn't blowing as strong by 4:30 P.M., so he attempted another flight. In the air, the wind kept catching the wings, but Art was able to handle the stress until a second puff of wind hit him. The airplane turned on edge and dropped. As it began to fall, Art fought the controls with all his strength, but they would not turn. He was falling, helplessly.

His mother was not there to pray for him, and he thought about that as he struggled with the controls. "I knew I would have to pray for myself," Art said. "I cried: O God, save me!"[26]

Less than five feet from the ground, he felt the machine right itself. Then, as he pulled back on the wheel with all his force and body, "the machine leveled and with one great swoop rose high into the air."[27]

Pictures taken by J. W. Patch, 4121 Indiana Avenue, of Art Smith's airplane at Driving Park in 1911, show the plane in the air (above) and interested spectators (at left).

A photograph taken in Driving Park in 1911. Courtesy: Stackhouse Collection.

The speed of the fall lifted the airplane into the air, as Art couldn't believe. It rose one hundred feet in one swoop. Sloping away from the field beneath him was a little creek. His airplane had touched the water as the machine lifted. But in the air, he couldn't make a half circle because of the direction of the wind, so he nosed the machine over and came down. The airplane raced across the field, veered, and tore off a wheel. Art got out, looked at the smashed chassis, and laughed. He was alive!

The men on the field were "white as dead men," Art said. They thought he had been killed. When they saw he was safe, they yelled and shouted for fifteen minutes. After the enthusiasm died down, the chairman of the finance committee looked at his watch and mentioned that Art had stayed in the air only five minutes. Then he told Art they would settle the contract at noon the next day in his office.[28] Naturally, Art tried to figure what percentage of $750 he had earned in his eight minutes in the air. Finally, he decided he would argue for the entire amount.

The next day, Beresford was deserted, and Art impatiently waited until noon. When the finance committee chairman arrived, yawning and rubbing his eyes, he asked Art how he wanted to be paid.

"Please give me currency," Art managed to say.

"Better make it a draft," the chairman said. "You don't mean you want to go back to Chicago with all that money?"

"If you don't mind, I would like to, yes," Art said.

Then the chairman handed over the money — one fifty-dollar bill and the rest in twenties. Seven hundred and fifty dollars.[29]

Art later wrote about that evening. "That night, for the first time in my life, I slept in a Pullman berth. I slept hard, for I was tired, but I woke as soon as it was light enough to see that money again. I spread it out on the blankets and looked at it. For months I knew the name of every bank that had issued one of those bills, and the name of its cashier. Seven hundred and fifty dollars!"[30]

Finally he had earned real money as an aviator.

6

New Heights—1911

With $750 in cash in his pocket, Art felt rich enough to buy the world! Best of all, he had enough money to take his father to the best oculist in Chicago. As soon as he arrived in Chicago, he made an appointment with the eye doctor, then wired his father to come. Art planned also to buy a ring for Aimee.

While Art waited for his father to arrive, he worked on his engine at the factory to make sure it was in good repair for his next exhibition, which was booked for July 12, 1911, in Elkhart, Indiana. It didn't take him long to discover the cause of his engine problems. The main bearings of his two-cycle motor, which he had used continuously for two years, were so badly worn that the gas leaked from the crankshaft instead of being forced into the cylinders.[1] When he showed the machine to his fellow mechanics, they couldn't believe he'd been flying that way all summer.

A beautiful new six-cylinder, four-cycle Kirkham engine, priced at $1,650, had arrived at the Mills factory. Art wanted it. He almost could feel the sensation of flying an airplane with the Kirkham motor; there would be no sickening, sinking sensation that he felt with his old engine.[2]

He decided to show the president of Mills Aviators his old motor and ask if he could borrow the new motor for his Elkhart flight. His argument was that he should use the Kirkham since he was the only aviator available to fly because the other aviators were in hospitals or tied up with wrecked machines.

The president refused. Instead, he offered to sell the motor to Art if he would make a down payment of $700 with the rest in installments. Art refused. He needed his money for his father's eye appointment. Art said he argued his case the entire day. He finally got the president to consent to lend him the motor. "Everything seemed to be coming my way at last. I remember I did little dance steps and whistled all the time I was waiting for the train," Art wrote.[3]

On the way to the oculist, Art and his father discussed his Beresford success and talked about the construction costs of different big buildings in Chicago. What they didn't do was discuss the eye appointment; however, both were excited. They arrived for the appointment an hour early.

For Art, the wait seemed interminable. Finally his father came out of the office accompanied by the oculist. From their expressions, Art couldn't tell a thing. After they left, his father turned to him and said, "It's all right, Art. Don't feel bad. He says nothing can be done."[4]

Art took his father to the hotel and returned to see the oculist and asked if there was any chance he could have saved his father's eyes had he brought his father sooner. The reply was negative. "The sunstroke Dad had suffered while he was working so hard had injured the nerves of the eyes. He would never be able to see again."[5] Again the doctor said that nothing could be done.

It was something of a consolation to know he couldn't have done anything more, but Art was heartbroken for his father. He returned to the hotel and found his father, "sitting there quite serene."[6] After talking about the situation, his father told him how proud and glad he and his mother were about Art's success and flying career. Then his father asked to go back to Fort Wayne.

Art said that although his father never voiced a word of complaint or expressed self-pity, he knew his father had to give up all hope of realizing his dreams. "I know," Art said, "because I have worked hard to realize my own ambitions."[7] It was an unspoken bond of understanding between father and son that Art never forgot.

After achieving success in San Francisco in 1915, Art told a reporter about his father. "Dad and Mother are living now on a beautiful little ten-acre place near Fort Wayne. All I can spare of the money I earn by flying at the Exposition is going back there to improve the place and make Dad as happy and comfortable as possible. It is all I can do for him."[8]

In 1911, however, as Art worked on his Kirkham motor, getting it ready to ship to Elkhart, he promised himself he would give his father everything he possibly could, "all the rest of my life. I know that all I can do, will never be as much to him as the one thing I wanted to give him, and never can."[9]

To Art's delight, Aimee and his mother came to Elkhart to see his exhibition. He met them at the train and took them to see the new motor. Neither had seen Art make a real exhibition flight, so they were excited. "We had a great time that evening," Art said. "I had real money in my pocket, and I took them to the best hotel in town."[10]

The next morning a large crowd was at the exhibition, the air was steady, and the new motor was in fine shape. When Art started the engine, it ran beautifully. When Art pulled back on the controls, " the machine fairly leaped into the air."[11] The machine, with its sixty-horsepower motor, responded to his every touch. When he pulled back, the plane rose like a bird. When he turned the rudder, the plane wheeled around on one corner instantly. When he pushed the controls, she dived. It was the first time, he said, that he knew what real flying was.

Flying in this manner was more than adventure. It was an experience of being at one with nature. Seated in the open with clean, fresh winds hitting his face, he felt free, enjoying the glorious space. He stayed up over half an hour, swinging around in great curves, flying higher and higher, and swooping down in long, smooth glides.

Unfortunately, when he landed, he had not anticipated the power of his new motor. The airplane ran across the field and smashed into the fence. He spent that evening doing repairs.

Word spread about Art's flying, and the next day, the crowds were even bigger. He made two flights and enjoyed every minute of each. His share of the gate receipts for the two days was $145.75. It made him feel "like a millionaire."[12]

When he said goodbye to his mother, he tucked a roll of bills into her pocketbook and told her not to worry about money ever again. Then he shipped his airplane to Hillsdale, Michigan, where he was booked for two flights the following week.

This scrapbook clipping shows Ida Smith standing by the steps of the house Art purchased for his parents. She is holding a broken propeller from his wrecked plane, in which a clock is mounted. The propeller clock was given to Al Wertman, and Herb Wertman recalled that it was a family keepsake. Courtesy: Greater Fort Wayne Aviation Museum. Photographer Don Goss.

Hillsdale also was a success for Art, and the managers begged him to stay an additional day. Because he was already booked to give an exhibition in Adrian, fifty miles away, he declined. As he was dismantling the machine, the managers came and urged him to stay. Again he declined. They insisted. They offered him a bonus. He compromised. Art said he compromised because he conceived the idea that instead of shipping his airplane to Adrian, he would fly it there. Flying would get him to Adrian in time. He told the managers he would give a couple of flights the next morning. It was a bold idea.

The next morning, Art had wonderful crowds cheering him, and afterwards as planned, he headed for Adrian. Before leaving, the editor of the Hillsdale newspaper asked him if he would deliver some papers to a couple of neighboring towns. Art agreed, and the editor came out with bundles of newspapers and tied them to the airplane. It was a journalistic enterprise Art would not forget. It was a hot July day, and Art was exhilarated as he flew over woods and fields, now and then dropping a bundle of papers over various little towns. When he finished his deliveries, he decided to experiment with a high altitude flight. It was a bright day, clear and sunny, and he was having fun.[13]

At four thousand feet, it was cool. He pulled back on the controls and nosed the plane upward. At five thousand feet, a curious thing seemed to happen. The earth didn't appear flat but curved upward at the edges, reminding him of a gray-green bowl. He lifted the machine higher, up to fifty-five hundred feet. The higher he went, the deeper the bowl seemed. He craned his neck to try to see over the bowl's rim. By then, almost numb with cold and aware that his gasoline wouldn't last much longer, he headed down in long, smooth swoops. Looking at the earth again, it appeared flat.[14]

By the time he landed in Adrian, he was chilled to the bone although the crowds were sweltering in the July heat. It was a glorious experience, a day, he said, when he learned about the density of the air. The explanation was that at the surface of the earth, air density is at its greatest. Light waves entering this dense medium are deflected by it, just as they are in entering water. The effect is similar to how a spoon or flower stem seems bent where it enters the water, if looked at from a certain angle. The earth looks bent in the same way when an aviator looks down at it, except that the density of the air, increasing gradually, gives it a curved effect instead of a sharp angle. Art described it as an uncanny feeling the first time an aviator sees the earth turned into a bowl, rising all around him.[15]

At Adrian, the manager of Mills Aviators showed him a contract for a flying exhibition at Deadwood, South Dakota. The show would pay $1,250, and he wanted Art to sign. He also offered to let Art rent the Kirkham motor, but Art didn't want to rent the motor. After a long discussion about the rental fee, which Art felt was too high, they struck a deal. Art would sign the contract if he could buy the motor with $700 as a first payment, and the rest on time. "Seven hundred dollars was almost every dollar I had," he said, "but I gave it to him."[16] Art was confident he would make enough money from the Adrian show to cover the cost.

Art made less than fifty dollars. On his first day in Adrian, he was able to give only a short flight because of rain. On the second day, the weather was so bad, Art's flight had to be cancelled. He barely had enough money to ship his airplane to Deadwood. He couldn't afford a Pullman. He arrived in Deadwood with less than four dollars.[17]

In South Dakota, his contract called for six flights of ten minutes each. If he could fulfill the contract, Art would make $1,250, and that would be enough to pay for the motor and get him to his next exhibition. He hoped and prayed for good weather.[18]

When Art arrived at the Deadwood station, he noticed that a large crowd had gathered and seemed to be waiting for someone. A touring car full of dignified-looking men was parked nearby, and there were colored flags and bunting decorating the streets, which added to the carnival atmosphere. Art wondered who the important person was who would be attending the exhibition. No one seemed to be waiting for him, so he crossed the platform and asked the ticket seller directions to the Business Men's Club.

The ticket seller, who also seemed to be watching for someone, was surprised. Then the ticket master asked if he was Art Smith. When I said 'yes,' he fairly leaped with surprise and excitement. Then I found that I was the important person they were all waiting for."[19]

Art was a treated as a celebrity. The mayor of Deadwood, a Mr. Franklin, had come to meet Art and with him some of "the biggest men in the city."[20] They escorted the young aviator to a luxurious car and took him for a ride. They showed him the majestic scenery of the Black Hills, then took him to the town's best hotel. After an elaborate luncheon, they drove him out to the aviation field. "I was so carried off my feet by this intoxicating reception that I said at once that I would fly there."[21]

Art spoke too soon. As he studied the field, he became apprehensive. Steep mountains surrounded every side of the field. If he could get off the ground, there would be no room to turn. It would be impossible to fly. Then, the men told him that in the past two of Curtiss's most famous flyers had been booked there and had refused to fly, but they were counting on his being able to do so.

Art was appalled. The men were upset. "There was no opening anywhere in that ring of mountains; they were like a rough wall around the field. There was not a chance in the world that I could fly there."[22]

Art sat on a box and tried to think. He didn't have enough money to get out of town. The only way he could get more money was to fly, and he could not fly. Finally he worked up enough courage to approach the Business Men's Club and formally tell them that he could not fly. They were stunned. The carnival had begun. Outside of their clubrooms, Art and the men already could hear the music and the crowd.

The mayor explained, "You simply can't refuse now. It's impossible. After getting the crowd here twice before — do you know what this means to us? I will have to sell my business and leave Deadwood." The others concurred, saying they would be ruined.[23] Art wrote that they talked for hours, and "I told them it would be suicide to take the machine off the ground in that field. I would not fly there."[24]

Finally, they gave up the argument. Art went to the hotel and counted his money. He had $1.90. The situation was a disaster. At three o'clock in the morning, the telephone rang. Mr. Franklin was on the wire. His automobile was downstairs, and he wanted Art to come down. The men would find a field that could be used.

Art's description of the trip and Mr. Franklin's driving is vivid. "It was a beautiful moonlit night. The car plunged up the steep mountain roads and raced along the very edge of precipices, so close that I looked over the fenders into canyons hundreds of feet deep. Every time we zipped around a corner, I expected the car to go over. The men with me were desperately intent on just one thing—finding an aviation field before morning."[25]

As the sky turned pink, they found a plateau, three miles from Deadwood. It was a field, half a mile long and fairly level. On all sides, the ground fell away, "sheer, to depths of hundreds of feet."[26]

Art decided if he could get the machine into the air before it raced over the edge, there would be room to turn before striking a mountain. He told the men he would fly there. His airplane was brought out to the plateau on a big carnival wagon. The first flight was scheduled for 4:30 in the afternoon. Art said he spent the day seeing that everything was ready. According to Art, "thousands of people climbed the mountains to the field."[27]

When Art started his plane, the machine raced across the plateau, and caught a strong wind blowing hard in the same direction. An airplane should start against the wind, Art said, in order to make enough speed to lift it. The plateau was small, and he crossed it in a second. As he was about to pitch over the edge, the plane caught the air. It was a slow, uneven climb because of the high altitude. Art pulled back on the controls and little by little got up to eight hundred feet. "The air was very bad — uneven, and tangled around the mountains and into canyons in dozens of cross-currents."[28]

Struggling with those wind forces, he made a complete circle without striking any of the mountains. Flying over the main valley, he could see the tree tops far below. Worried that he would not be able to land anywhere except the same small plateau, he brought the plane around, and as he did so, he was buffeted by hard gusts. Then he struck his first air hole, a strong downward current of air, almost a gale. Flying into an air hole, he said, gives the same sensation as plunging into a deep hole.

All the power of the airplane would not pull him across to steady air. He fell. Just above the plateau, the downward current spread out and cushioned his fall with solid air again. He landed ten feet from the edge.

Although "every mountain peak for miles was echoing applause," Art was shaking. He said it was the first applause he ever received that did not interest him.[29] Mr. Franklin and his committee were ecstatic. They had not witnessed merely a flight, Art said, but "the most spectacular one imaginable!"[30] He had been in the air only eight minutes, but he had flown. He had actually been off the ground in an airplane, and it was marvelous to the Black Hills people.

Art had five more flights on the contract.

He staked his airplane to the ground so that the wind wouldn't blow it off the plateau during the night. He left a man to watch the plane, and he and the committee raced down the mountain in Franklin's automobile. While Deadwood celebrated, Art telegraphed Aimee.

The next morning, although there were some clouds swirling around the tops of the mountains, the space over the plateau was clear. The air current was flowing steadily down the valley so Art took off, rose a thousand feet, and made two circles and a short glide. It was a flight he enjoyed. As he came in to land, however, an enormous cloud covered the plateau. "It looked as solid as a rock."[31] Without time to swerve, the airplane headed straight into the cloud. Art was sure the plane would crash into pieces against some gray mass of stone. He could see nothing and could not tell whether he was flying straight ahead or sidewise. "It was a nightmare," he said.

Then came blessed daylight. "I gasped — unconsciously, I had been holding my breath all that time."[32] The plateau was beside him. He turned and landed without a jar. Again the crowd went wild with excitement.

In the afternoon, Art's flight was cancelled because clouds covered the plateau. He wasn't sorry. He told the managers that the next day, he would try to fly from the plateau to Deadwood and land on the field originally chosen for his exhibition.

That afternoon as a diversion, a party of businessmen gave Art a tour of the Trojan mines showing him "every process of gold mining, from the ore to the smelters." In the cyanide mill, Art saw a pan filled with a mass that reminded him of black mush. Stirring his finger in it, he asked what it was. It was gold amalgam — thirty-eight thousand dollars' worth of gold —ready for smelting. Quickly taking out his finger, he wondered if he had twenty cents' worth under his fingernail.

"I would like to see some of that when it's smelted," he said. The men answered, laughing, "Maybe you will, sometime."[33]

That afternoon, the weather was clear, and Art made a good start from the plateau and headed down the canyon toward Deadwood. With no place to land in between, he *had* to succeed. There were down currents that made the machine tip unsteadily. He rose to get better air. At a thousand feet, he felt the great waves of air from the mountain range strike. Half a dozen times, he flew into heavy downward currents, hit an air hole, and fell.

"I fought my way down to Deadwood safely," Art said. "I reached the little aviation field. Then I nosed the machine over for a long glide down to it. Eight hundred feet from the ground my engine stopped. I set my teeth, and volplaned. Only one thing saved me — the air was steadier in that little pocket in the hills. I held the machine right side up. It landed ten feet from the sheer side of the mountain."[34]

It was a spectacular flight. There were whistles, automobile horns, bells, and a total uproar, but Art was exhausted. "I just sat there in the machine."[35]

When he examined his airplane, he found the trouble to be in the gasoline tank. When he tipped the machine forward for the long glide, the gasoline did not cover the outlet, and the engine was starved for gasoline. That had caused the engine to stop.

Art decided he would cancel the rest of the contract and accept half the money. In the carnival, he met Mr. Franklin and asked to discuss the matter. Art was invited to the Business Men's Club. He found the rooms crowded. Someone took him into a corner to show him a picture, and when he turned around, he found they had lined up their chairs and were all seated, facing him. "I felt queer," Art wrote.[36] Mr. Franklin began the festivities. Art's account says, "My knees shook. He was making a presentation speech. I could hardly stand. Then he opened the box and pinned a gold medal on my coat. Everyone cheered. They called, 'Speech! Speech!' I could not say a word."[37]

The medal was made from the gold he had seen at the Trojan mine. They had smelted it in a hurry, raced it to the jewelers, and worked all night on it. It was inscribed, "To the first aviator in the Black Hills. From the citizens of Deadwood."[38]

It was one of the proudest moments in Art's life. They also gave him a check for $1,250.

That night he sent Aimee a telegram "a yard long."[39]

7

Not on Calhoun Street — 1912

Before leaving Deadwood, Art went to the jeweler who made his medal and bought a solid silver spoon for Aimee. He had it engraved with the name of the place and the date and put in a little leather box. Art said it was the first time he was able to send her a real gift and that mailing it gave him a great feeling. Finally he could be like other boys who gave little gifts to their sweethearts.[1]

Art mailed a check to Mills Aviators for the balance due on his new motor and still had two hundred dollars, more than enough to cover his expenses to Wellman, Iowa, his next scheduled exhibition. Standing on the back platform of the train waving at the crowds, Art saw nothing but success ahead — success and Aimee. He felt that he had proved he could fly, that he could earn money enough to care for Aimee, and that Mr. Cour would no longer object to their marrying.

The people of Wellman, Iowa, were celebrating a Farmer's Homecoming when Art arrived. Everything went right for Art, and he gave three exhibition flights. The field was good, air conditions fine, and his new motor worked beautifully. Art started his first bank account by depositing $600 from his earnings, and he sent Aimee another spoon.[2]

One disconcerting note, however, was a letter he received from Aimee. She asked that he send her letters in care of Art's mother instead of to her address because her father was still strongly opposed to her marrying an aviator. She didn't want Art's letters to antagonize him further. She wrote that she hoped by the time Art returned, her father would have a change of heart.

From Wellman, Art went to Kansas City where he gave an exhibition at Overland Park. It was an interesting flight because he used a skill he had learned on his first flight to New Haven, Indiana. At three thousand feet, he shut off the engine and glided down. The crowd thought they were going to witness a terrible and fatal accident. When Art landed safely, they cheered for five minutes.[3]

48

After Kansas City, Art flew at numerous county fairs and small carnivals. After a time, he simply listed the locations— Beauregard, Montana; Table Rock, Nebraska; Clifton, Kansas; Clinton, Montana; and "a dozen other places."[4] His life became one of catching trains and "struggling with small-town ideas of an aviator's needs." At Havelock, Nebraska, for instance, he was shown the field he was supposed to use: a vacant lot, 50 by 100 feet, surrounded by buildings. Art told them it would have been a bad field for a hot-air balloon.[5]

Throughout the summer, Art continued giving his flying shows, making about three hundred dollars in every town. As his bank account increased, the only extravagance he allowed himself was to send Aimee souvenir spoons. He said that he often had a hard time in the small towns, where he would have to show the jewelers how to make the spoon. Sometimes he was ready to leave before he got it. After a time, the first question asked on reaching a place was, "Where is the best jeweler?"[6]

On October 10, 1914, Art Smith gave an exhibition at the baseball park in Al Wertman's hometown of Auburn, Indiana. Sprightly red lapel tags were printed and sold in advance that stated, "I have paid to see Art Smith fly at Auburn, Indiana, Saturday, October 10. Money refunded if no flight."[7]

Seventy-eight years later, Teddy Walters of Auburn, recalled the event, as the "thrill of a lifetime." At age nine, Teddy cajoled his mother out of a quarter, ran

A postcard Art sent to his parents from Texas. Message reads: "Dear Folks, Got all the money here. Started off the street at the picknick [*sic*] grounds. This was taken just as I was getting up first time Friday. Gee, but this little machine flyes [*sic*] fine. Up Friday 17 minutes, 2,800 ft. Saturday 10 min., 1,700 ft. On to Marshall, Texas & Lawton. Write you tomorrow from Marshall. Art." Courtesy: James Wigner.

the full distance from his home east of town, paid at the gate, and got in where he could touch the flying marvel. "I would have died if I hadn't been able to touch that plane," he said.[8]

The crowd looked, touched, and marveled. Art took off, buzzed the town, looped another loop or two, and landed again. It could be repeated as often as it remained productive.

Willard Maxwell, a six-year-old from nearby St. Joe, Indiana, also saw Art's exhibition. Years later, he wrote about the experience in his memoirs. Poor weather caused two unsuccessful attempts to get the airplane back in the air before a final success. In spite of the day being "an unpromising day," townspeople turned out in large numbers.

At the appointed hour, Art's plane appeared overhead, executed its breathtaking turns and incredibly, settled onto the field. People paid twenty-five cents a ticket to enter the board-fenced baseball field where the Birdboy's Curtiss-type pusher biplane was parked. The tickets were printed, courtesy of two political candidates, and the Victor Joe Cigar Co., which by then was owned by Art's lifelong friend and mechanic, Al Wertman. The advertised candidates were H.O. Williams for County Recorder and John P. Hoff for Sheriff, as well as Victor Joe and National Speaker cigars.[9]

A number of aviation meets and competitions were scheduled in Chicago in early fall and Art wanted to participate, but to do so, he would have to cancel his Corning, Iowa, engagement. That contract would pay $850. It was a tough decision, but Art decided in favor of Corning. His airplane was old and had been in "more than sixty accidents."[10] If it failed in Chicago, he would have nothing. If he flew in Corning, he was assured of some pay. Every dollar he made would take him closer to home and to Aimee.

In Corning, the weather was clear and the air was steady; however, as Art started a spiral on his last flight, his

Admission ticket issued for the Auburn, Indiana, exhibition. Courtesy: Wertman-Stackhouse.

engine began to skip. Then his power failed. At the same time, a strong air current hit him. He was at two thousand feet. He nosed the machine over and glided down. When he landed, he discovered that one engine valve had broken.

While waiting for a new valve before heading to his next exhibition in Middleburn, West Virginia, Art went home for two days. Aimee and his mother met him at the train station.

Aimee was wearing a long skirt and had her hair "done up." She seemed so grown-up, he hardly knew her. "She was just the same girl, though, jolly and full of fun. We certainly were glad to see each other," Art said.[11]

Supper was festive with his mother bringing out jams and jellies. His father beamed and asked dozens of questions. Art showed them his bankbook and the medal he received in Deadwood. Afterwards, he and Aimee went for a walk. It was a lovely night, and he asked her to marry him when he returned from Virginia. Aimee had been lonely for Art and wanted to marry him, but she did not want to displease her parents. She agreed that she would marry Art if he could persuade her parents.

It was a hope.

The next morning, Art went to a jeweler's shop and asked to see solitaire diamond rings. The clerk showed him one for $30.00. Art asked to see finer ones. The clerk then showed him one for $40.00. Art then asked if he could see "a tray of your very best ones."[12] The clerk brought out a tray, and Art picked out the ring with the biggest stone. Taking off the ring from his little finger that Aimee had once given him, he handed it to the jeweler. "Cut the diamond ring to that size, right away," he said. "I will go down to the bank and get you the money. How much is it?"[13] The ring cost $200.

When he paid for the ring, he was the proudest boy in Fort Wayne. Leaving the shop, he planned to head for Aimee's house, but just outside the store, he ran into her.

He was so excited, he blurted out, "Oh, Aimee! Here's the ring!"

She gave him an odd look, then realized what he was doing.

"Oh, Art! On Calhoun Street!"

For a moment, Art thought she was going to cry, and he didn't know what to do. Then she laughed and put the box in her pocketbook. She wouldn't look at the ring or let him put it on her finger. "Oh, no! Not on Calhoun Street!" she kept saying. Art felt "any place" was romantic enough, but, he wrote, "Girls are different."[14]

Before leaving to fulfill his engagement in West Virginia, Art put the ring on Aimee's finger. The evening was bittersweet, however, for she then took off the ring and put it on a ribbon around her neck. She told Art she would wear the ring that way until he had spoken to her father.

It was hard to say goodbye.

In Middleburn, Art learned that his flight was to take place at Sisterville, a small town ten miles away from the railway station. His airplane was hauled from Middleburn to Sisterville on a wagon, and he followed on horseback.

The field was almost as bad as the one in Deadwood. It lay on a sloping hillside surrounded by wild mountain country. People had come long distances. As Art said, "Engaging a real aviator from Chicago was a big enterprise for that small town. I did not want to disappoint them if I could possibly help it."[15] He decided to attempt a flight, the last scheduled for the season. It was one he would not soon forget.

As he started from the highest point in the field, he ran the machine down the hill and rose just in time to clear the trees. He then flew up to a good height and came around in a spiral. As he was circling to bring down the airplane, the engine began to skip. A valve had broken.

He could not drive the plane upward with weakened power. He began to sink into a ravine, with trees on both sides and a brook in the bottom. There was no landing spot, either in the ravine or on the sides. He had to fly straight ahead. Art said that fortunately he was headed downhill, so he pushed forward on the controls to escape the branches of the trees. As they brushed his plane, "from every side birds flew out in panic."[16]

He roared through the gulch, curving and turning, desperately nursing the airplane. Finally, he came out into the main valley. It was below Sisterville. In order to get back to Sisterville, he tried to work the plane high enough to miss the houses. He barely skimmed over the roofs. "I dodged a chimney by no more than a foot, swerved around the little church steeple, reached the field, and landed. I did not go up again."[17]

Art headed home for the winter. At last he had money in the bank, good clothes, and his debts paid, including what he owed Senator Fleming. He bought presents for his parents, and he took Aimee automobiling and to the movies. In appreciation for what Mr. Streetor and Mr. Sprague had done for him, he arranged to give them an exhibition in their park and pay them well. He then went to the printers and to the newspapers. Because they also had helped him in his earlier days, he "gave them big orders for printing and advertising space. It was a happy time," he said.[18]

One challenge lay ahead for Art — Aimee's father, Mr. Cour. Although he spent each afternoon and evening with Aimee and asked her to allow him to speak with her father, she urged him to wait. She said that she was afraid her father would forbid her to see Art and explained that if he did, she would not know what to do. She begged Art to not push the relationship.

Art, however, wanted to marry Aimee immediately. He did not like waiting to talk with her father. Finally, he agreed that he would wait to talk with Mr. Cour until after his exhibition flights in Driving Park.

The advertisements had worked. Every ticket was sold. Art was scheduled to fly two days, Saturday and Sunday, and he had advertised a sensational program — spirals, glides, volplaning, and carrying a passenger. One of the boys was eager to make a flight, and Art had agreed.

Saturday was a cool, clear, autumn day, and the air was steady. The program started on time, and Art kept the crowd sitting on the edge of their seats for two hours. He flew in great circles, dropped from two thousand feet in swirling spirals, went up again, shut off his engine and volplaned down. He enjoyed every minute of the exhibition. The engine was running smoothly, the air was perfect, and he knew his mother and Aimee were watching.

It was a heady moment. When he landed to pick up a passenger, he looked for the boy who had wanted to fly and couldn't find him. Not knowing what to do and not wanting to disappoint the crowd, he asked several young boys who were on the field near his mother and Aimee.

Although he assured them that they would be perfectly safe, none volunteered. Then Aimee spoke up, "I'll go with you."[19]

The extra seat was all built and ready. In a moment, Art had Aimee seated comfortably. When the crowd saw what was happening, they stood and cheered. Art got in his seat and started his engine, and the airplane raced down the track. "Just before we rose, I saw Mr. Cour running across the field," Art said. "I had not thought of him, but it was too late to stop."[20]

The flight was beautiful. About two hundred feet up, he glanced over his shoulder at Aimee and she smiled at him. Art flew higher to five hundred feet, made a wide circle, and came down. The machine landed without a jar, he said. There was a tense moment, however, when Art got out of the plane. Mr. Cour was waiting, his face white. He took Aimee's arm and without a word, walked her off the field. Art knew then that he had made the worst possible mistake in taking Aimee as his passenger. The crowd, however, was delighted.

After Art put away the airplane, he went to Mr. Cour's house. Aimee came running when Art knocked, but it was Mr. Cour who met him at the door. According to Art, Mr. Cour was so angry he could hardly speak. Although Art tried to apologize for taking Aimee on the flight without his permission, Mr. Cour would not listen. Art tried to explain that he wouldn't let anything happen to Aimee, that he cared for her and her safety, but Mr. Cour was furious. Art then told Aimee's father that they were engaged and he planned to marry Aimee as soon as possible.

When Art said that, Mr. Cour replied, "Marry her! Great Scott, how old are you?"[21]

Art told him he was nineteen and that they had been engaged a long time. He also tried to tell Mr. Cour that he was flying successfully, making good money, and they wanted to get married.

Mr. Cour answered that the idea was "preposterous." He said Art and Aimee were too young. He argued that flying was "too dangerous," and he "would not consider such a marriage for a minute."

"You can't marry Aimee now; that's final," Mr. Cour said. "Get into some other work, and come back in three years, and I may think about it."

Mr. Cour seemed to have no idea how long three years was, Art said. "There was no use arguing with him. I got up and went out."

Aimee was on the porch. When Art told her what her father said, she began to cry. "Oh Art! What on earth will we do?"

"We'll get married, anyway," Art said.[22]

Their conversation was interrupted. Mr. Cour came out and told Aimee she had to go into the house. Art went home to think.

The next day, Sunday, was to be Art's second exhibition at Driving Park. He went to Aimee's house to take her to the show. Mr. Cour was seated on the front porch reading the Sunday newspaper. The two again talked for a long time. Mr. Cour was firm, but fortunately, he wasn't angry. He argued that Art and Aimee were too young to marry, and that in any case, he would not allow his daughter to marry an aviator. He said Art would not be able to give her a home, that he could be killed at any time, and that she would never have a moment free from anxiety. Mr. Cour said that he liked Art "very much," and that he did not know of anyone "he would rather have Aimee marry if I would give up flying and wait three or four years."[23] Art had to leave for the park. Mr. Cour said he would bring Aimee to watch.

Again the weather was perfect for a flying exhibition. The air was clear and steady, and again for nearly two hours, Art gave his hometown crowd a sensational show. He did spirals, dips, and volplaning. The spectators cheered. He could see them throwing up their hats and jumping up and down. When he landed to take a passenger, they continued to cheer steadily. Aimee was with her father, waving from the grandstand.

Art's mother and father were on the field, beaming with pride. This time, Art asked his mother if she would fly with him. She suggested he take his father. His father was delighted. Art led him over to the machine, got him comfortably seated, and showed him how to hold on. Then Art got in and started his plane.

It was a wonderful moment. The young aviator and his father rose to about two hundred feet and circled the field. Passing the grandstand, Art saw something fluttering by his shoulder. Looking back quickly, he realized his father was waving to the crowd. Although his father could not see them, he knew where the grandstand was. Seeing his father beaming and enjoying the flight, Art flew higher and higher. When he passed a thousand feet, he glanced back. "He looked happier than I had seen him in months," Art said.[24] Art nosed the airplane over into a vertical dip and came down. They had been in the air nearly ten minutes. His father was enthusiastic. Art said he had never seen his father look so animated.

"It's great, Art! It's great!" he kept saying. "If I could I would build one myself and fly in it!"[25]

After the show, one of the boys helping Art as a "mechanician" was busy pushing the plane back into its tent. The boy said, "I suppose, now the season's over, you want the airplane taken down for the winter."

"No," Art said. "I may need it again."[26]

He then instructed the mechanic to put on new control wires and a new set of valves early the next morning and to fill the plane with oil and gasoline.

8

Elopement — 1912

That evening Art went to Aimee's house. He was still excited about how well his Fort Wayne exhibition had gone. Mrs. Cour said that Aimee was out with her sister and wouldn't be back until late. Aimee's mother had always liked Art, but Art could see she agreed with her husband about preventing their marriage.

Art returned home and spent the evening talking with his parents. He thought about how they had married young, and in spite of their hardships, had a good relationship. He entertained them by telling about funny experiences he'd had that summer, and he also told them about an offer he had received from the Kirkham factory in Savona, New York, to teach aviation in a school they were starting. He was undecided as to whether he should accept it or sign with the Mills Aviators for another season.[1]

Later that evening, he tried to telephone Aimee and was informed that she had gone to bed. For an entire day, he had not been able to talk with her.

In the night, however, the telephone rang. It was Aimee. She told him that her parents were planning to send her away.

Art was incredulous. "Where? When?"[2]

She said that her father planned to take her east to visit her aunt, and she would be gone all winter. Her parents thought it best to keep them apart for a while. She also told Art that her parents would not think of letting her marry anyone for three years. If she still wanted to marry when she was twenty-one, they promised her they would consent.

Art's answer was direct. "The only thing we can do is elope."

Aimee said they couldn't elope in Indiana because the law would require her father's consent. Nor did she think they could get to another state without his finding out.

55

"We'll elope in an airplane. Nothing can catch that," Art said. Then he asked, "Aimee, are you game?"[3] She was. But, she explained, the elopement would have to take place that week because her father planned to take her east the following Saturday.

Art said he would arrange everything.

The next morning, Art worked on his airplane and made sure everything was in order. He put in a new set of valves and tested the airplane thoroughly. He carefully planned the trip. They would fly to Hillsdale, Michigan, seventy miles north of Fort Wayne. It was the nearest point where they could be married quickly without Aimee's parents' consent.[4]

On Thursday night, Art called on Aimee. When he knocked, she answered the door. She slipped out with Art before anyone saw her. As the two walked down the street, Art told her that everything was ready. He asked her if she could get away and come to the airfield early on Friday.

She said she could. She explained that her parents were watching the trains for fear they would elope, but they had not thought of the airplane. They talked together for a minute, then Aimee's mother called her. As Aimee left, she assured Art she would be at the field on time.

The next morning, October 26, 1912, Art once again tested the plane, and this time, he found something wrong with the propeller. He telephoned Aimee and told her to wait until noon. Knowing the train for Hillsdale left the station at 11:30 A.M., he felt sure Aimee would be able to slip away because her parents wouldn't be watching her closely after that time.[5]

Art called his friend Al Wertman, who by this time was married and living in Auburn, a little town north of Fort Wayne, and told him he would be leaving in about an hour. He told his parents he was going to Driving Park to put a new cylinder in his engine. Will "Wimp" Peters, his mechanician, would help.

Aimee was on time. She carried a paper package with a new dress in it, and she insisted on taking it with her. Art said, "She said she did not mind eloping in an aeroplane, but she declared she would be married in a new waist."[6]

Art fastened her package to one of the wings. He put Aimee in the extra seat and wrapped her in one of his big red sweaters. Then he fastened her skirts around her ankles with tire tape.

Will Peters later said that "Miss Cour had innocently asked to go along and did."[7] Will saw the two off on their biggest flight, but not until Art had a photographer record the event for posterity.[8]

In a field on the outskirts of Fort Wayne, Art taxied his machine and slowly lifted off. His plan was to follow the tracks of the Lake Shore Railroad to Hillsdale.

The engine ran smoothly with an even roar. It was a lovely fall day, and the few white clouds in the sky seemed motionless. The weather was warm and mellow, and the air was steady. Art said the airplane rose like a bird. Below them, a light haze over the countryside made everything beautiful. [9]

In order to talk with each other while they flew, Art had made a speaking tube four feet long with an improvised megaphone attachment at each end. He said his mechanician had been wild with curiosity about the contrivance all week wondering how it would work. As soon as Art leveled the machine, he called to Aimee through the tube. Unfortunately, she couldn't hear a word. The roar of the engine made his invention useless.

Holding the machine with one hand, Art turned and looked at her. She smiled. She was rosy and happy in his red sweater. He leaned still farther back and kissed her.[10]

They hoped to reach Hillsdale by one o'clock and be married before anyone in Fort Wayne missed them. Six minutes into the flight, however, around Huntertown, Indiana, the engine began to skip badly. Realizing that he couldn't fly it farther with any degree of safety, Art looked for a place to land. Seeing a smooth meadow ahead, he nosed the airplane over and landed. To test the engine, he and Aimee pushed the airplane across the field and braced the front wheel against a fence so that it wouldn't run away when he started the propeller. When he tested the valves, he found one of them was broken. They were about fourteen miles from Fort Wayne.[11]

Art was convinced Aimee would want to back out of the plan. Instead Aimee said, "Certainly not." Then he asked if she would like to go by train. Again she countered that she wasn't going to quit because of one accident, and, besides, they had started by airplane and if they went by train, her father might overtake them. "There never was another girl like Aimee," Art said, "She was game to the very core."[12]

They walked to a nearby farmhouse where Art telephoned his mechanician and told him to bring another valve and to say nothing to anyone. Then Art telephoned Al Wertman. In their excitement, neither Aimee nor Art had eaten breakfast, and it was past noon. They bought some bread, milk, and a few apples from the farmer and went back to the meadow. They spread the red sweater on the grass in the shade of a big tree and shared a picnic.[13]

About half past two, Al Wertman and Bill Fitzsimmons, who a few years later also would become a pilot, arrived bringing parts. Art said that at first Al was amazed to find Aimee with Art, then he began to laugh. Al said, "I bet you two are eloping to Hillsdale."[14] Art and Aimee made them promise to keep their plans secret, and Art asked Al to bring his wife to Hillsdale that evening and join them for a wedding supper.

In a few minutes, the young men installed the valve. Around three o'clock, Art and Aimee once again got into their seats. With no fuselage to speak of, the plane was simply a framework of pipe and steel wires with a seat and steering wheel in front and, two feet behind the pilot's head, a big radiator that cooled the engine. The wings were of varnished silk stretched over a framework of spruce. A propeller in the rear pushed the machine forward. It was patterned after the pusher-type biplane invented by Glenn Curtiss in 1908, and Art was familiar with its every part. With Al waving his hat from the meadow, the only worry Art and Aimee had was that somehow her father might have been alerted. They felt pretty sure, however, that the speed of the airplane would get them to Hillsdale before the next train could arrive.[15]

Art soon soared to an elevation of 1500 feet and flew over brilliant autumn woods and yellow fields. They saw Lake James in the distance, and "it looked like a silver patch among the trees." Pointing to a bird circling a hundred feet below them, Art laughed and wondered if it might be the same bird they'd watched four years before.[16]

Both Art and "Honeybug," as he affectionately called Aimee, were cramped and numb from the cold wind, but both were happy. Art said he reached back and took Aimee's hand. They were excited, but she could not have been comfortable with her head jammed against the sharp fins of the radiator.

Art was familiar with the terrain around Hillsdale because he'd given an exhibition there the previous June. He watched for the small lake east of the town. When he saw a tiny flicker of silver fifteen miles away, he turned the airplane toward it and squeezed Aimee's hand. Whether or not Art had alerted news reporters, no one knows for sure, but on the ground, telegraph operators at the ten railroad stations along the route clacked out to each other the exact times the biplane passed overhead. The railroad operators marveled over his speed, as Art made the final fifty-five miles in exactly one hour — nearly a mile a minute. The young couple hurtled along the line, buzzed Auburn as a salute to Al (even though he wasn't yet home), and flew on.[17]

On the edge of town, Art headed for a large, smooth field that was a part of the Hillsdale College campus. West of the field, he leaned against his controls to turn the machine in that direction. The ailerons didn't work. A flange of a pulley had broken, and the control wire was jammed. The ailerons, the small flaps that balance the airplane, were useless. Without them, the gentlest puff of wind would mean a wreck. One reporter theorized that Art probably wasn't able to handle the controls well because his feet and hands were numb from the cold.

Art said, "It was the most terrible moment I ever spent in an airplane."[18]

He gripped the wheel. The plane tipped to the left, and instantly he pushed to the right. He nosed the machine over and down. Art said that on a curve, flying faster, an airplane rises, so when he pushed to the right, the curve threw the left plane up again. The machine righted itself, hesitated, and tipped to the right. Art then swung to the left. His swing leveled the wings for an instant, and then they tipped over the other way. Art curved back. There was no time to choose a landing place, and there was one chance in a hundred that he could keep the airplane right side up and land anywhere.

The wings tipped again, and Art caught them just in time with a curve in the opposite direction. Below them was a bare field. The airplane was swinging in half circles over what seemed like hard earth. They were coming down fast, and Art did his best to keep the wings level until they reached the field.

He swung the machine to the right, to the left, then to the right. Short of the landing field, the plane flipped over. The cornfield, instead of being hard, was soft, and the plane's front wheels mired in the ground. The airplane turned completely over and smashed. Both Art and Aimee were thrown free.[19]

Reports differ about who saw them first. The *Hillsdale Daily* reported that there was a party of well-wishers waiting and watching in excitement, and that those spectators rushed to the crash site to find the "Smash-up Kid" nearly buried in the loose soil and his betrothed lying unconscious fifteen feet away.[20] Art, however, said a driver delivering a mattress for a furniture store was the first person to reach them. In any event, the driver raced over, calling for help. He and his helpers thought the two were dead. They put Art and Aimee on the mattress.[21]

Four hours later, when Art recovered, he was in a hotel room. One newspaper reported, "they took the couple to the Smith Hotel," then quipped, "they DO have Smiths in Hillsdale."[22] Al Wertman was nearby and frantic. Art was wrapped in bandages "from head to foot." When Art asked about Aimee, he was afraid he would be told that Aimee was dead. Al told him Aimee had been conscious several times. Art demanded to see her.[23]

Art was put in a rocking chair and pushed down the hall to Aimee's room. She was conscious, but "white as her pillow. Even her lips where white, and there were bandages around her head and over her cheek."

Seeing Art, she smiled and said, "Hello, Art."

"Are you all right, Aimee?" Art asked.

Her answer was reassuring. She said that she certainly was.

Someone in the room asked if they still wanted to be married.

"Do you, Aimee?" Art asked.

"Of course, if you do." She held out her hand.

Art's plane after the disastrous 1912 elopement flight. Courtesy: Allen County–Fort Wayne Historical Society & Museum.

Art said that someone pushed his rocker nearer to her so he could take her hand. The chair struck her bed. "She screamed and fainted." Art said that he supposed the jar was too much for both of them because then, he fainted too.[24]

About an hour later, Art recovered consciousness. He was lying on the bed beside Aimee. The room was full of people, and the minister was there. Aimee had recovered sooner than Art, and someone had given her papers to sign. Art said that he wasn't sure who found the county clerk at that hour or who got the license or who paid for it.[25]

Art and Aimee had hoped the Rev. W. F. Jerome, an Episcopal minister, would perform their marriage, but he was unavailable because he was addressing a women's suffrage meeting in nearby Litchfield, Michigan. Someone secured the services of the Rev. C.E. Thomas of the Presbyterian Church. The substitute minister asked them if they were ready, and they said they were. It was said that Art was able to stand for the ceremony, but that Aimee could not. Reverend Thomas "united them as man and wife," with Al and Lucille Wertman as witnesses.[26]

Dr. W. H. Sawyer, a professor at the University of Michigan, and Dr. R. F. Green, who were attending them, joined in the ceremony along with a nurse. One of the doctors placed Aimee's hand in Art's, and the ceremony proceeded. Also present was Congressman J.M.C. Smith of Charlotte, Michigan, who happened to be in Hillsdale at the time.[27]

The reporter for the *Hillsdale Daily* wrote, "At eleven that night, as they lay together on a bed of pain, Art and Aimee were married."[28] After the vows were said, Congressman Smith gave the couple a coffee urn.[29] The doctors urged everyone to leave because Aimee and Art were suffering from their cuts and bruises and needed to be kept quiet.

Art said, "I did not hear much of the ceremony." While the doctors were talking, in walked Aimee's father, her mother, and my mother."[30] But a number of newspapers reported that it was not until Sunday night at 8:20 P.M. that their parents arrived. They had been met by Will Peters and were taken "to the children's suite of rooms." When the door opened and "in walked Mrs. Alexander Cour and Mrs. James Smith,"[31] Art and Aimee stopped their talking and laughing. It was an emotional meeting. Art and Aimee's parents were so glad their children were alive, they forgave them.

The citizens of Hillsdale were excited that Art and Aimee had selected their town for their historic elopement and would not hear of the young couple leaving without a proper celebration. A committee was formed to plan a party. Wrote one reporter, "Every man, woman, and child in Hillsdale was a friend of Smith's."[32]

Art and Aimee's elopement was historic — recorded as the world's first aerial elopement. Many years later in 1989, Larry Massie retold the *Hillsdale Daily's* October 28, 1912, event. Art Smith, "a twenty-year-old stunt pilot from Fort Wayne, employed by the Mills Exhibition Company in Chicago, yearned to do something no other aviator had ever done"— elope using an airplane. Because of the number of airplanes Art had crashed and wrecked, it was no wonder that the Cours didn't want their nineteen-year-old, "pretty and fashionably plump" daughter "cavorting around the skies with the Smash-up Kid."[33]

The *Hillsdale Daily*, however, said that the bride's parents didn't hear about the marriage until the next morning, and "wired their forgiveness to the happy couple," urging them "to return by train and leave their former means of travel" in Hillsdale.[34]

Art said that when Aimee's parents arrived, "Mr. Cour walked in and went straight to Aimee and tried to find out how badly she was hurt. His voice shook so that he could hardly speak."

Aimee said, "We're married, Papa; don't be cross." Then she began to cry.[35] Art said he had never seen Aimee cry before, and he tried to sit up to console her but a doctor put his hand on his forehead and he couldn't. So relieved was Mr. Cour that Aimee was unharmed, he said, "It's all right; it's all right."[36]

The Cours had brought their family doctor with them. Art's mother and the Hillsdale doctors got Art into the next room and held a conference about his condition. The doctors wanted to give Art a hypodermic, but Art didn't want it because he was afraid he would go to sleep before he heard what the Fort Wayne doctors had to say about Aimee.

It took them a long time to decide. Finally, one came in and announced that "the muscles of the young lady's back are badly torn. She also has a sprained ankle and a dislocated shoulder, but she will get well." He was stern and seemed reluctant to tell Art that Aimee would get well.[37]

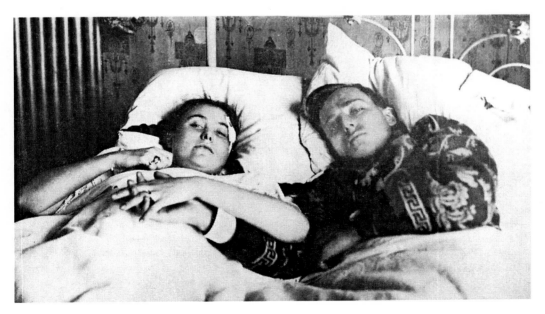

Though bandaged and wracked with pain, newlyweds Art and Aimee nonetheless posed for wedding pictures the day after they said their vows. Many of the photographs were printed on postcards and sold to souvenir hunters. Courtesy Allen County–Fort Wayne Historical Society & Museum.

Art was given a hypodermic and he went to sleep. When he woke up, he was informed he had bruises and a badly sprained left ankle and leg and had barely escaped a serious concussion of the brain.[38]

Aware of the value of publicity, Art arranged for a reenactment of the ceremony for the purpose of having souvenir postcards made. By that time Al and Lucille Wertman had left, so Art conscripted two strangers to pose as witnesses for the benefit of the photographer. The photograph shows the newlyweds bandaged and wracked with pain, holding hands and lying in bed. It was a fake wedding photograph that delighted the public but disgruntled Lucille. Hubert Stackhouse, who knew the Wertman family, commented, "Lucille was always a bit huffy the rest of her life about that picture."[39]

There was no hospital in Hillsdale, a community of about five thousand, so the Smiths stayed at the hotel for three weeks. By then, Art was up on crutches. Aimee traveled back to Fort Wayne on a cot in a train baggage car. Before she left, however, she told reporters, "I am not the least bit afraid to fly with Art, but I do not expect to do so again."[40]

Her father, somewhat reconciled to the marriage, would not allow them to stay anywhere else except at his house while in Fort Wayne. Art said, "He has never been altogether content with my being an aviator, but he has not actively opposed it except once — the winter I built my machine for fancy flying."[41]

Two weeks later, while Art was still on crutches, one of his friends insisted that he accompany him downtown. In front of the jewelry store where Art bought Aimee's ring, his friend stopped and pointed to something in the window. There Art saw a beautiful diamond-set gold medal engraved with an airplane. Art's friend then told him that the citizens of Fort Wayne had made up a subscription list and bought the medal and that it was going to be presented to Art.

Art said he was so overcome that he could hardly wait to get home and tell Aimee about it. It was an unforgettable moment.

9

Hometown Celebrity — 1913

A week later at a mass meeting in Temple Theater, the medal was formally presented to Fort Wayne's "Birdboy." When Art was invited to the grand presentation, he insisted on having Aimee present, so the family turned a taxicab into an ambulance and took her. "The whole population of Fort Wayne was in the street cheering while we carried Aimee across the sidewalk." The crowd followed the couple into the theater and cheered again. "We were in a box, Aimee surrounded by pillows, and I with my crutches, so pleased [that] I did not know what to do."[1]

Art said he knew that he would be asked to give some sort of speech, so all week he and Aimee had worked on one. "It was a fine speech," he said, "but when the city attorney came out on the stage and said I was a hero and my home city delighted to honor me, and then handed me the medal over the edge of the box, I forgot all I meant to say." Never at a total loss for words, however, the charismatic young aviator managed to thank them all. "It was the proudest moment of my life," he said, "there in the box with my wife beside me, and all Fort Wayne proud of me because I had at last succeeded in flying. It was good to see Dad's face, too, and Mother's."[2] It was one of Art's best memories.

Expenses while he and Aimee were hurt, however, had eaten up most of Art's bank account, and Art needed to make money immediately. He began considering several attractive offers from a number of booking agencies to give some straight flying exhibitions.

Looping-the-loop had never been done in America at that time, but Art had read about Aldophe Pegoud doing loop-the-loops in France. He was eager to experiment "along the same line" and do "fancy flying," as stunt flying was termed. He talked it over with Aimee, but she was unwilling for him to try it. Even if she had agreed, Art would not have been able to do fancy flying because his plane was damaged. It had been completely wrecked in the elopement flight. Had it not been wrecked, it still would have been impossible for Art to do stunt flying because fancy flying demanded a different kind of machine. The project of rebuilding his plane took most of the winter.

In the spring, Art and Aimee headed out on a second exhibition tour. The tour was an adventure. The honeymooners traveled through all the states where Art had flown the previous year, visiting little towns in Missouri, Nebraska, Arkansas, and Texas. Again Art gave an exhibition in Kansas City. In the big towns, they lived in the best hotels. In the little towns, they roughed it. "Aimee is the jolliest of companions," Art said. "Things never look so blue that she can't find something to laugh about."[3]

It was a wonderful summer for the Smiths. The young couple not only saw the country but also different lifestyles. Art talked about some of those places. For instance, Norden, Nebraska, was located twenty-five miles from the railroad station, and Art and Aimee were driven the whole distance in a buggy drawn by "a poor, gaunt livery horse." On their trip, they passed five little sod houses. Norden had offered to pay $650 for Art's flights. When they arrived, they were amazed to find the town had only one hundred and five inhabitants, but all that night "people poured into the town" from remote areas. Some came on foot, others on hayracks, farm wagons, horses, and mules. Some traveled nearly a hundred miles.

After marrying Art, Aimee (or "Honeybug," as Art affectionately called her), often accompanied him on his travels. Courtesy: Wertman-Stackhouse.

"I gave them my best work," Art said.[4]

After Norden, the couple traveled to South Dakota. Between engagements, Art took Aimee to see Deadwood, where he had been so royally treated the previous year. Before they had gone three blocks from the train station, someone recognized Art.

"After that, the town was ours," Art wrote.

Aimee and Art were treated as celebrities by the people in Deadwood. Art showed Aimee the plateau from which he'd flown and the mine that had furnished the gold for his medal. They left the town on a special train, especially arranged by the citizens so that he could spend more time with them before leaving for his next exhibition.[5]

For the first time since the couple eloped, Art took Aimee up in the airplane when they were in Carthage, Illinois. They stayed in the air fifteen minutes, and it was such a beautiful flight that Art said he hoped Aimee would be inclined to change her mind about letting him try stunt flying.

When French parachutist and aviator Aldophe Pegoud looped-the-loop in September of that year, Art read everything he could find about Pegoud's technique. Art was determined that he could master the stunt. That night, again Art brought up the subject of fancy flying. He explained that they had made enough money to pay for a machine designed especially for stunt flying and they also had enough in the bank to meet expenses until he learned how to loop-the-loop. Once he learned to loop-the-loop, he would be able to make even more money. He told Aimee that he already had experienced the principle of looping-the-loop, and it was one that had saved him in his two sidewise falls. He explained that the same principle would make aviation safe when it was understood and recognized. "A principle of mechanics never changes," he said, "it can always be depended on."[6]

Aimee's answer was predictable. She laughed, then said that "she must be like a *principle* then, for she had not changed. She did not want me to risk fancy flying."[7]

Art was aware that, like his wife, many people had the wrong idea about fancy flyers. People considered fancy flyers to be merely circus performers risking their lives for money until something went wrong and they were killed. Art thought otherwise. In his opinion, stunt flyers "are those who do the real work in aviation. There is no value in breaking records—long-distance records, altitude records, and speed records—until the plane has been proved practical."[8]

Meanwhile Art gave exhibitions throughout Illinois, after which the young couple traveled to Arkansas for a number of exhibitions, then turned north. Late that fall, Art and Aimee finished the season with an engagement in Durant, Oklahoma. While in Durant, Art read about Lincoln Beachey who had started flying the loop-the-loop in America.[9] After Art's flight that day, he talked with Aimee about Lincoln Beachey and the loop-the-loops. "I did not ask her opinion," he said. Instead, Art told her he would not attempt fancy flying as long as she objected, but he knew she would tell him when she changed her mind.

That night, she woke Art up and asked how badly did he want to do fancy flying. He told her. "And is it safe—you're sure of that?" she asked.

ART SMITH, WIFE
AND
"BABY"

A typical souvenir postcard. Courtesy: Wertman-Stackhouse.

"I certainly am," was Art's reply.

"Well, you always have done what you said you would. If you want so much to loop-the-loop, I am willing," she said.[10]

They caught the first train home. Art didn't waste a minute before beginning work on the new plane. He also continued his studies, undertaking the study of fancy flying as he had studied straight flying. "I thought out every principle involved," he said.[11]

The two perilous falls Art had survived — at his first benefit and at the one at Beresford, South Dakota — helped him. On both occasions, he had figured out what had saved him and how it had been done. In both of them, he had literally fallen sidewise, with apparently nothing to save him, but before he struck the ground, the machine had swung into a vertical dive. By pulling back on the controls, he had swung the airplane into safe flight. Those two close escapes gave him the key to safety in aviation — the rudder. "It acts like the feathers on an arrow, and pulls the machine into a head-on fall," he said.[12]

He built his new plane with that principle in mind. The rudder was twice the size normally used, and it was mounted fully three feet from the body of the machine to give greater leverage. Every part of the plane was two or three times heavier and stronger than usual, in order to withstand the greater strain. The building of his new plane continued during the winter, and by the time it was finished, the bank account was running low. Again, Art had to make money immediately.

DeLloyd Thompson had followed Lincoln Beachey doing fancy flying through-out America, and in May 1913, Thompson gave an exhibition of fancy flying in Fort

Wayne. Art watched his work in the air and saw looping performed for the first time. After the show, Thompson and Art talked. Thompson inspected Art's new machine, then he said that "the plane would not do the work."

Art argued, saying Thompson was wrong. "She will not only do straight looping; she will do the sidewise roll."[13] Thompson said Art was crazy and that he would kill himself if he tried it that way. Art's propeller wasn't working well, so he didn't want to attempt doing a loop for Thompson. Art said that Thompson left Fort Wayne still declaring that his theories would not work.

The next week, testing a new propeller, Art climbed to two thousand feet in the air and attempted his first loop. Twice the engine stopped in the air, and he dropped hundreds of feet before making a complete, end-over-end circle. He was ecstatic. While testing his theories, he had looped his first loop.[14]

As his confidence and reputation grew, Art explained his theories to interested people and asked them to consider questions such as, "What good does it do to fly up to twenty-six thousand feet, if when you come down a gust of wind at one hundred feet will wreck the machine? What is gained by making a speed of one hundred and twenty-five miles an hour, so long as a disabled engine means death to the aviator?"[15]

Then he would tell them that stunt flyers demonstrated that aviation was safe. "Before we began work, a certain degree of tilt to the planes was dangerous," he said. He then explained the following principle.

> Two degrees farther and the aviator was gone. I am proving every time I fly...that when the machine tilts those two more degrees, it is possible to let it roll on over and still land safely. I am proving it not once, but hundreds of times, under all air conditions. I am proving that nothing — nothing — can happen to a sound airplane in the air which will kill the aviator if he keeps his head and handles his machine according to definite principles.[16]

Art believed that fancy flyers not only tested the limits of aviation, but that their contributions were valuable. "With the principles established by fancy flyers we can now attack problems of speed and altitude with the knowledge that the aeroplane is practical and safe," he said.[17]

With Art's successes and growing fame, it didn't take long before he was booked for acrobatic flying throughout the summer. He tested his theories over and over, and each time they proved airworthy. He and Aimee traveled throughout the Middle West, entertaining and exciting both young and old. In Lawton, Oklahoma, a fifteen-year-old boy named Wiley Post witnessed one of Art's exhibitions and was so impressed, he was inspired to a life in aviation.[18]

Born in Grand Plain, Texas, Post was a farmer before he became an aviator. He suffered an eye injury while working at oil drilling in 1924, and with part of his insurance money, he bought an old airplane and learned to fly. In 1930, he won the Los Angeles–Chicago air derby, and the next year, with Harold Gatty, flew around the world. In 1933, Post became the first man to fly alone around the world in the record time of seven days, eighteen hours, and forty-nine minutes.[19]

For Art and Aimee, the summer of 1913 was a blur of exhibitions, travel, fun, and success. Art bought Aimee a little runabout, and the couple often motored from town to town, shipping the airplane by train. One unsung hero during those times was Art's uncle, Edgar E. Johnson. After each exhibition, Johnson had to disassemble the airplane, pack it and ship it to the next exhibition, and then reassemble it again at the next location. Johnson must be given credit for doing this task over and over again, without seeking the limelight or objecting when Art garnered all the publicity.[20]

For the first time in his life, Art felt free from pressing financial worries. He bought his father and mother a comfortable home with ten acres of land to replace the house they lost, and he showered Aimee with gifts. But again, Art postponed competing for the big prizes. To build an airplane for altitude or speed work would cost from $5,000 to $6,000, and because of its special constructions, such an airplane wouldn't be usable for other work. High-speed machines, for instance, required wings of such small surface they would hardly permit volplaning. Although money was no longer a concern, Art did not want to invest in an airplane that could be used for only one type of flying.[21] Moreover, Art was in demand for barnstorming, first with the Mills Aviators and then, in 1915–1916, with the Lincoln Beachey air circus.

Art Smith, "the Smash-up Kid," became known as the "Bird Boy of Fort

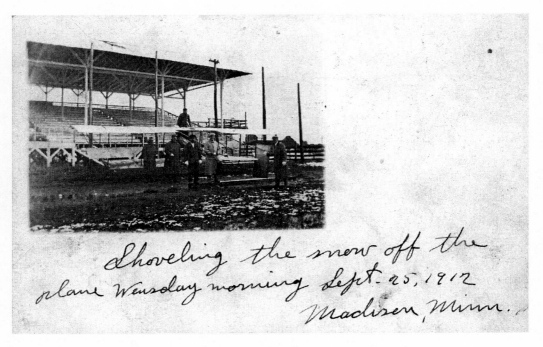

Shoveling the snow off the plane Wensday morning Sept. 25, 1912 Madison, Minn.

Postcard from Art to Al Wertman. Courtesy: Wertman-Stackhouse.

Wayne."[22] Not only was Art their hometown hero but a national celebrity. Newspapers published articles about his tours and exhibitions, his medals and honors, the money he was making, and his opinions about aviation, politics, and technology. The story of how his family mortgaged their home for $1,800 so he could buy materials for his first plane and how Art had succeeded in building an airplane after many mishaps, was told and retold.

10

Fame — 1913–1914

Newspaper headlines touted Art Smith as an intrepid, daredevil aviator, and people flocked to see his exhibitions. Photographers liked taking pictures of him because he was extremely photogenic. His glowing smile and youthfulness charmed the public. Reporters liked to interview him because he was talkative and friendly. One commented that whereas the famous stunt pilot Lincoln Beachey was "quiet and morose," Art was just the opposite.[1] They celebrated Art's adventurous spirit, and quoted his observations and comments. People liked being around Art. His charisma attracted young and old, men and women.

Art played his role well. People are not interested in me, he once said. They are interested in my flying. "When the crowd on the ground holds its breath, or shrieks, or wildly cheers, it is not because Art Smith is playing a dangerous game with Death up there in the clouds. It is because over their heads a man just like themselves is mastering the dangers of an almost unknown element. My triumphs are not personal. They are new triumphs for all mankind."[2]

These words were probably the most modest comments Art ever uttered. Perhaps Art was being humble. Or merely clever. Either way, whether it was his engaging smile, his amiability, his daring flying, or a combination of all three, Art Smith was a sensation.

Art and Aimee regularly sent postcards to Al and Lucille Wertman. One card postmarked January 1913, reads, "Dear Friend, Everybody is happy here. I am anxious to get to Auburn again. Hope it will be soon. We will get there but can't say when. Mrs. Honeybug Smith."[3]

Another card reads (with the original spelling intact), "Hello Al, Swell weather today. Fine flying. Made 21 flights today. 2nd time down the field went down to Daylors and stoped in soft ground. Rest of trips stoped meadow. Highest about 100 ft.

Two postcards that Art sent to Al Wertman. Courtesy: Wertman-Stackhouse.

Look like a payday befor long. Art." Yet another card reads, "Dear Old Pal, This is a new craft. How dose look? Gee! But it flyes fine. Have had wings up 1,000 feet and brought him down in a 3 turn and then he can run it himself. Am awful busy and will write you later. Yours, Art."[4] Sometimes the message was not limited to news about the airplane. "Dear Friends, I am resting real easy today but Art is sick to his stomach and has a headache. We want to go home before next week this time. Sorry we don't write more often, but it is so tiresome. Write to us. Mr. & Mrs. Art Smith."[5] Even at the pinnacle of his success, Art stayed in touch with his family and friends, sending letters, photographs, and postcards.

Because Al and Lucille Wertman were Art and Aimee's best friends, it wasn't difficult to get Art Smith to arrange an exhibition in Auburn, Indiana, between his other bookings. The news and events surrounding his Auburn exhibitions serve as one example of what happened in hundreds of towns and cities throughout the Midwest. Articles and headlines advertised upcoming shows, theorized about weather conditions, and presented apologies when shows had to be postponed.

On October 12, 1911, the Auburn newspaper carried the following headline: "Fort Wayne Aviator May Fly to Auburn."[6] Art had made his first successful flight to New Haven the previous Tuesday, and nearby towns were abuzz with excitement. It wasn't until 1914, however, that Art actually gave an exhibition in Auburn.

On October 5, 1914, a news article announced, "Contract for Art Smith is Signed." The sub-headline read, "Fort Wayne's Birdboy Will Fly at the Athletic Ball Grounds in Auburn, Sat. Oct, 10." The contract stated that Art Smith "shall make five loops, and unless such a feat is accomplished, the terms of his contract will not have been complied with." In return, Art required a guarantee of $300. His request was granted.[7] He cancelled an exhibition in Hamilton, Ohio, for October 10, in order to accommodate his Auburn friends.

THE DIVE IN HOME.　　ART. SMITH, MILLS AVIATOR.

Postcard from Art to Al Wertman. Message: "Well I guess we showed 'em up some didn't we. Gee, but it was a great ride. Wish I could have had you along. Art." Courtesy: Wertman-Stackhouse.

The Automobile Dealers Association in Cincinnati had contracted Art to give an exhibition flight, so the plan was that Art would travel from Ohio to Angola, Indiana, for the Angola district fair (Angola is about fifty miles north of Fort Wayne and about twenty miles north of Auburn). Although Auburn wanted Art for their district fair, a clause in the Angola contract stated that Art would not fly "at a nearer spot [to Fort Wayne] than Angola" until after the fair. Consequently, Auburn scheduled Art for the following week, Saturday, October 10, 1914.[8]

The Auburn newspaper ran huge ads about the Birdboy's upcoming show. The Auburn City Band would provide music and not only would Art demonstrate his flying skills, he would give a talk to explain his plane. Admission tickets would be twenty-five cents. Because of the weight of his machine, Art let it be known that he would take up no passengers.

Merchants distributed 10,000 bills (posters) in a thirty-mile radius of the town. Sponsoring merchants ran ads for the big day, offering discounts and shopping inducements. Adolf J. Schloss, a dry-goods store, offered ladies' ready-to-wear items and rugs. Nine by twelve rugs that generally sold for $22.50 would go for $19.95. E.O. Little Jewelers advertised jewelry, Edison phonographs, and Victor talking machines. The F.J. Nebelung Company offered seal, plush coats for $25.00 and Buster Brown school shoes from $1.50 to $3.00. Schaab & Brothers Company would sell fine men's suits regularly priced at $18.00 for $14.75.[9]

To entice spectators to see the exhibition, the article gave a long account about how as a boy, Art had dreamed of building and flying an airplane, and took no lessons, yet because of his determination and inventiveness, had succeeded. The story detailed the events surrounding the elopement, Art's relationship with the Cours, and facts about Art's family. In short, it was the sort of article, like hundreds of other clippings about a celebrity, that people cut out and saved in their scrapbooks.

In Angola, however, Art had an accident with his plane. "Birdman at Angola Had Narrow Escape When Levers of Craft Failed To Work," read the Auburn headline.[10] Some five thousand people at the Angola fair were disappointed. The news also disappointed the Auburn merchants because the Angola accident made it necessary to postpone the Auburn show. Art stopped by Auburn on Friday evening and discussed the situation with members of the Loyal Order of Moose, his Auburn sponsor. Repairs had to be made before he could fly again, and there was nothing that he could do except postpone the show.

"Flying Exhibition Must Be Postponed," read the news headline.[11] The merchants put out a block announcement that read: "Owing to breaking of machinery, Smith, the Birdman, COULD NOT make his flight last Saturday. Arrangements were immediately made for his appearance here on October 17th. Special inducements offered for last Saturday will therefore hold good for next Saturday. We hope to see an immense crowd."[12] The accompanying article told how Art Smith had broken his motor at Angola and wouldn't be able to fly in Auburn until October 17.

The following week the merchants and sponsors again featured the event. Again there were huge ads announcing the Birdboy's show. "In every respect the plans for the flying exhibition by Art Smith Saturday are in accordance with those announced for the delayed event last week," a prominent member of the Loyal Order of Moose Lodge announced in the newspaper, adding that "close to thirty officers would be on the grounds to preserve order." The article went on to say that "Mr. Smith needs no introduction to Auburn people, many of whom have seen him in sensational flying stunts either at Fort Wayne or on the opening day of the Angola fair last week."[13] The plans were that the Auburn event would be "in the nature of a general gala day, which the merchants of the city have termed 'Art Smith Day.'"

On Friday afternoon, Art Smith arrived in his plane. He landed in the park and secured the airplane in front of the grandstand. "The descension marked the first in the annals of the city that a flight had been made there," stated the paper, and it gave youngsters the thrill of a lifetime. Art left two men in charge of the plane until the following day, and police made sure that no one could enter the park.

The exhibition was scheduled for 3:00 P.M. Extra policemen were on hand. On Saturday morning, the weather was nice, but by noon clouds darkened the sky. Even so, thousands jammed the ballfield and streets, housetops and buildings to see the aviator perform. Art got into his airplane and ascended. He was in the air only two minutes when he was forced to descend on account of a broken rocker arm.[14] He promised to return the following Saturday. Purchased tickets would be good for the next exhibition.

The following week the newspaper carried the feature, "Smith Desirous of Flying Here Again."[15] Despite the previous "great disappointments," Art was quoted as saying that "He Will Fully Redeem Himself." The article went on to explain that on the previous occasions, weather or an accident had prevented him from flying in Auburn. "All doubt relative to a return date for Art Smith for Auburn was cleared away at 1:30 Wednesday afternoon when the signatures of Mr. Smith and the members of the Loyal Order of Moose committee were affixed to a contract whereby the Birdboy will appear in Auburn Saturday afternoon."[16]

The article explained that Smith "would show the spectators ... an exhibition that will be even more thrilling than the one planned for last Saturday afternoon." It went on to comment that Smith "appreciates the fact that his misfortune here Saturday was a keen disappointment to the people of Auburn and vicinity and he says he will fully redeem himself Saturday afternoon and will give them an exhibition that will equal if not surpass, any he has given heretofore."[17]

Before his show, Smith would "lecture on the subject 'The Practical Good of Looping the Loop.'" The talk was designed to "put to flight the fallacy that there is no practical side to the sensational loop-the-loop, the accomplishment of which has been one of his big cards this season."[18]

The news article also detailed how Smith and his wife and mechanicians stopped in Auburn while en route to Hillsdale for a Thursday and Friday exhibition. According to the newspaper, "The Birdboy is negotiating for a number of flights in the south this winter and an agent will endeavor to book him for a number of exhibitions in Cuba. He has at this time extra parts for his biplane and should a similar accident to that of Saturday befall him next Saturday, he will be fully capable to cope with the situation."[19]

Another article commented that "the young aviator … neither drinks, smokes, chews or uses profane language." It pronounced Art Smith to be twenty-three years of age, and added that from "an early age, he showed a great disposition and desire to try difficult feats of daring, as he is absolutely fearless and he has great stick-to-itive powers and no obstacle is too large for him to undertake and he always succeeds."[20] Although Art didn't smoke, Al Wertman had a cigar manufactured that he named "The Hi Flier," and he used Art Smith's picture on the wrapping.

When Art did fly, the newspaper gave the following account.

> For fifteen minutes, Art Smith, of Fort Wayne, the famous young aviator, thrilled hundreds of spectators by his sensational loop-the-loop, spirals, side rolls, upside-down flying and figure eights at an altitude from eight hundred to eighteen hundred feet over the Auburn Athletic baseball grounds Saturday afternoon.
> Smith said a few days ago "The third time's the charm," and those who witnessed his flying Saturday will agree that he was right.
> A sharp breeze fanned the ballpark and spectators in overcoats and familiar winter togs stood patiently expecting at any minute to see the biplane leave the ground. At 3:04 their patience was rewarded.
> Smith's mechanician started the propeller to whirling and in a twinkling of an eye the biplane and its young master were skipping like a bird across the grounds in a northwesterly direction. He left the ground at a point only about three hundred feet from where he started.
> For several seconds, the machine climbed higher and higher and when an altitude of about eighteen hundred feet was reached, Smith made three successful loops.[21]

When his exhibition was completed, Art flew to a point nearly over the west fence of the grounds and at a height of about a thousand feet, "and en route to this point and during the first few seconds after his arrival, turned eleven loops, flew upside down for a considerable distance and negotiated a number of pretty side rolls and figure eights."[22] One spectator who had witnessed the Birdboy at Cincinnati and had another time seen the work of Beachey said that in his opinion, "Smith is the greatest American aviator in the business."[23]

The people virtually swamped Art the moment he climbed from his machine, and not the least enthusiastic of the throng was Aimee Smith, who witnessed the latest accomplishment of her husband from an automobile that occupied an advantageous position inside the board fence enclosure.

The newspaper reported, "Smith alighted at nearly the exact spot from which he started. When the machine was taken to the crates, Chester Hodge, of the Loyal Order of Moose Lodge, announced that Saturday night Smith would be made a member of the Auburn Loyal Order of Moose as a token of the esteem in which he is held by the members of the Auburn lodge."[24]

"Smith has in no way been responsible for his failure to fly at Auburn as at first announced," wrote the reporter. "He felt more keenly than anyone else, it seems, the disappointment Auburn people, and out of town spectators as well, had suffered. He was anxious to give as good an exhibition here as possible and this he did."[25]

Notwithstanding the fact that the famous young aviator had disappointed the crowds on two previous Saturdays, a large crowd attended that afternoon to see the flight. The weather was bad, and that kept many away who feared that Art might not make his flight. The ballpark was filled with spectators and on all the buildings of the city there were large numbers out to see the flight. Then the journalist added, "To say that all were immensely pleased with the flight was to say the least."[26]

11

The San Francisco Exposition — 1915

In celebration of the completion of the Panama Canal and in commemoration of the four hundredth anniversary of the discovery of the Pacific Ocean by the explorer Balboa, the United States held a world's fair. After several years of campaigning and negotiating, the contest to be the host city was between San Francisco and New Orleans. President Taft chose San Francisco. It took three years to construct the six-hundred-and-thirty-five-acre fair, which opened with great fanfare in February of 1915. Its attractions dazzled visitors until its close on December 4. Thousands of people came to see displays and exhibits of agricultural and industrial innovations, contests, concerts, flying exhibitions, and the Tower of Jewels, which was forty-three stories high. Much of the activity took place in the area called the Marina, over which aviators thrilled spectators with daredevil acrobatics and flying exhibitions.[1]

Lincoln Beachey was one of the many featured attractions. He was probably the most popular hero of his times, and his flying exhibitions cost enormous sums of money. A consortium of one hundred newspaper reporters declared Lincoln Beachey to be "the eighth wonder of the world."[2] Beachey's impact on aviation cannot be underestimated. He developed many of the basic fundamentals of flying. He was the first person to fly upside down, the first man in America to loop-the-loop, the first to tail-slide on purpose, the first to figure out how to pull out of a spin, the first man to fly over hundreds of American cities, and the first to point his machine straight down and drop vertically until maximum velocity was reached. His fame and achievements inspired thousands of people to invest their lives in aviation.[3]

Art could not have imagined that someday newspapers would call him "the comet of the air" who "out–Beachied Beachey."[4] That accolade came to Art in 1915,

The Tower of Jewels at the San Francisco Panama Pacific
Exposition. Courtesy: James Wigner.

shortly after Beachey died when his plane crashed at the Panama Pacific Exposition. When Beachey's plane crashed, he drowned near the Golden Gate. Suddenly the Exposition committee needed to find a replacement aviator.

At the time, there were only three American aviators other than Art who were looping the loop: DeLloyd Thompson, "Charley" Niles, and a Chicago girl named Katherine Stinson.[5] Beachey's death gave Art the opportunity to take center stage, and he "took San Francisco by storm" with his spectacular flying, skywriting, and his night shows. His flying talent commanded the sky with displays of fireworks, colored lights, and blazing trails of smoke. One account stated, "Art Smith [is] now absolutely acknowledged as the world's greatest aviator.

Beginning at the Panama Exposition an almost unknown boy, he quickly surpassed Lincoln Beachey by a series of stunts so daring that they threw Beachey's flying in the shade."[6] Art proved that he was equal to the challenge of entertaining the Exposition visitors.

The story of how Art became an international celebrity at the San Francisco Exposition is included in his autobiography, *The Story of Art Smith*, a souvenir booklet, edited by Rose Wilder Lane. The booklet, published in 1915, is subtitled *The Autobiography of the Boy Aviator*, and it appeared as a serial in the San Francisco *Bulletin*. As Art's flying captured the imagination of the public, the ninety-four-page booklet, which cost twenty-five cents, sold like hotcakes.

On August 13, 1915, the San Francisco *Bulletin* stated, "The story of Art Smith, the wonderful young aviator, which was printed in serial form ... two months ago ... has sold with such extraordinary rapidity that by far the greater part of the edition has been already exhausted." The book was "available at all book stores here and across the bay."[7] It documented Art's version of how grit and determination contributed to his success. Wrote one reporter, "It has assumed its place as the classic narrative of aviation. No book ever written sums up so well the thrills, the dangers, the failures, the problems, the triumphs, the romance of the aviator's life."[8]

In twenty-nine short chapters, Art told how he first became interested in flying, worked to build a plane, survived several crashes, and ultimately succeeded. Again playing the role of a prodigy, he said, "I celebrated my twenty-first birthday by signing my San Francisco contract ... just five years since the time I had watched the bird flying over James Lake. I am flying now over the domes and towers of the world's greatest Exposition."[9]

Art explained in his autobiography that earlier that year, E.A. Moross gave a flying exhibition in Fort Wayne, and after the show, he and Moross talked about night flying using an illuminated machine. Both were excited about the possibility, but it was Art who began working on the idea immediately. He made several night flights with the machine outlined in lights. Then it occurred to him to use fireworks in order to leave a blazing trail of light across the sky. He tried the technique and found a Chicago firm that would make a special brand of fireworks suitable for the purpose.

"Using them, I first began the spectacular night flights which I am doing at the Exposition," he wrote.[10] Getting the contract for the Exposition depended on those night flights, because it was hard to convince the Exposition people by letter that he could do the things he claimed. He was given two trial night flights by the Exposition committee to prove himself. His manager, Billy Bastar, insisted he could do it. Both were confident that his flights would be an irresistible argument to win the contract.

Art first met William Bastar in Chicago when Charley Whitmer, who was sailing to Russia to teach the Czar's officers how to fly, introduced them. Art said that when he walked in Billy's office after the stenographer took in his card, Billy asked, "Where's Mr. Smith?" He had taken Art for a messenger.[11] "I did not look old enough to fit his idea of Art Smith, the aviator. It was an awkward moment," Art said.[12] The two, however, became good friends, and it was Billy who encouraged Art to try out for the San Francisco show.

The Exposition Committee set Art's trial schedule: a day flight on Saturday, April 3, and his night flights on Sunday, April 4. Art and Billy reached San Francisco late Friday night, but the plane didn't arrive until Saturday. Then he and Billy discovered that the schedule had been changed. The night flight was to take place that very evening, and Art's special fireworks had not arrived. "It was an anxious day," Art said.[13]

According to Art, the narrowest escape he ever had in the air occurred on his first flight in San Francisco. The machine was wrecked that night, but he and Billy managed to conceal that fact.

But before that happened, while the machine was being set up, Art and Billy spent the day scouring San Francisco looking for fireworks. Late in the afternoon, they found some among the Exposition supplies. "We wired them to the airplane in great haste. I was concerned about the air conditions here, and spent most of the afternoon watching the clouds for indications of them."[14]

Art with mechanicians and business associates at the Panama Pacific Exposition. William "Billy" Bastar was Art's manager. Courtesy: James Wigner.

The flight was to take place at 11:30 P.M. When Art reached the field, a high wind was blowing. It looked like a bad night in the air. He said, "The machine was all ready, the fireworks connected. I looked it over carefully and started."[15]

He drove the machine down the Marina for the first time and lifted it into the air. Everything depended on that flight. "Close to the surface," he said, "the currents were swift and uncertain, but I flew through them, watching the machine carefully. I passed a thousand feet, fifteen hundred, two thousand. Then I encountered a curious thing — the air was warm. Just when I should have felt the first keen cold of the upper air; the wind against my face was almost hot. The air was still too, with the close, oppressive stillness of a hot summer day on the ground."[16]

Over San Francisco, Smith discovered, the air conditions were different from other places. "The surface air, warmed by the sun, rises above the cold ocean breeze, and lies like a great calm lake, about two thousand feet from the earth. It is always still, not a current disturbs it. The surface winds over the sea do not reach so high."[17]

It seemed unreal to be flying at two thousand feet in warm air. The machine flew steadily upward. He flew with every bit of skill he had, aware that he was flying directly over the spot where Lincoln Beachey had had his fatal accident the previous month. He remembered the opinion among eastern aviators that the extraordinary air currents above the Golden Gate were responsible for Beachey's fall.

After he passed twenty-five hundred feet and neared three thousand, the time came to do the loops. Art pressed the button to start the white glare of the magnesium lights. They responded instantly. He then dropped the machine into a vertical dip.

Two hundred feet below, he pushed the controls into the first loop and touched the button for the trailing "comet tail." The airplane went end-over-end in a perfect circle, curving up through the propeller draft with a great jolt. Art then dropped into the vertical dip and touched the second fireworks button.

Art said he heard a terrific explosion as the machine fell forward into the second loop and as the engine stopped for a fraction of a second before picking up again. The machine quivered and a piece of the framework hurtled through the air, barely missing his cheek. He threw all his strength on the controls. The machine responded and swung around and up again. Just before it came right side up, there was another explosion. He heard it above the roar of the engine. The fireworks were wrecking the airplane. He had to land.

He nosed the machine over and down. "Right beside me," he said, "I heard another sharp report. Fire blazed in my face. My coat was in flames." He held the machine steady and came roaring down.[18]

Art was wearing goggles that protected his eyes. He held his breath. Ten feet from the Marina, there was another explosion. The plane shook violently, but Art was able to land.

Tearing off his overcoat, Billy ran to the plane and flung it over the blazing machine, smothering the flames. Art said, "I beat the fire from my clothes."[19]

Art was convinced he had blown all chances with the Exposition officials. In his autobiography, he said the trailing edge of both wings was blown off clear to the windbeam and the supports were shattered.

There is no proof that the situation was that dramatic; however, Art believed that if the fireworks had exploded, nothing would have saved him. He was angry with himself because he had gone into the air without first testing the fireworks. Instead of the Roman-candle types, which he generally used, these were giant cannon crackers, twelve inches long. Wired tight to the framework of the machine, they had exploded like bombs.

He blamed himself, saying there was no excuse for such recklessness. "An aviator should take no evidence but his own positive knowledge of every part of his machine. I had taken the word of another man for the safety of the fireworks."[20] He went home leaving Billy to talk with the Exposition officials.

The Exposition committee offered Art a contract. In San Francisco, Art's loop-the-loops were a sensation. Beachey's flying had been a huge attraction, but nothing was as thrilling as Art's daring feats, especially his night shows. Night after night, crowds came to watch Art's flying. Photographers were never satisfied with one picture. Newspapers ran picture after picture of Art doing aerial loops, dips, and death-defying night displays.

Long articles were devoted to how Art accomplished his daredevil flights, especially his loop-the-loops that were captured on film by photographers. Art said, "A good illustration of my whole life is in the way I first looped-the-loop. It was after I had got through most of my early difficulties with no money, no teachers, without ever seeing another aeroplane, against every opposition, I had built my first machine and learned to fly in it."[21]

"I had made a success in straight flying," he said. "I was testing a new propeller.

It worked all right. So I turned the machine upward and flew straight up into the air. There was a bank of clouds above me — it was a gray day, down on the earth. I flew up through them, and came out into bright sunlight, about two thousand five hundred or three thousand five hundred feet high."

He said that from below, the clouds were gray and forbidding, but looking down on them, they were fleecy and shimmering like white silk. "They curled and shifted under me. The sky was bright blue overhead, full of sunshine. I decided to practice a loop."[22]

He pushed the wheel over hard. "Just as the plane stood on edge, the engine stopped."[23] The only thing that keeps a machine off the ground, he explained, is air resistance under the horizontal wings.

"When the engine stopped, half a ton's weight of wood and iron, with me strapped to it, fell like a dropped brick. Six hundred feet below I managed to catch the air with the wings. The momentum of the fall gave me a little speed. I swung the machine upward again, on this speed, preparatory to volplaning back to earth. As I tilted her upward, the engine started. I swung up into the blue sky with that engine humming along as sweet as ever."[24]

As he swung around in a circle above the clouds, he tried to figure out what had happened. Nothing was wrong with the engine. After a time, he decided to try it again. "With all my strength I pushed the wheel over. The machine stood on edge; the engine stopped. Again I dropped." This time, he was ready. "I caught the support of the air again in about four hundred feet, swung upward — the engine started."[25]

After the second time, he flew back and forth until he thought through the problem. "When the machine is on end the gasoline in-take fails. The engine stops. The only thing that starts it again is that upward swing." He reasoned that if the machine picks up on the upward swing, all he needed was sufficient momentum to turn the machine completely over and swing her upward. "That was it — the momentum!"[26]

He flew five hundred feet higher, pushed the machine over into a vertical dip, and dropped clean. "When I judged the momentum was great enough," he said, "I rammed the wheel over with all my might. The machine turned completely over in a beautiful curve; the engine picked up, and the plane made its loop."[27] His theories were sound. After he performed his first loop for the crowd, he said, "I flew about in great curves in the clear air, and under the sunny sky. I was happy."[28]

Since he had been booked all that summer for fancy flying exhibitions, he had many opportunities to test his theories. "They proved good," he said. "They are now so thoroughly established that no aviator need wreck his machine no matter how bad the air may be, if he keeps his head and the control wires hold. An aeroplane will not fall more than three or four hundred feet before it comes into a position where skillful work will save it."[29]

Art told his admiring San Francisco public that the day he first experimented with his loop-the-loops, no one had known he'd gone up to practice doing them except Aimee. She had watched the machine turn edgewise, roll over and over in side-

Spectacular night scene of Art's flying over the Panama Pacific Exposition. Courtesy: Greater Fort Wayne Aviation Museum. Photographer Don Goss.

wise curves, and tumble down through the clouds and land. He said when he landed "without a jar," Aimee ran across the field, and "we hugged each other like two kids." Art then commented, "It is a great thing for an aviator to have a game wife like Aimee."[30]

Asked how he came to use special effects, Art said the previous year, when he and Aimee were talking about the advanced construction in machines that stay on the ground, such as a motorcycle that makes a speed of one hundred miles an hour with a fifteen-horsepower motor as compared to the airplane that makes only sixty miles with its eighty horsepower motor, he told Aimee that he predicted a time when there would be planes with better engines, with propellers that would allow a proportion between speed and power similar to that of the motorcycle. "The possibilities of aerial navigation cannot even be imagined now," he said. Art said that as he and his wife talked about aviation, Aimee, "who saw the poetry and romance of things quicker than I do," suggested "a picture of the night sky, full of airplanes brightly lighted." Art said her idea was appealing and it intrigued him.[31]

Perhaps aware that the first telephone connection made between the United

States and Japan had occurred that same year (1915),[32] Art said, "Some day, it [flying] will be no more thrilling than using a telephone. Within a short time —five years per- haps— licenses for airplanes will be issued as licenses for automobiles are issued now. Then a change will begin in human life — a change so tremendous we can not even imagine it today."[33] His comments were visionary. He theorized that aviation not only would change world commerce, but also world politics.

Foreign governments invited him to give flying exhibitions and offered him opportunities to join their air forces. Certainly they wanted to showcase his superb flying, but more than that, they were anxious to learn as much as they could about aviation techniques. As Art's fame grew, important political figures of the nation courted his favor and asked to be photographed with him.

Art enjoyed the limelight.

12

King of the Air — 1915

For four months Art's aerobatics, death spirals, and night flights with phosphorus fireworks captivated the crowds. He was called "a boy aviator," "a beardless wonder," "an intrepid daredevil," and "the most daring aviator of all times." Reporters seemed hard-pressed to find enough superlatives to detail how Art "electrified" the crowds as "the greatest entertainment feature" of the Exposition. They wrote, "His aerials feats have astounded aeronautical enthusiasts"; they headlined him as "King of the Air."[1]

Some accounts describe how the crowds reacted. "Strong men gasped, women swooned, and motherly types scolded," but everyone wanted to shake his hand, talk to him, or be photographed with the Birdboy.[2]

One reporter wrote, "The story of Art Smith's life, brief though it has been, would make the tales of the old time yellow-back literature turn a sickly green with envy."[3] Other reports described his feats. One eyewitness gave the following account:

> On his opening day at Frisco, Smith eclipsed anything ever seen here. Looping the loop was a small part of his act. Rising, he drove his bronze-colored biplane into the teeth of a thirty-mile gale far out over the Golden Gate. Suddenly he seemed to lose control. His machine tumbled over and over, backward and forward. Twenty-one times he looped the loop. The crowd gasped. Then he thrilled everyone in earnest. He dropped his biplane to within 1,000 feet of the ground. Suddenly it caught its side to the wind. A gust caught it and the crowd groaned. It seemed that he was about to meet the fate of Lincoln Beachey. His machine tumbled about in the wind like a box kite with the string cut. Over and over it flopped and rolled. Then it suddenly righted itself, and the aviator, with a long graceful glide, landed within ten feet of the starting point.[4]

Art did not disappoint the crowds. Reporters wrote about "the slim young man who was about five feet six inches, not at all as you would picture the man whom you have heard to have done such marvelous feats in a heavier-than-air machine at 2,000 to 3,000 feet altitude." They talked about how Art would "rock his machine like a boat in a swell as he ascended to the height where his gyrations were fairly safe," and they raved about his illuminated skywriting. When the Shriners were guests of the Exposition, "he out-heralded himself when spectators were able to follow the words he traced, in letters of fire in the air, that spelled 'Shriners.'"[5]

News accounts of Art's San Francisco daily successes appeared not only in his hometown paper, but in papers throughout the Midwest. His hometown newspaper reported that Duke's Clothing Company had received photographs of Art, which were displayed in their store. "One of them is an enlargement of the birdboy, the face itself showing about two feet high and the hand as large as a man's head. He is seated in the machine, and wears his million-dollar smile that won't come off. The other is a picture of Art flying over the Tower of Jewels, and the reflection of his machine is shown in the lake below."[6]

Even though he was a star attraction and a celebrity, Art kept in touch with his family and friends back home, not only keeping them abreast of his activities, but also staying involved in their lives. The following telegraph from the Exposition grounds was written at the height of his public acclaim:

A telegram to Mr. and Mrs. Al Wertman Auburn, Indiana. YOURS CARDS RECEIVED AIMEE AND MYSELF. JOIN IN SENDING OUR VERY BEST WISHES AND HEARTIEST CONGRATULATIONS OUR SINCERE HOPES ARE THAT BOTH LU AND MIKE ARE STILL DOING WELL. AM FLYING MOST EVERY DAY AND OFTEN AT NIGHT AND WILL BE THINKING OF YOU MORE THAN EVER. ART 7:18 A.M.[7]

Art demonstrates the controls of his plane to an admirer at the Panama Pacific Exhibition. Courtesy: Greater Fort Wayne Aviation Museum. Photographer Don Goss.

Meanwhile, throngs in San Francisco paid to catch a

glimpse of him. Others watched from rooftops. One account states, "Tot Watching Smith Fly Falls to Death." Three-year-old Zilda Bagani and some other children had climbed to the roof of a building on Filbert Street to watch one of Art's afternoon flights. In her excitement, Zilda plunged three stories to the ground and was instantly killed.[8] The news article about the little girl's death is included in Art's scrapbook along with articles and clippings about his exhibitions.

Back home in Indiana, the city of Fort Wayne carried the headline "Pride of Fort Wayne Given Ovation," and the Commercial Club and the Fort Wayne Rotary Club made plans to honor Art when he returned.[9]

Meanwhile, the advertised program for the Exposition was that attractions would begin at 9:30 A.M., when people could view the Liberty Bell, which on August 3, 1915, was on display in the Pennsylvania building. On that day, at noon, the Boston Band performed in concert at Fillmore Bandstand, followed by an organ recital in Festival Hall.

At 1:00 P.M., the Exposition Orchestra performed at Old Faithful Inn, and at 2:00 P.M., the U.S. Marines held a dress parade in front of the Tower of Jewels. The Ford Motor Band performed at the same time at the Palace of Transportation. The Philippine Constabulary Band played at the Court of the Universe at 2:30 P.M., while the United States Marine Band performed at the Palace of Liberal Arts.

At 3:00 P.M., the featured attraction of the day was Art Smith's airplane flight from the Marina. While Art prepared to fly, the Marimba Band played at the Guatemala Pavilion, Buddha's day ceremonies were held in the Palace of Education, and there was *tea dansant* in the ballroom at the California building.

In the evening at Old Faithful Inn, the Exposition Orchestra performed before Pi Kappa Alpha day ceremonies. The Boston Band and the Ford Motor Band also gave evening concerts. The evening attraction was the illumination of the grounds at 7:45 P.M.[10] Afterwards, there were more band concerts and exhibitions.

Art's evening flights were given press coverage unlike any other performance. The July 30, 1915, *Oakland Inquirer* caught the fantastic performance on film, a journalistic first. The *pièce de résistance* was of Art flying his plane at night. It shows the night sky and a descending ribbon of smoke attached to a gnat-like plane, finishing the flight at low level over the blazing lights of the Exposition. It carried a large photograph with the following headline: "Remarkable Night Picture of Aviator Art Smith Machine and Display Caught by Camera Man." The accompanying caption reads: "This remarkable night photograph shows Art Smith and biplane in a spectacular midair gyration. It is the first successful attempt of the camera man to register on a photoplate, both the stream of fire Smith leaves behind and the machine in which he flies, together with the wonderful lighting of the exposition. Photo critics agree this is one of the best pictures yet secured."[11]

The photograph was made from a single timed exposure, and it made history. The camera shutter was open during the period of flight, the first photographic record of an airplane's course ever made on a single negative.[12] The picture was carried in newspapers around the world. It was said that the photograph was a fitting tribute to the best aviator of his kind.

Remarkable photographic record of an airplane's course made on a single negative. Courtesy: Wertman-Stackhouse.

One of Art's stunts was called the "dippy twist," termed by *The San Francisco Examiner* as "the most spectacular, daring and difficult feat ever attempted by the Exposition aviator." The dippy twist, wrote the reporter, "began at a height of three thousand five hundred feet and descended to fifteen hundred feet as Art made seven perfect loops, finishing out with a flash-like-cork-screw spiral. The biplane spins like a top as it bores downward with the speed of a falling meteor."[13]

Nothing such as Art's flying had ever been seen. "When Smith alighted from his plane, the crowd was in an uproar and guards were brushed aside. There was a mad rush made for Smith and his biplane, flowers were tossed on the aeroplane, on Smith's baby auto, and on Smith himself."[14] One question they wanted answered was, what were his sensations during his mad twist?

Art said, "The earth seems to become a jumbled mass of color. While making the swift revolutions, I lose all sense of location. I try only to keep account of the number of twists. Too many would cause me to lose consciousness. I never make over eight." He explained, "Eight are enough. A few more would have a tendency to make the spectator search for 'sea legs.'"[15]

Art said that he invented his dippy twist in Clarinda, Iowa. He explained that he made his first twist while he was flying over the state insane asylum in Clarinda. "Because it was over the asylum, the newspaper men christened it the 'dippy twist.'"[16]

Another stunt that delighted the crowd was when Art dropped a bomb that exploded about three hundred feet from the ground, sending forth hundreds of tiny colored lights.

It was at the 1915 Exposition that a long, very close friendship developed between Billy Parker and Smith. According to Parker, "Art Smith was positively the finest exhibition flier who ever lived."[17] In a phone conversation that Bob McComb had with Billy Parker in April of 1969, for information about the "Birdboy of Fort Wayne" for the *OX5 News*, Parker said, "Art took his plane to three thousand feet and dove it straight to the ground, pulling out at the last instant, flying level for a moment and then entering a steep climb. Name Beachey and Smith, and you've named them all."[18]

In spite of all the attention Art received, he remained loyal to his old friends and chums. He and Aimee sent messages via postcards and telegrams. Most of their messages were similar. They wrote that although they were enjoying their celebrity status, they missed their friends and hoped to see them soon.

In California, Art was toasted and entertained. One account states that he was "welcomed by 75,000 friends."[19] He was photographed with lovely women. He led the grand march at a local ball. He visited orphanages, and he gave a blind boy the thrill of his life when he helped the boy feel the contours of his airplane with his fingers.[20] He became an ardent Santa Clara baseball fan and on one occasion threw

Art waves to crowds during a parade at the Panama Pacific International Exposition in 1915. Courtesy: Allen County–Fort Wayne Historical Society & Museum.

out the opening ball and helped umpire the game. He was featured with a Miss Medina Mervin at a fund-raiser at Olympia Club Minstrel Show.[21] He demonstrated his machine to movie personalities Miss Marguerite Snow and Francis X. Bushman.[22] In a ceremony, he dropped a wreath from his airplane to the memory of Lincoln Beachey.[23] He loved to race "baby cars" [racers] and acquired an Auto Association Racing Driver's Register. He was often photographed with admirers around his cars. The day's attraction on Thanksgiving Day, in addition to his flying exhibition, was that "Miss Marie Templeton, an ardent speed enthusiast," would be his "mechanician." On the given day, she changed a tire on the racer, as the crowd cheered.[24]

He teamed with the Grain Dealers as a Santa Claus for their annual Christmas tree for orphans.[25] He dropped coupons from his airplane which could be redeemed for candy and toys. Charlie Chaplin wished him "Success and Good Luck,"[26] and Charlie Foy signed his photograph, "To a real fellow and a swell pal, Art Smith, from Your Pal."[27]

The newspapers focused on Art, but from time to time they would write about him from his wife's perspective. "Does Mrs. Aviator Get Excited When Art Smith Goes A-Soaring," was the subject of one article. The response given was that "she does not, but she's interested."[28]

Aimee was good-natured and sociable and most of the time enjoyed watching and seeing her husband with reporters and city officials. One photograph in *The San Francisco Examiner* shows Art being escorted with his wife to the Exposition. Art is seated on the back of a convertible waving his cap to the crowds while Aimee, dressed in a fashionable hat and fur coat, looks out at the crowd from her place in the back seat. The accompanying article stated that "all along the line of march, women waved handkerchiefs, men and boys united in crying 'Hello Art,' and all joined in hearty applause."[29]

Aimee willingly posed with her husband for photographers; however, she often found herself on the sidelines. She began spending time visiting or talking with Art's mechanicians. With them, she said she felt more comfortable. She said they were more realistic about Art's celebrity status than the adoring San Francisco crowds that clamored about him.

Art was quoted and photographed, and he was toasted and entertained in some of the finest homes of the city. Dignitaries, beautiful women, and ardent fans read everything they could about the personable young celebrity, including the fact that he received one thousand dollars for an afternoon flight and fifteen hundred dollars for an evening flight.[30] It was no wonder that he was approached by businessmen and showmen eager to discuss investment ideas or have him sign contracts for flying exhibitions. He used many of those occasions to discuss American military air-preparedness.

But with celebrity status came problems Art could not have imagined.

Women admirers flocked around Art, and newspapers began to link Art's name with a number of them; however, most accounts support the fact that Art simply was enjoying the notoriety of being a celebrity. He was photographed with beauty queens, driving his Willys-Knight Touring Car, and posing for ads. He was offered as much as $30,000 for an exhibition. Women requested that he take them on airplane rides. Some asked to fly with him in the Exposition. He took his mother up for her first flight instead.[31]

As the summer's flying engagement came to an end, the city of San Francisco planned a gala celebration. Sunday, August 8, 1915, was designated "Art Smith Day." One newspaper lamented that "in less than eighty-four waking hours," the young aviator, who for four months "has thrilled the people of this city by his loops and dives and twists, will have folded his tent like the Arabs and as quietly stolen away, leaving only a memory."[32]

Cartoons also celebrated his four-month suc-

A well-dressed Art Smith prepares for a flight. Courtesy: Wertman-Stackhouse.

cess. One reads, "He's A-Leaving Us." It shows a larger-than-life, smiling Smith wearing a crown of Olympic laurel leaves, holding a suitcase in one hand, an airplane tucked under one arm and his souvenir booklet under the other. A dapper-looking man wearing a coat marked S.F. (San Francisco) stands waving his hat across from Smith, saying, "Good Luck to you, Art, you've done fine!"[33]

An "Art Smith Testimonial Fund" was established to honor the slim boy aviator, and a *Chronicle* article pronounced, "He's going away next Sunday, and he shouldn't have to leave empty-handed." Headquarters for the fund were set up on the mezzanine floor of the St. Francis Hotel and at the Great Northern building with James F. Kerr and Robert Edgar Long handling the project. Joining them in planning an appropriate honor were Senator James D. Phelan, Mayor James Rolph, William H. Crocker, Augustine Post, W. N. Moore, Horatio Anasagasti, Charles Cole, Blythe H. Henderson, Major-General Arthur Murray, Rear-Admiral Charles F. Pond, J.R. Barker, and Father D.J. Kavanaugh.[34]

To mark his last day, Art announced that he would perform three flights instead of two. One would occur at five o'clock, one at five-thirty, and one at eleven o'clock in the evening. For each flight, he would include a variation on the loop-the-loop that he had modified and fly the "falling leaf" stunt, a thrilling effect. In the afternoon, Art broke his own record by looping-the-loop in midair twenty-two times. For the first two flights, he had used a new machine, but on his third flight, he used his old machine. Directly over the transport docks, the young aviator began his downward swoops, loops, and side flops. Before reaching the one thousand feet level, he looped nineteen consecutive loops. He then put on three more for good measure. "Sweeping out over the bay, he then looped three times, circled the field, and made a perfect landing. That night during his illuminated flight, a dazzling display of flaming phosphorus, he wrote "Goodbye" in colored smoke in the sky.[35]

One newspaper stated, "Lord Richard Plantaganet Neville, who saw Smith fly for the first time seemed to express the sentiment of the crowd when he told the boy birdman, 'You are one of the marvels of this great Exposition.'"[36] Among the spectators was Silvio Pettirossi, the Argentine aviator, who was scheduled to take Art's place. Watching Art, Pettirossi said, "He is a wonder."[37]

Practically all the events of the day and evening on August 8, 1915, centered around the departure of the young airman — an Art Smith band concert, medal presentations, and even "a ceremony where the people of San Francisco will do the 'Human Camel' honor."[38] There were parties and dances. Employees of the Pacific KisselKar Branch gave Smith a "Kissel Komet," a miniature KisselKar equipped with a Harley-Davidson motorcycle engine. They said it was Smith's enthusiasm over the real car that was responsible for their gift. The little car was reported capable of seventy miles an hour.[39]

More than seventy thousand persons gathered on the esplanade to watch the 5:30 flight. Afterwards, Exposition officials waited for the playful spirit to subside so they could present Smith with a commemorative bronze medal.

Thornwell Mullally, Director of the Exposition, spoke of Art's courage, coolness, and judgment. He then took "the boy in his arms and held him up so all in the crowd might see."[40] One account of his speech said:

> "I cannot express what is way down here," Art answered, pointing to his left breast. "When I came to San Francisco sixteen weeks ago, I was practically unknown. Mr. Mullally says that while here I have flown into the hearts of generous big-hearted lovable San Francisco.... My greatest regret is that I must now fly out of those same hearts, for a time at least. I love every one of you, for San Franciscans have certainly been wonderfully kind and hospitable during the sixteen weeks I have been here. I hope to come back in October."[41]

Art's farewell was a strange mixture of frolic and emotion. "Just around the corner from the smile that habitually covers the lad's face lurked a tear," wrote one reporter, "yet shortly before the afternoon presentation, Smith amused the crowds by driving madly up and down the aviation field in a 'baby' auto that he designed for his own use and helped assemble." The report stated, "He appeared to enjoy the new plaything more than he did his aerial craft. Round and round the field, he sped, hat in hand, waving goodbye to the crowds."[42]

After his evening flight, Mayor Rolph held another presentation at the Marina Cafe on the Zone. Before an overflowing crowd, he gave Art a handsome gold medal studded with precious stones created by Ivan Berry of Walton and Company of Grant Avenue. It was a memento, he said, of Art's stay and "a lasting emblem of appreciation of his remarkable ability as a flyer."[43] The assembled crowd cheered as Art stood on a table and thanked them.

The "Smith Farewell" was one of the greatest demonstrations recorded at the Exposition. Reserve guards were called upon to manage the throngs. "The crowd seemed mad," reported the *Examiner*.[44] A testament to the affection San Francisco held for Art is apparent in a verse written by Jack Burroughs, entitled "So Long, Art," which appeared on August 4, 1915, in *The Bulletin*.

> The dauntless Bowman looks in vain
> To mark your comet flight,
> And see the scattered star-dust stain
> The curtains of the night.
> The tracings of the fiery brand
> No longer rend the Veil;
> The shadow of an unseen hand
> Obliterates the trail.
>
> We miss your motor's droning hum
> Above the rippled bay;
> New echoes from the reaches come
> Along the trackless way;
> New heroes to your wreath aspire
> On the billows of the Blue;
> New sailors brave the Storm King's ire —
> But none more brave than you.
>
> Old friend, goodby! Your pathway leads
> Along the cloud-flanked trail
> We'll cheer you as your star recedes
> In the swish of a comet's tail.
> And when you're winning greener bays
> In the sky's blue, starry main,
> For the sake of other, older days
> Come see us once again![45]

Shortly after his Panama Pacific triumph, Art said, "The greatest barrier between people is distance."[46] Certainly, the young boy from Fort Wayne would never have

William "Buffalo Bill" Cody presented Art with a pin, reportedly made from the first gold nugget Buffalo Bill ever found. Courtesy: Allen County–Fort Wayne Historical Society & Museum.

imagined that some day President Theodore Roosevelt or William "Buffalo Bill" Cody, who was his boyhood idol, would be one of his fans. When Buffalo Bill attended the Exposition, Art knew about it and hoped to have a chance to meet him. He loved to tell the story about meeting Buffalo Bill in San Francisco.

"I always greatly admired Colonel Cody," he said. "I suppose every American boy admires him, but he was my hero. While I was working on my first airplane, on the Buffalo Bill circus grounds, I used to think about him often. Every time I felt discouraged, I remembered him and went to work harder. To me he stands for the men who have succeeded in spite of every difficulty."[47]

Art said that when he came down after "a long, difficult flight," he saw a group of people waiting at one end of the Marina. While he was still in the airplane, Buffalo Bill came up. "I was so pleased, I could hardly shake hands with him. Then he said that as an American, he was proud of the work I was doing in the air. He took a pin from his coat. I found out later it was made from the first gold nugget he had ever found, and was fastened to a gold bar, which had been presented to him by King Edward. He had worn it for twenty-five years."[48]

Buffalo Bill said, "Here, I want to give this to you." He then pinned it to Art's coat. "I was glad I was still strapped to my machine," Art said. "I couldn't have stood up while that pin was being hung on me. That was one of the very finest tributes I have ever received."[49]

13

San Diego, Other Towns, and Headlines—1915

California was a golden time for Art and his bride of three years. His aerial feats were the talk of the state, and photographs of his daredevil aerobatics sold newspapers and features. Photographs show Art behind the wheel of his machine, his radiant smile fairly shining off the pages. They, along with accompanying articles, were used for advance publicity for his flights. Most of the articles begin with such phrases as: "Art Smith, the most daring aviator of all time," "Art Smith, the boy aviator who is proving..." "Art Smith, the intrepid aviator," or "Art Smith, the youthful Indiana aviator."[1]

After San Francisco, Art squeezed in two flights at San Diego on August 11–12. As in San Francisco, he and "Honeybug" were the toast of the city. His contract provided that he would not fly anywhere on the coast that season after his engagement in San Francisco except at San Diego, so it was the only other exhibition Art gave before heading south and east for a number of shows and state fairs.[2]

In his publicity articles, Art's age continued to be distorted by two to five years, probably because he was well aware of the value of being considered a prodigy. It seemed that every word uttered by the "boy prodigy" was considered worthy of quotation.

In old scrapbooks, article after article features the "the boy wonder" and quotes his observations and comments, not only about flying but also about the weather, his machine, and even military preparedness. While Art was giving his sensational shows in San Francisco, the San Diego *Union* ran a column on July 25, 1915, entitled "We Are Still Inclined to Believe The Marvelous," tweaking the adoring public for their tendency to believe almost anything Art said.

"The world is as ready as it has ever been to believe what it wants to believe," the columnist wrote, and went on to report that Art said he had seen a second sunset at nine o'clock post meridiem.[3] The writer continued his observations, putting Art's name in quotations, as if to chide his readers.

> I don't know whether the reporters believed "Art" Smith or not, but I do know that they printed his "observation" as they print everything else "Art" Smith says to them; and when the populace read it in the papers on the following morning everybody believed it — everybody except the astronomers, the mathematicians, and other chronic skeptics who are hardly convinced that they are alive and confess with unblushing humility that they don't know why. The astronomers and mathematicians, however knew better, they knew that "Art" Smith had either been deceived by the hallucination of his own senses or that he was deliberately catering to the reporters' love of the unusual and the marvelous. Two sunsets in one day! That was a headline to flush the classic brow of the Exposition assignment man with pride and to make the man on the police beat eat his heart out in envy.[4]

The column concluded with a paragraph entitled "Why He Didn't See It":

> The astronomers, mathematicians, and other learned savants knew that when "Art" Smith thought he was looking at that "sunset," or cogitating the sort of yarn he would tell the reporters waiting for him on the Marina, the sun was in its zenith somewhere over Canton in China, latitude 22:14 north, longitude 105 east, and that the horizon of its effulgence was about 1050 miles distant from San Francisco northwest. To see anything 1050 miles from San Francisco the aviator would have to rise to an altitude of 154 miles; but "Art," inadvertently, perhaps, says he only "made 5000 feet," which is less than a mile. No doubt if he had been a learned savant instead of a mere hippodroming flying-machine man, he would have gone the limit in his tale to the reporters.[5]

The writer added that in his opinion Art had observed the fog glow of Point Bonita light or, possibly, he mistook the rays from the Farallone light for the vanishing twilight of the noonday sun in Kwang-tung. "I am not a learned moonshee in either astronomy or mathematics, but I am positive that 'Art' Smith didn't even see the reflection of the arc lights from Honolulu town," wrote the agitated columnist. "But why should we cavil at a little thing like that?" he continued. "It was Barnum, I think, who said the American people like to be humbugged; and there is no doubt whatever that if the American people could be deprived of their credulity half the joy of living would thereby be denied to them. And think of the slump that would ensue in the gold brick industry and the traffic of the politicians!"[6]

The column was not enough to dissuade the public from believing what they wanted to believe. Viewers again dubbed Art "King of the Air," and a columnist

Opposite: These photographs were used for hundreds of publicity articles. Courtesy: Wertman-Stackhouse.

reported that "Smith has turned over thirty loops in succession in one flight, a feat which has never been approached by any other aviator. Nor does he loop-the-loop in the customary way. His machine looks like a falling leaf when executing the loops, and the last loop has been executed as near as three hundred feet from the ground."[7]

When Art went to San Diego, the newspaper that earlier had chided the San Francisco public for believing everything Art said carried the headline "Art Smith Will Arrive Tonight." The article began, "He's coming tonight. He'll dip the dip, loop-the-loop, write 'San Diego' in the sky in a fiery trail, and do other unheard of stunts in his airplane."[8]

The article provided information about parking directions both at the north gate and the west gates. Parking cost twenty-five cents a space for automobiles, and arrangements were provided for owners of automobiles to arrive close to the tractor field, where the flights were to be held, so they wouldn't have to walk more than a very short distance. "The wonderful boy aviator will give exhibitions of his 'aerial insanity' both tomorrow and Thursday at 4:00 and 9:00 P.M., the night flights to be marked by trails of fire."[9]

The account also stated, "At all performances Smith will lecture on aviation and explain his machine, which is of his own design, and show how he fastens himself in it for his upside down flying, his loops and other hair-raising stunts in the air."[10]

Another newspaper carried an article about Art's insurance. It was headlined: "Birdboy Pays Big Price for Policy, Which Insures Family $10,000.00, If Death Snatches Him From the Sky." The writer posed the question, "If you were a life insurance agent, would you write a policy on the life of Birdboy, Art Smith?"[11]

The article concluded that Art was not a good risk for an insurance agent. "Aviators are considered about as undesirable risks as torpedo gun-pointers in a submarine," wrote the columnist. "Art is twenty-three years of age and on account of his hazardous occupation pays about ten times the premium charged for insuring those content to follow saner and safer occupations." Art's insurance was a straight life policy of $10,000.00, which "Smith pays in yearly premiums" and is "large enough to insure that his wife need not worry about financial troubles should the 'intrepid sky-pilot crash to the earth.'"[12]

Crowds came out to see the youthful aviator who promised to write "San Diego" in his fiery display over the city. They were not disappointed. Art gave them four spectacular shows, and the newspapers gave their readers features and background details about everything from Art's early flying attempts and his elopement to how the exhibition and Art's contract were arranged through H.F. McGarvie, Art's representative. Even McGarvie's comments were worthy enough to be quoted. "McGarvie, having just returned from the northern exposition, says there is not much fuss about this boy aviator — he is always on time and up and away on the minute, as advertised."[13]

Art amazed the San Diego public with his flying. He gave two afternoon flights and two night flights. "His afternoon flights, loops, and dives are punctuated in the sky by streaks of gray smoke from a number of smoke pots attached to his machine. At night, his aerial acrobatics feats are emblazoned on the sky by comet-like streams of blazing fire," stated the newspaper.[14]

He flew his airplane in "long curving loops until he was about three or four thousand feet in the heavens, and the purr of his motor could scarcely be heard." He then flew east, "his machine outlined in red lights against the sky. When he passed between clouds drifting in from the sea and the black sky above him, only the dim reflection of his machine could be seen. He was nearly three thousand feet up when he started his first loop and brought the first gasp from the crowd."[15]

Seven times in succession, Art flung his airplane in wide circles, while behind him, streamed a continuous line of fire. Occasionally a burst of brilliant fireworks flashed out against the sky. So rapid did the machine swoop around in loops that "circles of fire were left for seconds etched on the sky."[16]

Art wasn't timid. He lolled sideways and spiraled and all the time the stream of red fire poured out in his trail. It was a spectacle that made "every person in the vast crowd hold his breath. The sheer beauty and unearthliness of it all was impressive. It blotted out for the moment the terrible risks the boy was taking."[17]

Art made his flying seem easy. He landed as "an Exposition dove of peace would alight on the broad, smooth dome of William J. Bryan, and when he did so, the crowd gave vent to admiration in a shout."[18]

In the afternoon flight, it seemed that the "boy had gone mad." His machine dipped and curved and hesitated and tangoed sidewise, onward and backward. "A kite in a gale of wind could not act more insanely." Over the crowd and not more than five hundred feet high, he rolled over sideways, "somersaulted forward and backward, and then rolled across the wind like a barrel going down stairs."[19]

One person was quoted as asking a mechanic, "What in the name of Heaven is that?" The answer was: "That is what Smith calls 'aerial insanity,' doing stunts close enough to stir the feathers on women's hats."[20] Art kept his show going for a "full five minutes while people with weak valves shut their eyes. He came down looking as though he had just stepped out of an ice cream parlour, grinning like a boy."[21] Newspapers near and far reported the details of Art's San Diego exhibition.

When Art had arrived in San Diego, one of his first questions was, "Where can I get a Dodge Brothers car?"[22]

When informed, Art applied at the C.W. McCabe Company on 1132 First Street. He told the people at the agency he knew something about Dodge cars because he had purchased one for his mother in Fort Wayne about six months earlier, and he liked the car so well, he wanted to rent one while he was in San Diego.[23]

Reporters announced that it was deemed unusual for anyone to rent a car but Mr. McCabe was convinced. He rolled a brand new Dodge from the salesroom floor to be placed at Art's disposal. The Omaha *Bee* wrote, "Aviator Smith Chooses Dodge Car For Pleasure While in San Diego." An accompanying photograph showed Art in the Dodge automobile. The article stated, "It was parked in such a way that behind it can be seen Smith's own airplane in which most startling stunts were done over the exposition grounds." The two machines were "Smith's pet machines, one on earth and the other in the air."[24]

When Art left San Diego, he sent McCabe a $50.00 check, "rent for three days," with the accompanying note:

> I probably could have used some other car without paying rent but I con-
> sider the Dodge service good enough to pay for. By way of a compliment
> to what I consider the greatest light car in the market today, let me add that
> it has a wonderful motor. Its accessibility is one big feature. It has the proper
> proportion of power to weight and its design and spring make for easy rid-
> ing.[25]

Many different promotions made the San Diego exhibitions memorable. One unlikely combination that resulted in record-breaking attendance was a Sunday gathering and flying exhibition that featured Art Smith and Billy Sunday. The arrangement was negotiated by a number of ministers, and it was advertised as an exhibition of "aviation's most daring exponent" and "the famous aerobatic evangelist."[26]

The *Los Angeles Examiner* reported about Art's San Diego show and said, "The marvelous manner in which Smith literally hurtles his machine into the loops, side twists, and spirals has never been equalled by any aviator that ever plied the air lanes in America or Europe."[27]

After San Diego, Art and Aimee visited Des Moines and then Mason City, giving flights at the State Fair and the North Iowa Fair. Familiar shots of Art at the wheel of his airplane were used for advance publicity of his flights. His boyish smile shines from the front page of countless newspapers. Exactly the same text was used for most of the annunciatory articles; more than twenty examples in one scrapbook begin, "Art Smith, the most daring..." and another twenty or more begin "Art Smith, the boy aviator who is proving...."[28] He was billed as the most wonderful exhibition of the century, as well as the highest paid single attraction in America. Art knew the value of publicity, and he deliberately continued to distort his age by two to five years. He was able to get by with this deception because of his boyish appearance, his spirit of enthusiasm, and the fact that his public would have believed almost anything he said.

Art posed for pictures, advertised the Underwood typewriter, and played Santa Claus. Money was no longer a concern. According to one source, the average annual income in 1915, was $1,267, and Art was sometimes making ten times that much for a single flying exhibition.[29] That year, he gave his father a player piano for Christmas. Later he gave his parents a farm and sixty-five hens.[30]

It was during this time in his life that Art developed a keen interest in auto racing. Many of his exhibitions began to include race car attractions. He hired a number of young men to drive his cars, and he loved to race one of his "baby speedsters" against them. Sometimes his drivers raced Art's "baby cars" while he flew loop-the-loops above them. On other occasions Art would fly his plane in time with the cars below or race against them to a finish line. Sometimes after he completed his flying, he would make a trip or two around the racetracks in his automobile. In photograph after photograph, there are scenes of Art's "the line-up," his time-trials, and his cars on their "road tests." One postcard reads, "the Mercedes turning a mile in sixty flat."[31]

At various places on his tour, he was a guest of honor in luxurious homes and with celebrities. When people asked to fly with him, it was news. When Marie Vandenberg's mother wouldn't allow her daughter to fly with Art, newspapers ran feature stories.[32]

Through page after page in old scrapbooks, Art and Aimee's adventures and exhibitions during the summer of 1915 continue as a lovely, profitable blur. Throughout August, September, and October, there were performances in Huron, Aberdeen, Watertown, Sioux Falls, Butte, Beresford (a second time), Des Moines at the State Fair, and Mason City. He swept and swooped through the high plains, approximately fifty bookings in seventy-five days.[33]

Art was honored, interviewed, photographed, quoted, and entertained. He was informal and approachable. He spoke at service clubs and Chamber of Commerce luncheons, often shedding his coat and asking his audience to do likewise. He talked about his mishaps as well as his successes.

He held his audience spellbound each time he told the story of how in Des Moines his machine "fell from thirty feet at the State Fair grounds" and wrecked. Fortunately, he was uninjured. He explained that he ran into a string of electric wires as he was "leaving the grounds."[34] He explained aviation techniques to his audiences and discussed his new engine and his "baby cars." His new engine was a six-cylinder Curtiss-type biplane with a seventy-five horsepower motor. He discussed internal combustion engines lubricated with Zerolene, and said, "I use Zerolene because I have found it gives perfect lubrication."[35]

Indeed, Art was a friend of motors. "If a thing hasn't a motor connected with it," reported one paper, "he's not interested. It is for that reason he constructed a baby automobile for himself, which already has made a record of nearly a mile a minute. When Smith isn't aviating, he's running his baby."[36]

He joined the Aero Reserve and offered his services to the government. On the tail of his biplane, he painted stars and stripes and underneath them the words, "Art Smith, U.S. Aero Reserves."[37] In Mason City, he had his bronze-colored biplane repainted red, white, and blue.[38]

When he appeared at the Clarinda Fair in South Dakota, the newspaper wrote that he was the most wonderful exhibitor of the century and the highest paid single attraction in America. They also reported that it would be necessary for Art to have "an electric socket at either end of the flying field, one that will stand a two-thousand watt lamp. He has to have the lamp in order to see his landing."[39]

All across the country, Art's flying was termed to be the most sensational form of aerial insanity and his stunts surpassed anything ever known in the time of air machines. His schedule was posted in newspaper after newspaper. For instance, his Middle West schedule was as follows: August 17–21: Mason City; August 25–26: Clarinda; August 27–September 3: Des Moines; September 6–11: Hamlin; September 16–17:

These photographs show Art racing airplane against his baby cars. He did this in San Francisco as well as in Japan. Courtesy: Wertman-Stackhouse and Greater Fort Wayne Museum.

Huron; September 19: Sioux City; September 27–October 1: Trenton; October 16–31: Dallas.[40] He dazzled New York, Richmond, Virginia and New Orleans. In New York he flew loops and glides over the Hudson River. In New Orleans, he "accomplished a feat never before executed — that of flying at night in an illuminated airplane and looping-the-loop at that."[41] He "wowed blasé Chicago," and "everywhere, people marveled at his flying skill. He actually writes his name in the sky with some sort of lighting display."[42]

Several articles include references to the fact that while in California he was a guest speaker at a number of Rotary Clubs. It was no wonder, then, that while en route to a flying exhibition from Illinois, he was met in Fort Wayne at the train station by a group of men from the Fort Wayne Commercial Club and the Fort Wayne Rotary Club, where there on the platform in the rain he was welcomed as a member of Rotary International.[43]

During this time Art had selected San Francisco to serve as his home base, but his trips took him all over the country. His repertoire for the South Dakota State Fair in Huron (September 16 –17) was:

1. ten loop-the-loops in absolute succession from three thousand feet;
2. a vertical drop from two thousand feet down to landing;

Postcard Art sent to Al Wertman written from Trenton, Missouri. Message reads: "Got away with 2 flights–2 days and $750 here. They were well pleased. This was a landing. I am going into K.C. [Kansas City] to make a gas baloon trip Sunday. A young K.C. aviator, who has never been up in a baloon, and I expect to ride her to the very limit 20 to 30 hours. Keep a lookout if the wind is from this direction about Monday morning. We may be over that way. Next to Corning, Iowa. Art. 10-11-12." Courtesy: Wertman-Stackhouse.

3. a wing slide, in which the machine is rolled sideways until the wings point up and down, then fall sideways;

4. a tail slide, in which the machine is flown straight up until it stalls, then falls backward, tail first;

5. fly upside down;

6. do straight and spiral turns, looping the loop at one thousand feet with hands off the steering wheel and arms outstretched.[44]

Art performed his show flawlessly, making his machine look like a falling leaf, and turning his loops so that his airplane tumbled about in the wind like a kite. Newspapers claimed that Art had out-performed Beachey.[45] Every loop and spiral glide was clearly outlined against the blue by spiraling streamers of white vapor, which most folks thought was the exhaust from the engine, but which was actually a carefully designed system of smoke pots made by the Thearle-Pain Fireworks people.[46]

He made his flying appear easy, but in truth, there were many frightening moments. On one occasion, after a crash, he was overheard telling Aimee, "Stuff a handkerchief in your mouth. Do anything but don't scream."[47]

How could Art survive such acrobatics? The San Diego *Union*, Monday, August 3, 1915, issue devoted an article to Art's good luck charm. Whereas Ty Cobb carried a peachstone in his pocket and Tod Sloan had an old jockey's cap, it said Art's good luck charm was "the strangest one ever carried — it is a hospital patient's chart, — Art Smith's chart."[48]

The explanation was that when Art regained his consciousness in a hospital after his first crash in Fort Wayne, the first words he heard were from a nurse who said, "I don't believe his temperature is as high today." When Art left the hospital, he took his chart. "Now it is folded up in a small packet about the size of a parcel post stamp for convenience. When he goes up, people will see him feel into his pocket for this charm." That explained why sometimes spectators were heard saying, "Art's temperature is going up" or "Art's temperature is coming down."[49]

Everywhere Art went, the press mobbed him and women flocked to be near him. Art was an enthusiastic dancer, and he and Aimee often led the grand march at balls. As a celebrity, women wanted to dance with Art, and many said it was good luck just to touch him. Women asked him to take them up in his plane, and many times, he did.[50] Sometimes Art would give one of his medals to an adoring fan.

Tucked in his scrapbook amid clippings about his 1915 successes, however, is a prayer written on a torn piece of paper in simple handwriting. It reads:

Prayer
To be ever conscious of my unity with God,
To listen to His voice, and hear no other call,
To separate all error from my thoughts of Man,
To see Him only as my Father in age;
To show Him reverence and share with Him my holiest treasures,

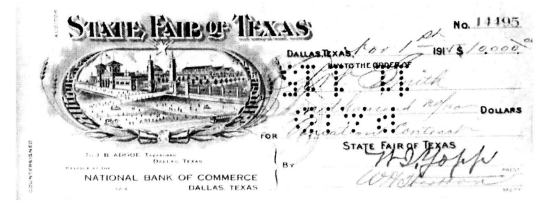

Photograph of the $10,000 check Art received for his exhibition at the Texas State Fair. Courtesy: Greater Fort Wayne Aviation Museum. Photographers Don Goss and Tony Napier.

> To keep my mental home a sacred place, golden with gratitude,
> Redolent with love, while with purity and cleansed from this flesh.
> To send no thoughts into the world that will not bless or cheer,
> Or purify or heal
> To have no aim but to make earth a fairer holier place and
> To rise each day into.... [unfinished][51]

Perhaps it was because of the difficulties of being a celebrity or the constant traveling, but during the fall of 1915, the young lovers' dream began to unravel. Even so, Art and Aimee celebrated their third anniversary in Dallas, Texas, at a private dinner hosted by Otto Herold, manager of the Oriental Hotel. Newspapers reported the details. A private dining room was decorated with American beauty roses and ferns, and there was "a wedding cake, above which hanging by a red ribbon was a tiny red airplane." Eddie Vaughn, one of the honored guests, served as toastmaster. Art gave his wife a diamond in return for a kiss. After the dinner, Art drove around the hotel in his "Comet Racer, which had an eleven horsepower engine, which would run about one mile per hour." The newspaper headlined the event: "Aviator Sells Valuable Diamond For A Kiss."[52]

Even so, the strain was too much for the couple.

14

A Celebrity in Japan — 1916

While he was performing in San Francisco at the Panama Pacific Exposition, Art became acquainted with a number of visitors and officials from Japan. They found him personable and likable, and he was charmed by them. On November 9, 1915, Art took up the Japanese flag on one of his flights "in honor of the new Mikado who ascends the Japanese throne tomorrow," and when he reached three thousand feet off the ground, he released the parachute to which it was attached.[1] It was a memorable ceremony. It was one of a number of occasions whereby the Japanese people and Art began to forge a lovely friendship.

As Art's fame spread around the globe, foreign governments vied with each other to obtain him for their aviation corps.[2] In the spring of 1916, the government of Japan offered Art $10,000 for a series of exhibitions to be held in Japan.[3] The government was not only interested in giving its citizens a view of Art's spectacular flying, they also wanted Art's services as a consultant and teacher.

During the time this offer was being extended, Art and Aimee's marriage became deeply troubled. On December 28, 1915, Aimee left California and returned to Fort Wayne to be with her parents.[4] Soon headlines were ablaze with the news that Art Smith was seeking a divorce from his wife. In Kendallville, Indiana, people read the details. "On the eve of his departure from San Francisco to Japan, Art filed suit for divorce from Aimee Cour in a divorce complaint filed secretly. Smith charged his wife with cruelty, declaring that her actions for the last two years have undermined his health."[5]

Another newspaper stated that Aimee was in Fort Wayne with her parents "and didn't know of his divorce suit until notified today by the newspapers in Fort Wayne."[6] Yet another newspaper explained that "just at noon as the young aviator set sail for Japan to teach Mikado's aviators," his attorney, Harry T. Stafford, filed the divorce papers.[7]

Since Art and Aimee were no longer together, Art asked Al Wertman to go to Japan with him, but Al declined. Lucille Wertman said, "We had been married only a short time, and he didn't want to leave me."[8]

Art sailed on the Chiyomaru for the Far East, accompanied by his plane, race cars, and five men to drive his "baby cars." Although the race drivers probably were not authorized representatives of the named companies, each wore a uniform on which the recognizable legend — Peugeot, Mercedes, Stutz, or Fiat — was emblazoned. The photograph of Art posing with his drivers has the following caption scrawled across the top: "My 'Baby Boys.'"[9]

The trip was a grand adventure. Souvenir postcards and photographs show Art hamming it up with the ship's crew and posing with the captain and passengers. One photograph that is typical of many shows Art dressed in suit, shirt, and tie, his cap on backward, in one of his speedsters, driving around on the ship's deck. Scrawled in ink on the picture is: "On the 48th lap on the Chiyo Maru."[10]

In Japan, as he did in San Francisco, Art dazzled his audiences. He was received

Although Art's drivers wore the names of automobile companies on their suits, it is unlikely they acted as authorized representatives. Courtesy: Wertman-Stackhouse.

Sir Bertrandis in Peugeot

Al Menasco

The lineup of Art's drivers, taken in 1916 in Japan. Courtesy: Wertman-Stackhouse.

by the technology-hungry Japanese as some sort of a flying god. Fascinated spectators included the Emperor, the Crown Prince, and the Prince's brothers. Art was granted special permission by the government to make his exhibitions above the palace, waiving a longstanding custom that no one could be "above" or higher than the Emperor.

One Japanese newspaper reported that when the "pyro-technic signal announced the opening of the program," the birdman took out his new machine and after minutely inspecting the machine and examining its motor, boarded the plane and made circular flights several times. He then ascended to a height of about 1,200 meters. At that altitude, Art carried out his favorite stunt of looping-the-loop. He repeated the loop ten times in quick succession, then followed them with a spiral flight. After making a few more stunts, he flew toward the Aoyama Itchome, where he made an almost perpendicular drop. When the plane came down to about fifty meters, Art "balanced the machine by a dexterous handling of the propeller and steering the craft toward the ground over the Military Staff College building, [and] ascended to the height of about one hundred meters, whence he descended to the ground by a perpendicular flight, amid the deafening cheers of the crowd."[11]

Opposite, top: Vic Bertrandias, one of Art's race drivers, who years later eulogized his friend. *Bottom*: Art taught Al Menasco, one of his race drivers, how to fly while they were in Japan in 1916. Courtesy: Wertman-Stackhouse.

Fire change on the 121st lap

While on his trip to Japan, Art often drove his baby car, "The Comet," around the ship's deck. Courtesy: Stackhouse Collection.

The Crown Prince and his two brothers, Princes Atsu and Takamatsu, attended by Lieutenant-General Nagaoka, some Court officials, and His Highness' school-mates, witnessed the flight from the Aoyama palace. While flying over the ground, Art sighted the Crown Prince watching his flight and twice took off his cap and bowed toward His Highness. This was recognized by the Crown Prince, who responded to the courtesy of the aviator "in an appropriate manner."[12]

Art's second flight was carried out in the afternoon. He ascended to a height of 1,100 meters and made several loops. "Then descending to the altitude of only four meters above the ground by spirals the birdman joined in a race with three small automobiles, circling the ground twice."[13] Afterwards, Art was honored with a monetary present from the Crown Prince, "through Lieutenant-General Nagaoka."[14]

Later, Art was presented with a medal of honor and a beautiful bouquet by the National Aviation Association. Students of the Kyoto Industrial School gave him another medal, and the "Jiji Shimpo" gave him yet another.[15] The newspaper said that "Mr. Smith's eyes were shining with tears of gratitude, and boarding one of his small automobiles circled the ground waving his cap to express his heartfelt thanks to the spectators."[16]

Art receives a gift from Matsumoto. Note baby car and airplane are in the background. Courtesy: James Wigner.

During the afternoon, there were a number of automobile races, after which Art gave another exhibition. Volplaning about thirty meters, Art made an ascent ... and on attaining a height of about one thousand meters, he made five loops and five over wings, and then descended to four hundred meters by a spiral flight. Descending farther by an overswing, Art made a "dead dive" from the altitude of three hundred meters. Again from the lower altitude, he raced with four small automobiles.[17]

It was estimated that a crowd numbered over 60,000. Among the spectators were Marchioness Matsukata, Admiral Baron Uriu, and Baroness Uriu, Fleet-Admiral Inouye, and Barons Mitsui and Goto.[18]

Art's night flight was historic. It was "the first night flight ever made in this country," reported the Japanese newspapers.[19] Again, dignitaries and members of the royal family were present. Art left the ground "on the machine illuminated first with red lights, which later changed to green, and attaining a height of one thousand meters, steered his course toward Akasaka-Mitsuke, returning to Aoyama some ten minutes later."[20] During the course of the show, he looped-the-loop eleven times, discharging magnesium fireworks in the air. At Asakusa, which was opened especially for the flight, Art was unable to perform his show because a searchlight was turned toward him and he was unable to see distinctly. Instead, he gave his exhibition over Hibiya Park. Unfortunately the sky was partially clouded over, and the loopings were sighted only two or three times, to the great disappointment of the spectators.

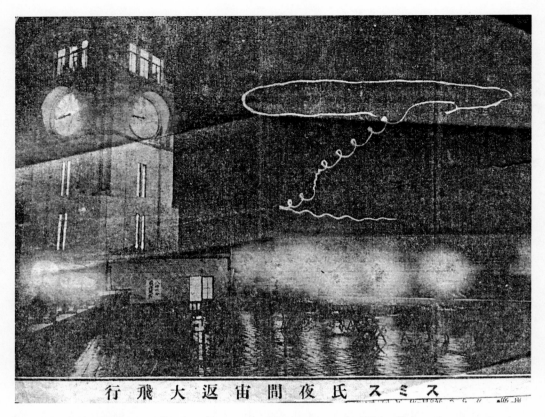

行飛大返宙間夜氏スミス

A Japanese newspaper clipping shows one of Art's spectacular night flights. Courtesy: Stackhouse Collection.

After the historic night event, Art drove to the Imperial Hotel in one of his small automobiles, hailed and cheered along the way by crowds lining the streets. People "invaded the hotel," reported the newspaper, and "gave him an enthusiastic banzai." Art later appeared on the balcony with two paper lanterns in his hands and waved them in response to the cheering of the crowd.[21]

Art was toasted and entertained by dignitaries and royalty. The Japanese evidently knew of Art's love for medals; it was said that medals meant more to Art than money. Just

Thirty-two diamonds grace the medal Art received from Count Okuma in Tokyo. Courtesy: James Wigner.

about everywhere he went, he was showered with commemorative gold medals. On his second arrival to Tokyo, a delegation from the Editors' Aviation Society met him at the station and presented him with a handsome, large gold medal. The Osaka Ashuri Newspaper Company gave him a gold medal, and the citizens of Nagoya gave him one that featured the crest of Nagoya, with a design of fish in inlaid enamel in the center. The inscription read, "Presented to Art Smith by citizens of Nagoya, April, 1916." Another gold medal had an engraving that read, "Presented to Art Smith April, 1916, in memory of his flight at Narus."[22]

After his Tokyo exhibitions, Count Okuma pinned a large and magnificent medallion on the chest of the daring young aviator. The design on the medal showed "a trail in the sky inlaid with thirty-two diamonds, symblematic of his flight in Tokyo in a wind storm when the velocity of the wind was thirty-two meters a second."[23] Later, Art quipped that had the wind been blowing at fifty meters a second there would have been fifty diamonds instead of thirty-two.

He gave the city a complimentary night flight.

Newspapermen could not resist saying that Art had received "so many medals that he cannot wear all at one time, and he is as happy as a school boy — charmingly and enthusiastically proud of them, and he fondles each one with a pride akin to love."[24]

Art enjoyed receiving and wearing his medals. He wrote a friend that no money could buy them from him. His letter was quoted in the Fort Wayne newspaper on June 8, 1916: "I will look like a Russian general when I get back and put on all my medals for you. Some of them are pinned on and some stuck on, and the others are to hang around my neck on a chain."[25] The article was accompanied by seven photographs, four of which were of his medals. Three other photographs show Art receiving a large wreath of flowers after a flight, being presented to a prince at Nagoya, and the wreck of one of his racecars.

One rare honor that Art received was that the Emperor

Art shows a few of the medals he received on his trip to Japan. Courtesy: Greater Fort Wayne Aviation Museum. Photographer Don Goss.

Art is wearing the medal he received from the National Aero Club of Japan. *Close-up at bottom*: It is gold and silver, with a ruby in the center. Courtesy: James Wigner.

gave him some packages of money. The newspaper explained, "The money is not of value to exceed six or seven dollars in our money, but the honor of having been presented with it by royalty is seldom held by anyone. Each package is bound with special cord and is sealed and addressed to Art Smith, the address being, of course, in Japanese."[26] Additionally, Art received the agreed upon honorarium for his exhibitions. It was rumored that the Japanese understood that his purse would go for alimony when he returned to America.

He also received a number of "beautiful vases and other things of value," including a gold embroidered screen made by "an admirer," which Art gave to his mother.[27]

In Ida Smith's and Herb Wertman's scrapbooks, there are numerous newspapers written in Japanese. They show photographs of his fireworks, throngs of spectators gazing upward, and Art smiling as he posed with a number of Japanese dignitaries.

An English newspaper gave an account of Art's Tokyo exhibition over the Nijubashi. "The Emperor of Japan and the Empress, holding in her arms the infant Prince, witnessed yesterday afternoon one of the best exhibitions Art Smith has given since his arrival in Japan. By permission of the Imperial Household, the American aviator circled the palace ground, looped-the-loop, and made his thrilling spiral drop for Their Majesties just over the Nijubashi."[28]

> This is the first time that any aviator has been honored by permission to give a special exhibition for the rulers of Japan…. The Emperor and Empress went out into the open space where the horses in the Imperial stables are exercised to see the flight. Both expressed extreme pleasure at the feats performed for their special benefit and were amazed at the remarkable control over his machines which Mr. Smith showed. General Nagaoka, president of the National Aviation Association, and Viscount Kaneko, who explained the evolution of the aviator's biplane, accompanied the Imperial pair.[29]

The account also gave details relative to how many meters Smith ascended on that particular flight, how many loop-the-loops he performed, and how many hundred feet he dropped as he did his downward spirals. The article stated, "Saturday morning, if the present schedule holds, the aviator and his party will leave for Northern Japan, where flights in most of the larger cities of that district have been arranged."[30]

One explanation for Art's popularity was that his "indifference to danger" was especially appealing to the Japanese belief in fatality. The Japanese had great admiration for anyone "who does not fear death," and they viewed Art's death-defying dips and loops as nothing but heroism.[31]

Many of the Japanese news articles that are pasted in Art's mother's scrapbook show photographs of Art's night flights. One shows Art's fancy flying appearing like a huge bright lasso against a black sky. To accomplish his night skywriting and loop-the-loops, Art used flaming phosphorus, which emitted a brilliant white light and an impressive plume of smoke. With fireworks spitting sparks from his reeling airplane, he flew rings of fire all over the black sky. In the daytime, Art employed smoke torches to mark his course, but at night, he came into his glory, "writing with a finger of fire across the clouds."[32]

The Japan Times called Art an "aerial wonder" and an "aerial torpedo." Many of the Japanese talked about his "jolly dances," and cheered lustily as he did his fancy stunts. Newspapers reported that "from Imperial Palace grounds, H.I.M., the Emperor was pleased to witness Smith's flights and admired the dexterous flight and aeronautical feats of the aviator."[33]

Another newspaper reported, "The most distinguished body of men that has ever gathered to do honor to an aviator in this country attended the banquet given in honor of Art Smith, the American birdman, at the Imperial Hotel last night."[34]

Guests at the banquet included Dr. Okuda, the mayor of Tokyo; Baron Eiichi Shibusawa, a prominent industrialist; General Nagaoka, president of the National

Dinner

given in honour of

Mr. Art Smith

By

Count Shigenobu Okuma,
President, the Imperial Aero Society of Japan

Baron Eiichi Shibusawa,
Chairman, the Advisory Council of the Japan
Society of New York

Lieut.-General Nagaoka,
President, the National Aviation Society

Buei Nakano,
Member of the Executive Committee, the
Japanese-American Relations Committee

The Imperial Hotel,
Tokyo, Japan
June 2, 1916

MENU

DINER DU 2 JUIN 1916

HORS D'OEUVRE VARIÉS

CONSOMMÉ À L'IMPERIAL

TRUITE SAUMONÉE À LA CHAMBORD

FILETS MIGNONS À LA MONTPENSIEP

ASPIC DE HOMARD EN BELLE-VUE

SORBET ROMAINE

ASPERGES SAUCE CRÈME

DINDE FARCIS

POUDING PRALINÉE

BOMBE VANILLE

FRIANDISES

MOKA

The front cover and inside of a menu from a gala banquet given in honor of Art Smith by the Japanese in 1916. Courtesy: James Wigner.

Aviation Association; professors from the Imperial University and "some of the greatest men of an Empire." Although the Japanese admired his skills, they also were interested in learning everything they could about Art's flying techniques, which would be useful to their military forces.[35] Not only did Art become the idol of the populace, but the Japanese army aviators hailed him as "their superior in the air…. They anxiously watch his every flight and are eager for his instructions and explanations."[36]

Art appreciated the Japanese culture, and he was a good tourist. One bill of sale, dated May 13, 1916, shows that in Tokyo he bought from one S. Nishimura, "Manufacturer of and Dealer in Embroideries, Cut-Velvets, and Silk Goods," a "one-piece embroidered four-folding screen, 'Chrysanthemum,' for 6700 yen."[37] It was one of many souvenirs Smith brought home.

Only once did Art have what he called a bad experience. On May 14, 1916, he was to make a flight in Osaka, but his arrival was delayed. When he did arrive, a mob of unbelievers, despite the national publicity about his feats, was on hand to greet him. As soon as Art appeared on the field, he was greeted with a chorus of jeers and a volley of brickbats. General Nagaoka stood in the plane and declared in the name of the king that the people should cease, but he, too, was the target of their anger.

Vic Bertrandias, who had accompanied Art to Japan, said, "It was a howling mob, lusting for God knows what, with stones and bricks flying everywhere." Art was standing in the plane trying to overcome some motor trouble. Art said, "Vic, if you ever believed in God, believe in Him now."[38] There was strong anti–American sentiment in the district, and as soon as he and Vic could manage it, they started the plane and flew away, leaving the angry mob. Art recalled, "A brick caught me and I carried away a big lump and a headache as a souvenir of that incident."[39]

Japanese officials were embarrassed that "the treasure of the United States" had suffered such indignity. Art excused the situation, however, and told them that he held no resentment about the Osaka attack because it had been a matter of "misunderstandings."[40] Interestingly enough, it was in Osaka where Art's letter in behalf of the YMCA protesting the opening Tobita Licensed Quarter was published.[41]

For his skills, Art received accolades in two languages and effusive accounts of his exploits. Next to the royal family, Art was easily the first man of Japan and the most talked about. Bernard J. Losh wrote that filial love and devotion is one of the bulwarks of the Japanese civilization. When the Japanese learned that as soon as Art had made money enough from his exhibition flights in Japan to do so, he had cabled it to a San Francisco automobile dealer with instructions to deliver a car to his parents, his act of devotion caused his popularity to grow by leaps and bounds.[42]

Although Art's Japanese tour was scheduled to last four months, a landing accident in Sapporo brought it to an abrupt end. Art's first flight on June 18, 1916, a Friday, was for two o'clock. After it was successfully completed, Art was presented with a handsome gold medal from the municipality of Sapporo. He then was scheduled to make a second flight at four o'clock, but because the weather was changing rapidly and a strong breeze was rising, Art decided that it would be best to make the ascent before the wind got stronger.

At 3:17 P.M., he started his engine and ran his plane along the ground for thirty meters before lifting off. He had hardly left earth when the engine stopped. Art attempted to glide to the ground, but he was unable to do so because of the risk of killing or wounding some of the spectators. He tried to turn the plane to the right, away from the crowd, but his propeller had stopped and with the gusting wind, the plane turned over. He fell about eighty feet with the right wing down.[43]

Fortunately, his injuries were not critical. His right thigh was fractured about a third of the way down from the hip, but it was said the break was a clean one. When the crash occurred, General Nagaoka, dean of the Sapporo Agricultural School and the Governor of the Hokkaido, rushed to the fallen biplane, followed by several Japanese physicians. Art insisted that he was fine, in spite of a severe nosebleed. In the end, however, and upon examination, Art was removed to the hospital. He also had suffered cuts on his leg and several bruises. Art's airplane was ruined, but fortunately not the engine.[44]

News that Art suffered a broken leg and that his plane was severely damaged made headlines around the world. The fact that he did not land in the crowd was considered by the Japanese as a heroic act, which added further to his name and his

Japanese fans cheer for Art during one of his tours. "With a good smile, they are saying Bunsi Bunsi" [*sic*]. Courtesy: Wertman-Stackhouse.

fame. As he lay in the hospital, he received coins from schoolchildren as well as letters and gifts from the purses of the rich.

On July 19, 1916, Mr. Zenjuro Horikoshi, representing Baron Shibuzawa and other promoters of the exhibitions, and General Nagaoka called on Art at the Imperial Hotel and presented him the sum of 7335 yen, which was the total amount of a fund collected "for the purpose of consoling Art after his injury in Sapporo."[45] The sum amounted to about $7,000 in American money.

Leaving his two biplanes in storage, Art returned to America, promising to go back to Japan the following year to fulfill his contracts.

15

Scandal, Surgery, and Business—1916–1917

Upon Art's return to America, newspaper articles continued their speculations about Art and Aimee's relationship. On March 3, 1916, the Waco *Morning News* headlines announced: "Art Smith Suing Wife for Divorce."[1] Art charged his wife with cruelty and said that his wife's affections were elsewhere. He said Aimee had "quit him and he was alleging desertion."[2] Aimee said her husband "was worth $100,000 and had an income of $1,000 a week," and that she planned to fight the divorce.[3] She accused Art of being a "swellhead," and Art accused her of having kissed a married man.

People who knew the couple took sides. Even though "Cigarettes, Cigars, Liquor Are Taboo For Birdboy," stated one headline, Art enjoyed dancing and partying.[4] Although he and Aimee were honored at gala balls, Art's increasing popularity strained the couple's relationship. Photographs showed him posing with female admirers.

Aimee was quoted, "He would do anything for publicity. He would stand on his head in the sky just to get a little front-page stuff. It's all I have seen for four years, and I am sick of it."[5] On another occasion, she said, "When I called Art a 'swelled-head,' he struck me. He wouldn't have done that when he was in Fort Wayne and possessed only $400.00 to his name. He was a regular fellow then."[6]

At first the three principals in the divorce triangle were Art, Aimee, and Paul Cooley. Art blamed Paul Cooley for some of his marital difficulties. Paul was an employee at the Exposition, who also had taken moving pictures of Art in Kendallville, Indiana. When asked about *her* indiscretions and the kiss she purportedly gave one of Art's mechanics, she said, "Well I met Mr. Cooley in San Francisco through

Art. I haven't seen him since. It's true that I kissed a married man in Fort Wayne, but Fort Wayne is just a small town and what I did is merely cut-up stuff."[7]

Even though many of Art Smith's acquaintances in Northeast Indiana at first didn't know about the separation, the scandal was fodder for California newspapers. Soon, news and gossip about Art and Aimee's relationship spread throughout America. Although Art's mother probably tried to keep the matter under cover, there is evidence that a number of clippings in Ida Smith's scrapbooks have been torn from the pages.

But the scandal didn't dissuade Art's fans. Nagaoka's diary of Art's exhibitions carried the following statement: "Hypocrites, luxuries, wines, cigarettes, and flatteries are the things Art Smith disliked most. It was for this reason that he was separated from his wife."[8]

In several articles about Art's exhibitions in Japan, it was reported that Mrs. Art Smith returned to Fort Wayne, where she obtained a quick divorce.[9] Actually that bit of news was not true. According to the best accounts, when Art filed for divorce Aimee *was* in Fort Wayne with her parents. She in turn filed for "an appearance in the case ... and obtained [from] Superior Judge Cabiness an injunction tying up all her husband's property until his divorce petition has been disposed." Her petition was a forecast of legal action on her part to demand a division of Art's estate and receive a large amount of alimony.[10] It was a horrible scandal that became worse.

Prior to leaving for Japan, Art dismissed Billy Kyle, one of his five mechanicians. Upon Art's return, however, he found a letter written by Aimee, which newspapers termed "Love Notes," that led Art to name four other men as recipients of his wife's affections.[11] In the letter, Aimee had written that "Harry H. Hardesty has blond hair, brown eyes, and is pretty good-looking. He treats me fine and seems to think a h—l of a lot more of me than Paul does, but I like Paul the best." She added, "Paul won't commit himself one way or the other." Her letter also mentioned Albert E. Beaumont, and "my blond baby."[12] A newspaper told the story with the headline: "Wife Busy on Earth While the Young Husband Goes Up in the Air."[13]

About that time, Art found out that he had been named as a "co-respondent in a cross complaint in the case of the William J. Caples divorce." Caples, the son of the millionaire Richard C. Caples of El Paso, said that he had been informed that "his wife confessed her love for Art Smith."[14] William Caples announced that he was going to name the aviator in his complaint.

Meanwhile, in Fort Wayne, Aimee's mother was "prostrated by the affair, declaring that she had no inkling that Art considered a divorce or that he had harbored suspicions that her daughter's conduct with other men should have been anything other than circumspect."[15]

Then the news came out that Art was planning to sue William Caples for slander for being named in his divorce case. Caples then declared that he had never "seen Smith except when he was flying, and he did not know of the relations, but [that] Mrs. Caples had frequently admired Art Smith for his bravery, daring, and good looks."[16]

Newspapers tried to interview the various parties. Different stories surfaced. Aimee said that their trouble started in a little candy store in San Francisco. It seems that Art and Aimee saw a photograph of Art that was priced at two dollars in the store window. Art sent the store a check for two dollars for his picture. Instead of sending him the photograph, the store framed the check and stuck it in the window along with the picture. Then they asked that Art buy another photograph and pay for it with cash. According to the newspaper, the following dialogue occurred:

"What do you think of that for crust and me?" Art asked Aimee.

Art then answered his own question. "I guess it's worth two dollars to have my check."

"Are you getting swell-headed," Aimee asked.

"No, but I am Art Smith, ain't I."

Aimee said, "That was the end. It disgusted me."[17]

That is when she made the statement that when she called Art a "swelled-head," he struck her. It was at the same time she said she had met Mr. Cooley through Art, but said she had not seen him since.[18] Meanwhile, newspapers reported that Mrs. William J. Caples declared, "I don't love Art Smith."[19] She said she had gone to a recent Pal's Club ball in the company of the aviator, but that was all. Mrs. Caples was seeking "one thousand dollars a month and a quarter of a million dollars from her husband's estate."[20]

Another paper came out with the facts that Paul Cooley, known as "Beau Brummel" by his friends, was a thirty-six year old widower living in Chicago, working for an artificial limb company.[21] A full-page article discussing the case and "aviation temperament" ran in the Sunday newspaper.[22] The article quoted Aimee as saying that "Art is a crank, perhaps the biggest crank in the world. After each flight he'd go into a rage and made my life miserable."[23]

Meanwhile, Art withdrew his divorce petition and re-filed it in order to verify that indeed he had established his legal residence in California.[24] Aimee, who was served papers in Fort Wayne on June 11, 1916, immediately filed a cross complaint. She demanded cash and announced, "I don't care what charges he makes as long as he is willing to settle the money question right with me."[25]

Much of this exchange and confusion took place while Art was in Japan. On one occasion, he received a cable from Aimee's lawyer notifying him of an order to pay alimony. He cabled back that he would respect the court's order. The Japanese sympathized with him. They announced in their newspapers that all the money Art was making from his exhibitions "must go for alimony to his wife."[26]

On February 1, 1917, however, Art appeared for his divorce trial. Aimee did not appear to contest the suit. Attorneys quickly worked out a settlement. It was reported that she received less than one thousand dollars. The divorce was granted on February 2, 1917.[27] Aimee remained in Indiana.

During this time, Art was undergoing surgery on his broken leg, recuperating, and making plans to return to Japan. The tour was scheduled to last six months. Art invited his mother to go to Japan with him, and she readily agreed. He had fallen in love with the Japanese people, and he was anxious to share his affection for their culture with his mother. Lieutenant-General Nagaoka Gaisha wrote in his book that Art "dislikes the gorgeous dresses of the American women and loves the plain and delicate kimono of the Japanese women, and has bought several kimonos and silks at Kyota for his mother."[28]

But Art could not return to Japan until he was well enough to travel. His left leg had been badly fractured in the accident, which had occurred on July 16, 1916, nine days after Aimee was served her divorce papers. In his mother's scrapbooks there are clippings about the accident and his return to America by way of Seattle.[29]

Art's plan was to have surgery done by Dr. John B. Murphy, a renowned surgeon from Chicago, but on August 12, 1916, the San Francisco *Bulletin* carried the headline, "Surgeon's Death is Blow to Art Smith."[30] Dr. Murphy had died unexpectedly of heart failure while at Mackinaw Island. "It is now feared Art may be permanently crippled," reported the article. Details were that Art's leg already had been set three times ... twice in Japan and one time while en route, and that "the bones had failed to set, and had drawn nearly one inch apart."[31] It was hoped that Dr. Murphy would be able to repair and reset the bones.

Suddenly Art had to find a new surgeon and make different plans. Late in August, a headline announced the news: "Yankee Airman Who Was Badly Injured in Japan Leaving Hospital."[32] Although Art was suffering from marital woes, not all news that year about his situation was bad. Happier news came on March 30, 1916, from Sacramento. He was informed that the John T. Montgomery Estate supported and granted his request for a license to build airplanes.[33] (Professor John J. Montgomery died in San Jose, California, on October 31, 1911.) Art was negotiating the start of a manufacturing business and was actively searching for a "large tract of land."[34] According to the license agreement, Art was to pay the Montgomery Estate a royalty on every airplane he built.

"Art Smith in Fight for Air Millions," reported the San Francisco *Examiner*.[35] The Sacramento *Bee* carried the news: "Intrepid Exposition Flyer Takes Stand for Montgomery Airplane Patents."[36] The controversy involved a lawsuit between the Wright-Martin combination and the John J. Montgomery Estate to determine who owned the rights to various airplane patents. It was contended that John J. Montgomery had the first rights as issued by the U.S. government. Many considered Montgomery to be the Father of Aviation because he had experimented with the principles of aeronautics at Santa Clara as early as 1880. His investigations were said to have antedated those of Lilienthal, Langley, and other persons. The Wright Brothers contested Montgomery's claim. Newspapers said the Wright Brothers' company "has endeavored, with much success, to collect a royalty from every airplane manufactured in the country."[37]

Art was granted his license to build airplanes. He announced that he had raised $1,000,000 capital to build an airplane factory and an army aviation school near San Francisco. His plan was that Detroit would make the motors, but the airplanes would be built at his facility.[38]

In November 3, 1916, Silvio Pettirossi was killed in a flying accident. "Exposition Aviators All Dead But Smith," stated one headline.[39] Lincoln Beachey, Charles Niles, Silas Christofferson were gone, and now Silvio A. Pettirossi. People clucked about Art's chances, and wondered if he were taking too many risks.

Newspapers reported that Ida Smith would meet Art in San Francisco in order to join him on his tour of Japan. One said she was "busily preparing for her trip, telling Father Smith not to forget to put out the cat at night and to feed the chickens."[40] It also said Art was expecting to build biplanes for commuter use and would be spending time with the Japanese army flying corps in order to teach them about weather and fitful air currents.[41] Reporters hinted that an Art Smith Company might be established in Japan.[42]

Art was accompanied by his mother, his race drivers, a number of friends, and William J. Gorham, a businessman with a wide acquaintance in Japan and the Far East. On February 5, 1917, the day Art sailed for his second tour of Japan, his divorce became final.[43]

16

A Second Trip to Japan — 1917

In Japan, Art and Ida Smith and their entourage, which included Al Menasco and Charley Imatsu, both of whom had accompanied Art on his first trip to Japan, were greeted enthusiastically. *The Japan Advertiser* carried the news, "Art Smith Is Back."[1] The article was accompanied by a photograph of Art and his mother on the pier holding huge baskets of flowers. The caption reads, "The American flying marvel, accompanied by his mother, reached Yokohama on the Siberia Maru Friday."[2]

Among other photographs and souvenir postcards from their trip are some of Art trying different oriental foods, wearing and showing off a kimono, holding a parasol, playing in a lake, taking a ride along "the pine-tree road" near Nikko, which is about seventy-five miles north of Tokyo, being presented with baskets of flowers by high school girls, sight-seeing, posing for photographs, and riding in a rickshaw.[3]

Art and his mother and entourage were treated like royalty. Crowds turned out to see his shows. One newspaper estimated seventy thousand spectators witnessed the Aoyama exhibition.[4] On April 26, 1917, *The Japan Advertiser,* Tokyo, covered one of Art's exhibitions. A photograph shows the Aoyama Parade Ground, another shows a picture of the flying machine, and a third one is of "the aviator and his mother."[5]

The top headline reads, "Art Smith Thrills Big Aoyama Crowd." A sub-headline announces, "American Birdman Shows Old-Time Skill in Exhibition Given in High Wind."[6] The article says that Art made two flights that day, one at two o'clock and another at four. Both times the crowd cheered as the "aviation wizard looped and swooped downward in spirals." The exhibition was declared to be one of Art Smith's best. "His mastery of his machine and his perfect self-control appear not to have been hurt in the least by the fall at Sapporo."[7]

Most of Tokyo suspended work that afternoon to give people the opportunity to watch the "little aviator do those marvelous tricks in the sky."[8] In streets through-

The Japanese had a strong affection for Art and often held ceremonies in his honor during his two tours in Japan. At Matsuye, Art and his mother were presented with a basket of flowers by the girls of the high school. Courtesy: Wertman-Stackhouse.

out the city, throngs gathered and watched. No charge was made for entrance to the grounds, and as early as ten o'clock the previous day, the public began to assemble. By noon the number exceeded fifty thousand. Soldiers from the First Division were among the spectators. The newspaper reported, "Ten thousand soldiers from regiments in Tokyo attended the flight in a body, and lined in front of the enclosure, making a human fence against the pressure of the public standing ten and twenty rows deep."[9]

After each flight, Art and his mother rode around the grounds in a motor car and were cheered by the crowd.[10] They were presented to Major-General Prince Kuni, one of the Princes of the Blood. With Baron Sakatani acting as interpreter, the aviator and his mother talked with Prince Kuni. The Prince presented Art with a wreath, inquired after his health, and expressed gladness to see him again in the condition to make such wonderful flights. The Prince made Art a present of money. The Imperial Aero Society presented flowers and wreaths to Art and honored guests. The Prince was keenly interested in aviation and asked him many questions about the technology of flying. Art had a wonderful time with the Prince, and before he made his second exhibition flight, brought his airplane in front of His Imperial Highness Prince Kuni and minutely explained the details and workings of his plane.[11]

Part of the pre-show publicity was that Art had not made any exhibition flights since he was injured in Sapporo the previous June, so crowds clamored to see Art, wondering if he looked the same. The *Advertiser* stated, "He was full of confidence, which was justified by the tremendous success of yesterday's flights."[12] It presented the following account of the flight:

> In seven minutes he rose to a height of four thousand feet, and lighting his two tails of fireworks, at once began to make perfect loops. After four successful loops, he showed his new tricks of turning halfway, wing over wing. He went through every other trick, which has made him so famous, and dropping from a height of over one thousand feet straight down, the machine came gracefully back to the ground.[13]

The first one to congratulate him on the successful flight was his mother, "to whose arms, he rushed as soon as he came out of his machine."[14] When Art was asked how he could make such a flight after so long a rest, he said, "The art of flying is similar to bicycling or swimming, and when one learns the art of flying once, one can never forget it, even though one does not practice for many months." The newspaper added that Art was "just as confident at the start of his first flight yesterday as if he had been flying every day."[15]

In the second flight, Art went higher than the first ascent, reaching five thousand feet in nine minutes. After making several loops, he started to make another loop, but instead, he suddenly stopped his engine and turned completely over headfirst toward the ground. "When his engine stopped and the machine was seen high in the air, making a complete somersault, a hush went through the crowd below, fearing that something might have happened to his machine, but the purring of the engine was soon heard again, and the suspense was over."[16]

As Art returned to his hotel that night, he was given a wild ovation by the spectators and by the public on the streets. That evening, he was the guest of honor at a dinner held at the Seiyoken Hotel given by the Imperial Aviation Association, under whose auspices the exhibition was held.[17]

Eighteen engagements, mostly in the southern and western parts of the country, were to be fulfilled. They were the ones that had been canceled the previous year because of Art's accident. "Whereas one day's flight exhibition in the United States brings him in from fifteen to twenty thousand dollars gold," reported an American newspaper, it was speculated that "his trip to Japan, which would last four to six months, would net him between seven and eight thousand dollars gold."[18] By this time to Art, money was incidental. He was more interested in flying, receiving accolades, accepting medals, and meeting celebrities. For instance, in May while in Japan, Art was delighted to meet Katherine Stinson, who also was giving flying exhibitions at Narus.[19]

In addition to Art's flying exhibitions, the report was that "the aviator, inventor and producer of motors and flying machines" was bringing business interests to Japan as well. There was "a whisper of big business connected with the aviator's return to the scene of his former triumphs." It was said that Art admitted when questioned by a reporter that he might remain in Japan for some time in connection with "interests."[20]

News reports stated that the Art Smith Company owned valuable patents and had perfected a new airplane motor, which was to be placed on the market. Reporters tried to ferret out details. Art was approached with offers to acquire the rights for his patents, and there were invitations for him to "personally oversee the launching of what will be equivalent to a Japan branch of the Art Smith Company of America."[21]

One report was that Art had been approached with a similar idea the previous year before he had left Japan; therefore, "He would have no trouble in making satisfactory arrangements for the establishment of a motor and airplane factory in this country." William Gorham was to oversee the business negotiations.[22]

Art was a hero and an idol in Japan. "You have *samurai* in America," commented

Art poses with a Japanese dignitary. Courtesy: Wertman-Stackhouse.

one Japanese of the old school after seeing Art do his tricks in a high gale.[23] His remark expressed better than anything the feeling of the Japanese toward Art. In addition to being presented with medals and gifts, Art and his mother were given many opportunities to speak to groups and tour the country. For instance, while Ida might visit with some children in a church, Art would be speaking at a service club or a business luncheon.

A large scrapbook in the Greater Fort Wayne Aviation Museum is devoted primarily to photographs of Art's second tour in Japan. There are photographs of him on the ship, posing with Japanese dignitaries, receiving medals, and planting a tree near the Japanese Aviator's Monument. There are photographs of Art visiting the Buddha statue at Karmakura and touring various cities and scenic places and palaces. One picture is of Art and his mother having tea at Ito Gofukuten Department Store and another picture is of them having dinner at the Imperial Hotel. Many are of Art and his drivers and a number of them show Art racing his airplane against the baby cars. Others photographs are of him swimming, having a picnic, and working on his plane. Many include Art's mother, beaming with pride, as she and Art receive flowers from delegations of school children or as she watches her son enjoying the company of young women dressed in their traditional kimonos.[24]

Art and his mother in "a morning shower in Tokyo." Courtesy: Wertman-Stackhouse.

Art breaks through streamers during his exhibit at Osaka. Courtesy: Wertman-Stackhouse.

The hanger at Osaka built especially for Art. Courtesy: Wertman-Stackhouse.

Art loved to talk. Sometimes he discussed his religious beliefs, sometimes he talked about his flying, but one subject about which he was passionate was the importance of military preparedness. Art advised the Japanese government about its need for aviation technology and pilot training.[25]

Art had been on the reserve list for a number of years, and he announced that he would return home at the first indication that he could be used to help the United States improve her aviation forces. He said he didn't believe that airmen would be needed, however, "until airplanes are used for defense purposes or in conjunction with war transportation."[26]

From Tokyo, Art and his mother headed for Osaka. Art was eager to give a memorable performance in Osaka because it was there where he had faced the angry mob. Art said he had taken great chances in Osaka the previous year because of the weather, because of a new machine with which he wasn't that well acquainted, and because of a badly adjusted propeller. On his second trip, he did not disappoint the spectators, and the people of Osaka were more than gracious to him. They had built a large open-sided but covered hangar especially for his airplane.[27]

At Nara, Toyama, and Oyama, Art encountered bad weather and heavy rains,

Above and opposite: Art takes passengers up for a ride. Courtesy: James Wigner.

but most of his stops were successful. That summer, *The Japan Advertiser* reprinted a short biographical article about Art's early adventures and flying experiences that had earlier appeared in the April issue of *The American Magazine*. It was entitled "Most Daring Youngster in America."[28] The article ended its report with the following observation, "He is interested in the problem of flying and landing backward, and in the commercial future of the airplane."[29]

By September of 1917, it was time to return to America. Art had fulfilled his contracts, and the war was three years old. It was reported in the American media that Art Smith, "who has been living in Japan is on his way home. He will stop in Honolulu for a few days and expects to reach Fort Wayne about the first of October."[30] A photograph taken in Honolulu shows Art waving and laughing with a crowd of admirers as he posed in one of his "baby cars" under a sign that reads, "Autos Not Allowed On Piers."[31]

Art's two trips to Japan brought him many moneymaking opportunities. But Art was no longer concerned with making money. He was interested in flying, entertaining, starting an aviation school, and spreading the word about his Christian Scientist beliefs. According to Vic Bertrandias, Art was an aviator by day and a preacher at night.[32]

Any notion of continuing the status quo came to an end, however, as war spread throughout Europe.

17

World War I and Military Preparedness — 1917–1921

While at the Panama Pacific Exposition, Art was able to use his influence and celebrity status to talk about the importance of airplanes for military and commercial uses. As he traveled to Japan and developed a following among government officials, he became even more outspoken.

A number of foreign governments, including England and Japan, wanted him to join their air corps or to serve as a consultant to their aviation programs. The Russian government cabled him with a request to join her forces. The French honored him with a similar invitation. He turned down the offers to teach aviation and said he "preferred to stay at home and loop-the-loop safely in America."[1]

But Art became an ardent spokesman for American preparedness in the air. He believed there was a need for the United States to train and equip pilots in case of aerial battle. He pledged to use his skill in the air for "my country, if she ever needs me."[2] The newspapers reported his comment: "All I can do in aviation — and I hope it will be a great deal — belongs to her [United States]."[3] Another paper quoted him as saying he "was ready to assist Uncle Sam at any time that his services may be required for national defense." The reporter went on to comment that "If he does this free of charge, he will be contributing a large sum to the Government, for which he is still too young to vote."[4] Although in actuality, Art was twenty-seven years old, again he chose not to refute the comment about his age.

"I do not believe in war," Art told one reporter. "With so many difficulties to conquer, with the whole air-sea still uncharted, why should we fight each other?"[5]

After the United States entered the war in April of 1917, Art left his stunt flying exhibitions and tried to enlist in the Army Air Corps. He was refused. Instead, Art received an appointment to train, test, and evaluate pilots. Some said the Army Air Corps refused him because he was too short; others said it was because of the effects of too many crashes.

In 1926, Lieutenant V. E. Bertrandias, an aviator at McCook Field who had been with Art in Japan, said that Art "deeply regretted that he was not allowed to go overseas in the air service during the war. Smith had his leg broken in a fall before the war and the air service would not accept him because one leg was shorter than the other."[6] Bertrandias's comments at Art's memorial service also are insightful. He said that

> during my services overseas, Art would write and often times mention how he would like to trade his career for the opportunity that I had been so fortunate to receive, and sometimes his letters were sad because he could not get over it. He pleaded and begged with the authorities, but the handicap the famous birdboy had was due to the fact that he was crippled. Very few people knew this. This accident happened while in Japan the latter part of 1916, while in a town named Sapporo. In making an exhibition flight his motor failed and in order to avoid killing a number of spectators it was only by a miracle of God that he was not killed himself. However, this sacrifice on his part resulted in a very serious crash. Among numerous injuries, his leg was broken at the hip. The injury did not heal properly, which resulted in his return to the United States and having an operation performed. In order to save the leg it was necessary to saw a part of the bone off, because of the fact that blood poison had set in. This left the leg, when healed … shorter than the other one, and it was for this reason that Art never wore a uniform.[7]

In photographs of Art Smith while on his second trip to Japan, there is no sign of such a severe handicap. Accounts verify that after his accident, Art did have a limp, but such a deformity as Bertrandias described seems exaggerated. He had surgery and his leg had healed. Snapshots and newspaper photographs show Art, always beaming his wide, photogenic Art-Smith smile, as he meets and poses with potentates, royalty, admiring crowds, friends, and his mother. He appeared to be in wonderful health.

At the outbreak of the war, Art went to Langley Field, Virginia, where he served his country in a civilian capacity as an instructor and test pilot. Later at McCook Field, Art was one of two men trained to fly "the De Bothezat helicopter, at the time considered an exceedingly promising invention."[8]

Among his prized possessions was a tiny button he received when he became a member of the United States Aviation Corps. He liked to show it off at Rotary and Press Club meetings and said it was one he particularly valued. He told his audiences that he pledged to use his skill in the air for America.[9]

At different times from 1917 until 1920, Art was stationed at Langley Field, Carruthers Field in Texas, and Wilbur Wright Field in Ohio. His primary duty was to train combat pilots in aviation techniques. In Dayton, Ohio, Art also did wartime duty as a test pilot. It was while he was stationed in Ohio that Art became a personal friend of Lieutenant John A. Macready, the famous transcontinental flyer who was in charge of McCook Field.[10]

When Art arrived at Carruthers Field, it was big news. The *Fort Worth Star-Telegram* carried the headline, "World's Most Spectacular Flier, Art Smith, Of Stunt Fame, Sent to Carruthers; He's Experimenting For Future Air Feats; Motors Must Be Bettered, He Says, To Make Flying More Popular."[11]

The interview was covered by Mae Biddison Benson, who wrote, "Art Smith is here!" She said "that the internationally famous civilian flier is an instructor at Carruthers Field and has brought with him all his boyish enthusiasm."[12] Art's comments were quoted extensively. "It's so wonderful to mount up and sail above the earth far away from the nasty chuckle of life," Art told a battery of reporters. Then he explained that when America entered the war, he went to Washington and offered his services in any capacity that they were pleased to use him.[13]

When he was asked about his duties at Carruthers, he said, "Just before the armistice was signed, this field sent out an SOS call for instructors. I was taken from the Langley Experimental Field and ordered here. So far my work has been to test the airworthiness of planes."[14]

Art said he was "assigned to Langley Field and later to the Wilbur Wright Field to work out special features that I had designed for my own Exposition planes. That's what I have been doing since the States entered the war."[15]

Actually, Art was involved in working and perfecting a number of designs that would assist in teaching pilots. One was a plan to construct steel towers from which would be suspended a steel cable. An airplane would be suspended from these cables with enough play for the student aviator to execute a number of maneuvers and at the same time feel safe.[16] Art also came up with a system of double controls for teaching students to fly, which, he said, "is a radical departure from methods formerly in use and which, if it meets expectations is sure to eliminate much of the danger of learning to fly an airplane."[17]

According to the old way of double controls, there was only one set of controlling surfaces. Art's invention was to have the plane be operated by two sets of controlling surfaces. The second set of controlling surfaces would be entirely separate and independent from the first, thereby allowing the instructor the use of one set and the student the use of the other. Art's invention so impressed the Army, that it was while at Dayton flying field he was allowed to install his improvement on one of the army training planes."[18] After Art installed his double controls, he was told to "try it."[19] In order to test his invention, Art flew from Dayton on the morning of December 8, and arrived at Carstrom Field, Arcadia, Florida, the following day, a distance of 1,178 miles. He did the trip in sixteen hours and eighteen minutes of actual flying time.[20] According to the account, Art's invention, "if as good as hoped ... probably will be adopted generally for all army training planes."[21]

When reporters asked Art questions about his inventions and his flying, he was eager to answer. One question was, "Is there a possibility of constructing an instruction plane that will more thoroughly acquaint the flier with the approach of a dangerous condition?"[22]

To that, the crack flier said, "I believe that most accidents are due to inexperience, and if a man is taught how to avoid the deadly tail spin, a position that it is impossible to overcome once the plane takes it, half the accidents will be avoided."[23]

To round out one interview, Smith reminisced about his start in flying, his Panama Pacific Exposition stunts and his various medals. He talked about his flying adventures in China, Japan, Korea, and Manchuria. Recalling his visits to Japan in 1916 and 1917, he said, "The cherry blossoms, the wisteria, and the chrysanthemums of Japan are more wonderful than they are reputed to be."[24]

The newspaper article was accompanied by photographs, including one of Art and one of his baby cars, which the reporter said "the famous flyer parks in hotel lobbies and rides around the ship deck."[25] When asked more about his "ground attraction" and his baby race cars, "equipped with Harley-Davidson racing motors and made of the most durable material procurable," Art said, "When America entered the war, I had no more use for my baby cars. I'm selling them all but one."[26]

Indeed, Art put all but one of his baby cars up for sale. His advertisement read: "On account of entering the airplane manufacturing business, I am going to dispose of my miniature racing cars at a cost of $700.00 and up. Can be seen at Magginis & Perkins, 116 Van Ness Avenue."[27]

When Art was asked if airplanes would ever become as common as automobiles, he answered as an astute politician, "I should say not until the motor is perfected so that the power will be more assured and less apt to fail in mid-air. When aviation does come into its own, I don't see why Texas shouldn't be the pioneer. The most wonderful landing places in this country are here on the broad open tracts. It's fine."[28]

At the end of the interview, Art said,

> Whew! Sure, I'm as enthusiastic as ever. I haven't lost one bit of my enthusiasm. When I was building my first plane, I did it with so much yearning that I was up before the sun and working long after dark. It's worth it. When you're up in the air you don't have to eat somebody else's dust for miles and miles, either...." When he was asked about his age, he humorously quipped that he was "a little over 20, but I've been 20 for about eight years.[29]

Art said he hated to think that all records in aeronautical work were held by foreigners. "America produces men as resourceful and as daring, but because of the lack of governmental support, we do not have the machines or money for our work. Other nations are developing the aeroplane because of its use in war.... France, Germany, England, and even China are more advanced in aeronautics than the United States."[30]

Art was more involved in military preparedness than merely giving interviews. He visited airplane factories and military facilities. On one occasion, he visited the United States military aerodrome at North Island, near San Diego. The day was windy, and Art found only two U.S. Government machines that were able to fly in such

Art visited military bases and became an ardent spokesman for American air preparedness. Courtesy: Wertman-Stackhouse.

weather. Only eight flying machines were equipped with motors and five machines had no motors attached. He reported to the media, "Talk about the government declaring war, why this unpreparedness in aviation is almost criminal. It should be made public."[31] He believed that lack of government support was the cause of America falling so far behind other nations in aviation.

Art said France had at least two thousand five hundred experienced aviators when the war broke out, whereas America had fewer than two hundred aviators who would be of any value to the army or navy should America become involved in a war and even fewer airplanes.[32] Hundreds of the French pilots were civilians, he said, but they were able to take their planes and use them for military purposes. In America, the planes would have to be redesigned. "The question of machines now in use in various parts of the country would never serve for military purposes. We would simply have to wait until the airplane factories built airplanes that could be used, and then, they would not be up to those at the disposal of the European armies."[33]

Art was eager for people to realize there were uses for aviation other than for military purposes. He said, "There are peaceful conquests for aeronautics far more valuable. There is a great new element to be won for the use of commerce and transportation."[34]

Art talked about his plane and called her "my lovin-gal," and added that "she was as sensitive as a filly." He was sure with her he could out-maneuver the military pilots in Europe, but he "didn't want the experience of being winged by one of those beautifully mounted new field guns that the Germans had introduced over there for the purpose of exterminating the Allied birdmen, whom they happen to discover flying promiscuously around those German breweries."[35]

In truth, he explained that his airplane could not be used for military purposes because it was designed for exhibition flying. For exhibition work, he had to sit out in the open in the front of the machine, whereas military planes had to be enclosed.

He said that New Orleans and Chicago critics had stamped him as an aerial lunatic, but he was no lunatic. He had been inspired, he said, to excel in all that was daring in aeronautics by Pegoud and Beachey. He was "now doing what Beachey—even Pegoud—had never dreamed of doing."[36] Becoming serious, Art went back to the topic of military preparedness. He felt strongly about the need for the U.S. Government "to wake up and train aviators along the same lines as what I am doing. They will never learn to master the air in times of danger until they learn to loop-the-loop and perform the more difficult maneuvers of aviation."[37]

Once when Theodore Roosevelt was with Art, his arm around the young aviator's shoulder, he said, "I would do anything with you, Art. You are flying for fun now, but you must be careful. We don't want you to be killed out here. Someday it may be your duty to be shot for your country."[38] Roosevelt's comment was said in jest, but Art *was* willing to fight and die for his country. He had tried to enlist and was turned down. Even so, he wanted to help his country. He notified Secretary of War Garrison that he was ready to serve his duty in preparing men to fly in the war.[39]

Former president Theodore Roosevelt was one of Art's many fans. Courtesy: Allen County–Fort Wayne Historical Society & Museum.

Art ended one interview saying that if he lived through his exhibitions and grew tired of the game, he "would settle down, build a fine flying boat for pleasure... — and own a great cross-country airstrip — in which to take my friends for a spin." Then he added, "Oh, I'll never tire of aviation this side of the grave, not me."[40]

18

The Mail Service and
Ohio Lights—1921–1926

Art helped inaugurate the night airmail service. After the war was over and following the establishment of the Airmail Service, the post office department made plans to begin night flying on the transcontinental route in 1921. The department needed experienced flyers. Art was a natural candidate.[1]

While he was still at McCook Field in Dayton, Ohio, Art became interested in the Airmail Service, so one day when he was in Washington, D.C., and had the opportunity, he dropped by the office of Carl Egge, Superintendent of the United States Airmail Service, and inquired about their night-flying plans. After their conversation, Art filed an application for employment.[2] Although he applied in 1921, the date of his appointment as a pilot with the Airmail Service is April 1, 1923. (Some accounts place Art as leaving Fort Wayne in 1920 and joining the Airmail Service in 1921; however, research substantiates the year as being 1923.) He qualified for his license at the Kirkham School in Savonna, New York, and his assignment was to be "the appointed pilot on the Cleveland-Chicago route, as part of the Eastern Division."[3]

Not long afterward, Art's parents sold their house in Fort Wayne and moved to Cleveland. They were totally dependent on Art, so it was logical that they would make their home at one end or the other of Art's route.

Before Art could fly for the Airmail Service, however, modifications had to be made on his DeHaviland plane. Because he was so short in stature (5'2" and 125 lbs.), it was necessary to rig some extensions to his rudder bar so his feet would reach the controls.[4]

Flying in an open cockpit was not only dangerous, it was bitterly cold. Art and pioneer aviator Guy P. Fitzsimmons, known as "Wild Bill" Fitzsimmons, often discussed how to improve matters. Fitzsimmons said:

> I got to know Art Smith well. I first started flying at Kokomo, Indiana, and
> moved to Auburn to work for Irv and Glen Rieke at their father's foundry.
> There I resumed flying during the early twenties. I often drove my Model
> T to Bryan to be there to welcome Art when he arrived from Chicago.
> Although Art wanted to talk more about religion than flying, I managed
> to glean from him many experiences he had had, which helped me in my
> own endeavors. One thing Art always dwelt on was how I managed to keep
> from freezing to death while returning to Auburn those cold winter nights
> in my flivver. I kept telling him that the side curtains helped and also that
> I had one of those new-fangled exhaust heaters installed that helped keep
> the frost out of my little roadster. Art only shook his head in wonderment
> at me. Meanwhile, I wondered how Art kept from freezing to death in his
> DeHaviland mail plane.[5]

What Art did was to rig up an exhaust-type heater shroud with heat generated
by his four-hundred horsepower Liberty engine. Then he would remove his winter
flying boots, stow them in the plane, and fly the route in his stocking feet. "This keeps
my feet warm as toast," Art said.[6]

Art also devised a cockpit cowl, something akin to what is used by modern com-
petitive kayak racers. Using heavy-weight canvas, he designed a sort of inner lining
that could be snapped close to his neck to keep windblast out of the open cockpit,
with only his head sticking out so he could see. Waco Taperwings, Stearmans, and
Pitcairn Mail Wings that were built years later, especially for use on the mail runs,
adopted Smith's idea in the use of this inner-cockpit lining.[7]

DeHaviland luminous instruments were not yet in use. In fact, flight instruments
were virtually unknown. The needle deflection on the altimeter of considerably less than
one inch represented one thousand feet. There was no such thing as a sensitive altimeter, but flyers would become curious as to readings of their critical engine instruments
and want to know how the water temperature was doing and if oil pressure was holding. According to Fitzsimmons, "Art would unsnap far enough to glimpse these by
use of a flashlight mounted inside the cockpit. Then he'd snap the lining shut again."[8]

It was during this time that Art became acquainted with young Charles Lindbergh, who had a brief stint as an airmail pilot.

Art's schedule was fairly routine. He would take off in his DeHaviland from the
lighted Cicero Avenue Field in Chicago. During the winter months, he would leave
after dark and land at the lighted Bryan, Ohio, Airmail Field. In Bryan, he had a cot,
where he would grab some hours of sleep, then take on more mail, and take off during the pre-dawn darkness. He would time his takeoff in such a way that he would
land at Cleveland's unlighted airport after daylight.[9]

Art's membership card for the Airmail Pilots of America features the following
quote: "Ships may land, and ships may crash, /But we fly on forever." This statement did not turn out to be true for Art.[10]

On February 12, 1926, the weather was cold, and while on his mail route, Art
encountered fog and icy conditions between Waterloo, Indiana, and Bryan, Ohio. It
is believed that he drifted north about five miles off course.[11]

Art's Air Mail Pilots of America membership card. Courtesy: Wertman-Stackhouse.

"Wild Bill" Fitzsimmons speculated that Art had been flying rather high as he encountered a heavy snowstorm en route from Chicago to Bryan. He gave the following account about Art's crash and untimely death.

> Letting down to a lower level when his elapsed time was estimated to put Art in the vicinity of Bryan, he obviously spotted lights which he thought might be those at Bryan Airmail Field. Not certain, however, he made a pass and gave the plane the gun to circle around and look things over again. The lighted area he had dragged happened to be a farmhouse, and the lights Art saw were the headlights of a few cars and lights around the house and barnyard where a party was in progress. At the far end of Art's pass were some woods, and on his second pass, Art hit the tallest tree in the forest, cutting a swath some two hundred feet through the woods. Authorities could not determine whether Art died in the crash or in the subsequent fire.[12]

That night Art was flying a new type of air mail plane, number 602, a Liberty-engine Curtiss "Carrier Pigeon."[13] Details about the Montpelier, Ohio, accident revealed that the roar of Art's engine on his first and second passes brought people out of the farmhouse, and as they heard the sound of the crash, they felt almost certain that the aviator had parachuted out of his plane beforehand. "They formed a search party and scoured neighboring fields calling aloud for signs of the surviving flier—little realizing that his body was burning up in the gasoline-drenched plane wreckage and fire—a fire much too hot to investigate closely. It was hours later—dawn or after—that closer investigation was made into the real devastation for it took many hours for the intense heat to dispel."[14]

A farmer named Brannon who lived near the scene told officials that he saw Art's plane circle around and around in the air, flying very low, as if to find some landmark that would help him to fix his location. Whether the farmer or the reporter made the following statement, it has no lack of dramatic detail: "Suddenly with a devilish roar and the crash of breaking branches the plane leaped into the woods, like some giant football player attacking an impregnable line. It rode through the tops of the trees, leaving an open lane behind it. Then it was overcome in the uneven struggle. It tipped over and plunged to the ground. Fire completed the havoc and the lone pilot."[15]

The farmer notified officials, including the coroner of Williams County, who rushed to the scene. Art's body was found pinned under the debris, and the metallic remnants of the plane were so tangled with the trees that it was hours before the body could be removed.

Cleveland airmail officials took charge of the investigation. Art's body was taken to Cleveland where brief services were planned for the following Tuesday morning before his remains would be taken to Fort Wayne, his boyhood home, for the final resting place.

A wave of shock spread immediately throughout the Tri-State area and beyond. The Birdboy — the spirit of adventure in so many people — was dead. Hundreds of curious people drove to the spot where the plane fell, requiring Howard B. Shaver, superintendent of the Cleveland airport who was investigating the cause of the accident, to rope off the area. The mail, which was almost totally destroyed, was taken to the Bryan post office.[16]

It was established that the searchlight at the Bryan field was working properly at the time of the accident, visible by persons at Montpelier, eight miles northwest. People speculated about the accident. Some thought fog caused Art to veer off course. Others blamed engine failure. The former superintendent of the Bryan airmail field, O. L. Woodson, head of an airplane manufacturing company, gave the most likely explanation. His theory was that the crash was caused by a coating of ice that enshrouded the plane, making it so heavy it would not rise. "I flew to the scene of the accident shortly after it occurred," he said. "The temperature then was about thirty degrees—just right to cause the mist to turn to ice and cling to the plane. It is my belief that the added weight of the ice made the plane so heavy it would not rise, and that this caused Smith to crash into the trees."[17]

Local boyhood friends of Art and ex-service men, realizing that Art was one of the outstanding and heroic figures of American aviation, began making plans for a public service at the cemetery. Fort Wayne officials began making plans to see their hero properly honored.

When Art's mother learned about the accident and her son's death, she was angry. Understandably inconsolable, she decreed that there would be no public funeral services. She walked back and forth in her small home in Cleveland, stopping time and again to gaze at the hundreds of trophies won by her son, repeating the sentence, "Would that I were dead instead of him."[18] Around her were cups of silver and gold, the gifts of kings, medals for bravery, and tokens of honor for services in extending man's conquest of the air. Displayed nearby was the likeness of Art, gorgeously embroidered on silk, the gift of the Orient that he had received in 1917. "She gave her son to the conquest of the air, and the conquest of the air has taken him from her," reported a Cleveland paper.[19]

A local real estate man and intimate friend of the Smith family, James S. Peddicord, made the following announcement: "Any persons who wish to join in paying the last earthly tribute to the famous Birdboy are invited to meet the Nickel Plate train at the station on Calhoun Street at ll:50 o'clock this noon and follow the body to the cemetery. Others are invited to join in the services at the grave. The burial will take place immediately after the arrival of the body in the city."[20]

On February 16, 1926, however, Fort Wayne's *Journal Gazette* carried the following headline: "Public Service For Art Smith." Underneath the main headline, a sub-headline reads, "Mother Consents to Allow Friends To Pay Final Tribute."[21]

19

Tributes—1926–1928

When Art's mother learned how much the people of Fort Wayne wanted to honor her son, she agreed to a short public service at the cemetery. A Christian Science reader would accompany the members of the Smith family from Cleveland to Fort Wayne to take charge of the services. As plans began to develop, an attempt was made to secure a couple of planes from the aviation field in Dayton to circle above the cemetery during the services.[1]

Al Wertman, William Schnorr, Albert Johnson, Edgar Johnson, Charles Stauffer, and Paul Hobrock were named as pallbearers.[2] Each had helped Art with his work at some phase of his career. Their sad duty was to meet the train and escort the body to its final resting place.

Within hours, county and city officials and the heads of various civic organizations publicly endorsed the idea of a permanent memorial to Smith. Judge Charles J. Ryan proclaimed that "Art Smith is one of the most outstanding citizens Fort Wayne has given to the world. No single flyer has contributed more to aviation than he did. The whole world is his debtor. In that he helped to make aviation practical, Fort Wayne cannot afford to do less than erect a permanent memorial in his honor."[3]

Other prominent citizens concurred, including the mayor, the president of the council of Jewish Women, the judge advocate of the Indiana American Legion and past commander of the Fort Wayne Legion post, and many others. Eli Siussman, county commissioner, said, "Few men of this community have done such important work. We should have something to perpetuate his memory that boys and girls of the future may know that Fort Wayne produced a real hero in Art Smith." Another commissioner said, "I have a lot of respect for a boy like Art Smith. He started out with nothing and did big things. He showed appreciation for what his father and mother did for him. Unlike him, many boys forget their parents when success comes."[4]

As people learned about the crash, disbelief spread throughout Northeast Indiana and then the world. People from far corners of the globe could hardly believe the news. The Emperor of Japan sent a telegram asking if it were true that the Birdboy who had delighted him a few years before indeed had died. When Orville Wright, co-inventor of the airplane, heard about the crash, he said, "Art was a fine fellow and a very able flyer, and I am shocked to learn of his death."[5]

For an entire week after the tragedy, area newspapers carried stories daily about Art Smith, repeating details about his first attempts to build an airplane, his many crashes, and his subsequent successes. A newspaper reporter summarized what many citizens knew: "From the time that he first started to fly, Smith has been known as a daredevil, and many of the tricks, familiar to every army aviator during the war, were performed by Smith to thrill the masses years before they were adopted as tests for military pilots."[6]

Articles were devoted to tributes, speculations about what caused the accident, the Smiths mortgaging their home, Art's blind father, his "sorrowing, suffering mother," and the funeral services. Even before funeral plans were finalized, there was a move to create some sort of appropriate Art Smith memorial. Charles Corneille, a former serviceman who had followed Art's career from the beginning, suggested the erection of a fitting memorial statue.[7]

Selected to serve on the committee were Mayor William C. Geake; Postmaster Harry Baals; Ross McCullough of the First National Bank; Charles R. Weatherhogg (the architect for whom Art worked as a young boy); John C. Trier, president of the board of park commissioners; Judge Sol A. Wood; Judge Charles W. Ryan; Oscar Foellinger; L. G. Ellingham; Attorney Clarence McNabb; Robert M. Feustel, president of the Fort Wayne Art School and Museum; Fred George; Chester I. Hall; Albert Schaaf; Paul Guild; Clarence Cornish and Earl Moss—both former army aviators; and James S. Peddicord.[8] All were of the opinion that the most logical and appropriate site for the monument was Memorial Park (Driving Park), where Art made his first flying experiments. An announcement about the memorial was placed in area newspapers.

On the morning of the services, the train arrived at 11:50 A.M. over the Nickel Plate Railroad from Cleveland and was greeted by thousands of citizens headed by Mayor Geake, Chief of Police Harry Kavanaugh, and Postmaster Harry Baals. Post Office employees, "all dressed in their gray uniforms," were present to pay tribute to a fellow who died "while speeding the mail." As the casket passed, they laid a wreath on it that bore the inscription, "To a Comrade in the Service."[9] Aviation Reserve Corps pilots from the government airfields at Cleveland and Bryan, Ohio, attended.

The coffin, carried by the six pallbearers, was draped with an American flag "as the government's conventional tribute to those who by their lives exemplify American traditions of fearlessness."[10] The cortege moved south on Calhoun Street to Berry Street, west on Berry to Rockhill, and then west on Main to Lindenwood Cemetery. Citizens lined the streets and took off their hats in respectful silence as the procession moved solemnly toward the cemetery. The following account of the service reveals the mood of the day:

> The organ which played his requiem was the propeller of an airplane from
> McCook Field, Dayton, Ohio, which dipped low over the grave as the ser-
> vice was ready to start. The plane dropped flowers, which descended with
> the silence of snowflakes upon the grave.
>
>   As the plane was directly over her head, Mrs. Smith held out her hands
> toward it as if to receive a homing pigeon. It was as though her fancy told
> her that the plane would bring her son back to her as another plane had so
> often done. Some words she said, but the meaning of them was lost upon
> the throng.[11]

The plane represented the Fort Wayne chapter of the National Aeronautic Association and was flown by Lieutenant Clarence Cornish, a former army aviator.[12] During the service, two airplanes of the DeHaviland type, piloted by government flyers
stationed at McCook Field, flew over Lindenwood Cemetery. The "roaring ships
swooped low over the grave and dropped their floral tributes from overhead as the
crowd stood in reverent awe with upturned faces. The machines then flew back in
two-plane formation over the cemetery trees and then vanished in the clouds, which
Fort Wayne's beloved aviator had loved so well."[13] Piloting the planes were Major Hale,
Lieutenant Victor E. Bertrandias, Lieutenant Bayord Johnson, and Lieutenant L.P.R.
Reese.[14]

Vic Bertrandias was with Art in San Francisco and in Japan in 1916, and Art
taught him to fly. As Vic flew one of the airplanes, paying his last tribute to his dear
friend, what happened seemed symbolic. Bernard J. Losh, writing an account of the
funeral, said, "It seems more than a coincidence that the bouquet of flowers he [Vic]
dropped from his airplane should flutter slowly down to earth and land on the coffin,
as it stood beside the yawning grave."[15]

Hundreds of people attended the simple but impressive service. A dignified
reader "with handsome snow-white hair that drifted above a tall brow" from the
Christian Science church announced that he would read Mrs. Mary Baker Eddy's
interpretation of the twenty-third Psalm. After the psalm, there was a reading of "the
scientific statement of being" from *Science and Health, with Keys to the Scriptures.*
The services closed with three verses of the third chapter of the First Epistle of St.
John. That was all.[16]

At the time of the service, the employees of the Rub-No-More Company lined
up outside the plant and stood for a minute in silent tribute to Art Smith. The Rub-
No-More building was located near Memorial Park, where Art made his first flying
attempts.[17] Thousands who could not attend sent messages of sympathy or paid tribute.

To mark the occasion and in honor of Art's memory, the Airmail Service inaugurated a new mail service route between Cleveland and Detroit, one hour before
the final rites were performed.[18] The pilots and airfield officials then went in a body
to wish "Godspeed to their comrade of the clouds for the last time."[19]

Following the funeral, scores of queries and endorsements were received by *The
Journal Gazette* about a suitable memorial. On Thursday, February 18, *The Journal*

Gazette carried two articles about Art. One was a feature about the Birdboy's parents that began with Art's father's comment, "They are making an Abraham Lincoln of him now." Art's father was absolutely crushed by his son's death, and his feelings vacillated between despair, bitterness, and pride. The reporter wrote that the Smiths would be moving back to Fort Wayne.[20]

The other article was headlined: "Smith Memorial Campaign Opened." It listed by name the first twelve contributors. Both *The Journal Gazette* and Robert M. Feustel donated $100 each. James S. Peddicord gave $25. There were five $10 donations, five $5 donations. Two were from a Friend, one from an Aviator, and one from Anonymous. The total received was $295.[21]

From that time on, the paper regularly carried the list of contributors and listed the amount each donated to the fund. By the end of the next day, the total was $859.50.[22] News about pledges, coins, checks, fund-raisers, and letters from the Boy Scout troops, labor unions, realtors, clubwomen, Friars Club, businesses, ministers, schools, and interested people made the front page on a regular basis. Often a donation was accompanied by a letter, which was published along with the contribution list. One typical letter is as follows: "Kindly accept my little contribution for the Art Smith memorial fund. I consider this move a fitting and proper tribute to Fort Wayne's greatest citizen, a young man who rose from the ranks and was ever a faithful citizen to his country and his city, who died as he lived, honorably."[23]

Some testimonials were long and eloquent, but always, each echoed the sentiments that accompanied the check sent by businessman Edgar H. Kilbourne for himself, his wife, and his daughter.

> This fund ought to be supported by every man, woman, and child in the city of Fort Wayne; a memorial of this kind is of inestimable value to our future generation, especially in view of the fact that it will bring back to our mind, so beautiful a character as Art Smith, who was profoundly devoted to his parents and to Fort Wayne, his hometown. He brought fame to us; now in return, let the people of this historical place return their gratitude and build that kind of memorial that Art Smith's name deserves.[24]

The kind of memorial that would be erected depended on the amount of money received. There would be no drive. All contributions were to be voluntary. The committee thought that a suitable memorial probably would cost between $5,000 and $10,000. A permanent organization to handle affairs connected with the memorial was established, and the committee expanded to include various community dignitaries. Robert M. Feustel stated that "it would be easy for a few men to go out and raise $5,000 or $10,000 ... but the greater good would come to the city if everyone who can afford to give anything, gave a small contribution."[25]

Stores and factories organized freewill offerings. Schoolchildren got involved. Members of the memorial committee gave talks at club luncheons and meetings. The Central Catholic High School Athletic Association proposed a basketball game between Central Catholic and either Central or South Side, with the proceeds to go to the Art Smith memorial fund.[26] Industrial concerns and their employees made contributions. The president of the One Hundred Percent Club announced that five percent of all the receipts from the seat sale for the Colonel William Mitchell lecture at the Shrine auditorium would go to the fund. The Packard Piano company employees gave $67, the Eta chapter of Phi Beta Psi sorority gave $5, the Rt. Rev. Msgr. J.H. Oechtering gave $2. By February 25, 1926, the total was $2,458.88.[27] By the end of February, the total was $3,344.58.[28] Large and small contributions came from towns and people throughout Northeast Indiana and from states as far away as Florida and California.

There was a citywide competition for plans and suggestions for the design of the memorial. Mr. Feustel was anxious that the memorial adequately symbolize Art Smith's unusual career. "It should be something artistic and dignified," he said, "so that it will not become obsolete with the change of public taste."[29] The basketball game benefit could not be held because according to the rules of the Indiana High School Athletic Association members of the association were only allowed to play twenty games per season. Since that was the case, the city schools contributed $158.76 to the fund.[30]

The memorial fund continued to grow, Art's parents moved back to Fort Wayne, and newspapers continued to carry testimonials to their Birdboy. James Novelli, a sculptor from New York, was selected to design a suitable monument.[31] Tucked in Ida Smith's scrapbooks were hundreds of news clipping and photographs about Art's flying career, his trips throughout the Midwest and Japan, some personal keepsakes, including a loose page on which was written a four-verse poem entitled "Mom," and several articles about the various amounts of the memorial fund.[32]

On August 10, 1927, America's flying hero Charles A. Lindbergh flew the *Spirit of St. Louis* over the city of Fort Wayne while en route from Indianapolis to Detroit. He was on a tour of the United States to encourage popular interest in aeronautics. "The Viking of the Air," as the newspaper called him, circled the outskirts of the city, then brought his plane over the business district and dropped a message in a white sack which landed at the corner of Main and Court street. He then circled the courthouse and headed northeast. His silver plane, which was accompanied by an escort plane, came within a short distance of Sweebrock field, then turned northeast. Although Art Smith's name was not mentioned in the message, Lindbergh had known Art while both were in the Airmail Service. Lindbergh's flight over Fort Wayne was taken by its citizens as his poignant tribute to the memory of the Fort Wayne Birdboy, called in the newspaper's account "one of the greatest and most famous flyers of his time."[33]

One year later, Fort Wayne was ready to unveil and dedicate its permanent memorial to Art Smith. The ceremony was set for 2:30 P.M. on August 15, 1928, at Memorial Park. Art's mother was asked to pull the cord to unveil the bronze and granite memorial erected to her son's memory. She would be escorted by Robert Feustel, who represented the citizens' committee, and Harry W. Baals, Fort Wayne postmaster, representing the postal department.[34]

Carl F. Egge, former superintendent of the airmail service at Cleveland, was invited to make a brief dedicatory address. W. E. Gillmore, brigadier-general of the Air Corps at Wright Field in Dayton, arranged for three army planes, piloted by Lieutenants Gardner, Lampton, and Niergarth, to arrive in time for the dedication. Wesley L. Smith, superintendent of the eastern division of the Airmail Service, sent word that he would attend with at least one airmail pilot. "We want to do our part in paying tribute to Art Smith, who was one of the best of the pioneer airmail pilots," he said. These four planes, accompanied by a local airplane piloted by Arch Alspach, carrying W. H. Schnorr, who was with Art during his sensational flights at the San Francisco exposition and also on his trip to Japan, were to fly low over the memorial and drop flowers.[35]

At the appointed time, before the eyes of a host of Art's admirers and to the majestic roar of airplane propellers, Art's mother walked through the crowd and pulled the cord that released the flag veiling the bronze symbol of her son's immortal achievement. Art Smith was accorded his most lasting honor. There was no pomp, but there was sincerity. The addresses were few and brief. There were many tears.[36]

Contrary to the opinion of some people who thought the monument should be a statue of Art "showing him at the age he finished his first plane, holding aloft in one hand a miniature copy of his first plane just about to leave his hand and the expression on his face showing his joy," and under it, the caption 'It Flies,'"[37] James Novelli designed a statue to represent "The Spirit of Flight." Atop a forty-foot shaft of Barre, Vermont, granite is a bronze statue of a youth with wings and a flying helmet, face looking upward, with feet barely touching a small globe. At the base of the huge shaft of granite are four tablets in bas-relief depicting the four stages of mail transportation. These four stages include the stage coach of olden days, the iron horse with a group of Indians looking on stolidly, the steamship and locomotive, and the airplane, the connecting link between the Atlantic and Pacific.[38]

The figure in bronze is eight feet high. The inscription on the bronze tablet at the base reads: "Erected in memory of Arthur R. Smith (1890–1926), pioneer aviator, who gave his life in the U. S. Airmail Service. By the citizens of Fort Wayne, A. D. 1926."[39] In modeling the figure of the aviator, Novelli encrusted part of the form with masses of clay to give the novel effect of clouds. The wings of the flyer are outstretched as if he is soaring through space, and that is the feeling that one gets when looking at the figure.[40]

Among those who attended the memorial service was S.A. Oliver of Los Angeles, representing Menasco Motors and Al Menasco who had accompanied Art Smith to Japan.[41] Just before the dedication and unveiling ceremony began, the two groups of planes flew over the park in formation. The first group was headed by an airmail plane piloted by Frank H. Burnside of the National Air Transport, Inc. Burnside was the pilot who took over Art's route after Art's death. Burnside's plane was a Douglas transport type with a Pratt & Whitney motor. The others in the group flew Douglas 0-2 army biplanes from Wright Field. Arch Alspach of the Wayne Flying Service flew a Stinson Detroiter monoplane.[42]

"The Spirit of Flight," a memorial to Art Smith, mail service flier, to be erected at Fort Wayne, Ind., home of the aviator who lost his life a year ago at Montpelier, O. (Dorr.)

Newspaper clipping of sculptor James Novelli with the memorial he designed to represent "The Spirit of Flight." Courtesy: Stackhouse Collection.

The second group was composed of lighter types of aircraft owned by local flyers. This formation was headed by Homer Stockert in a Travel-Air biplane. Others in the second group were Paul Hobrock, Ed Hadley, and Harold Preston, all flying Waco planes.[43]

Colonel David N. Foster, president of the park commissioners, presided. The invocation was given by the pastor of the Plymouth Congregational Church, after which Colonel Foster read the letter of the citizens' committee. Mayor Geake accepted the memorial on behalf of the city. He said Fort Wayne "was proud of this boy with a vision," and he hoped that the memorial would always serve as an inspiration to the youth not only of Fort Wayne, but also of the country, "teaching the lesson that faith, patience, and perseverance are the qualities that make for success in American life. May it stand as a memorial to Art Smith, who brought fame to our city and whose memory we revere in our hearts today, to testify to the qualities of that splendid youth who gave up his life in the service of his country — our world-famous Birdboy — Art Smith."[44]

After the speech, Art's parents were presented to the crowd, and an eight-year-old boy gave Art's mother a large bouquet of flowers that were grown in Memorial Park. Art's mother was escorted from the speaker's stand to the column where she unveiled the monument. On the stand with Mr. and Mrs. James Smith were several relatives, the mayor, Carl Egge, and other guests, and Al Wertman, Art's boyhood chum.[45]

In his address, Carl Egge, executive secretary of the National Air Pilots Association, said that Art had flown 176,078 miles while serving with the Airmail Service, "equivalent to more than seven times around the world. He was with us less than three years. He paid the price many are called upon to pay when engaged in pioneering."[46] [U.S. Air Mail internet statistics list Art's total miles flown as 103,735 and total hours flown as 1,047.][47]

"It is mingled joy and sorrow," Art's mother said, smiling through her tears, as people who admired her son came forward to clasp her hand.[48] She asked that the newspapers express to the general public her deep appreciation of the tribute, that Art's native city had paid her son. She wished she could thank everyone personally.

Robert Feustel, chairman of the committee that had selected the sculptor, also gave a speech. After a number of remarks about Art's early dreams, Feustel said,

> from this humble beginning, the record of the Birdboy reads like a magic tale. [Art was an] experienced flyer, night flyer, exhibition flyer, adviser of the flying department of the Japanese government, instructor to the combat flyers in the world war, and then, when peace came, one of the pioneer flyers in the airmail service where he lost his life in the performance of his duty on the night of February 12, 1926.[49]

"I will always believe that Art's death was a self-sacrifice," Lieutenant Bertrandias said. In his speech, he said:

> The fact that he was carrying much valuable mail and flying a brand new airplane of experimental type had everything to do with his action. He was in trouble and wanted to safely land the plane with its cargo. If Smith had thought only of his own life, he could have climbed high enough and jumped to safety with his parachute and left the ship and mail to destruction. He realized the situation and rather than desert the plane, he attempted to pull out of the difficulty and sacrificed his life in doing so. Had he jumped to safety, he would probably have been severely criticized. He died a martyr to the mail service.[50]

It was after the crowd began to leave that a poignant scene occurred. Art's mother led her almost stone-blind husband to the memorial statue and helped him feel with the tips of his fingers the words and designs that honored their son.

20

Smith Field and
Beyond — 1926 to the Present

Art Smith was buried in Lindenwood Cemetery not far from where, four years later, his friend and America's first ace in the Great War, Paul Baer, would be placed. When Baer's plane crashed on December 9, 1930, near Shanghai, China, he also was in the airmail service. Baer established airmail service in South America and later flew mail and passengers for Chinese Airway Federal, Inc.[1] Their mothers were friends and they grieved together.

Fort Wayne citizens found it difficult to forget their Birdboy, the pioneer aviator who not only had shared his adventurous spirit with the world but also had put their town on the map. From time to time, newspapers ran articles about "The Smash-up Kid," "Fort Wayne's Birdboy," and the "Intrepid Daredevil." A number of organizations honored Art by displaying his medals or memorabilia. For instance, on the same day that *The News-Sentinel* (Fort Wayne) covered the upcoming dedication of the new Masonic Temple on East Washington Blvd., it also ran a photograph of an exhibit of Art Smith's medals, stating that Art "was killed recently while flying a mail plane at night [and had gotten the medals] for his skill during the early days of aviation."[2] The photograph shows nearly fifty medals, including the embroidered photograph of Art that was presented to him by his Japanese admirers. Art had received fifty-eight medals in all. Some he gave to friends. Some have disappeared, and some belong to the Allen County-Fort Wayne Historical Society Museum.

Throughout the years, there were memorials, honors, and gestures of remembrance. One of the more significant ones was giving the name of Smith Field to an eighty-acre airfield. The field was on the Fred Buecker farm on Lima Road (Route 3)

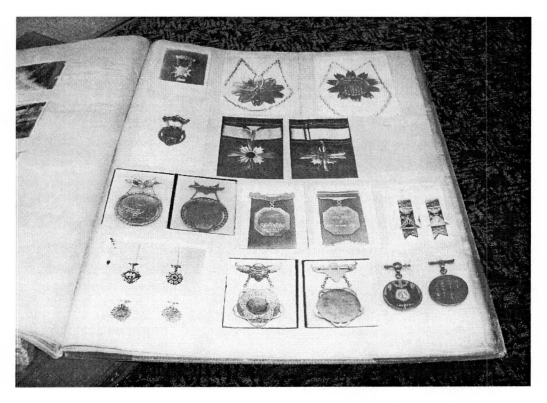

Art received fifty-eight medals. Shown on this page of his mother's scrapbook are photographs of ten. Courtesy: Greater Fort Wayne Aviation Museum. Photographer Don Goss.

on the north side of Fort Wayne.[3] The history of how it came to be named "Smith Field" is a story in itself.

At first, the field was known as Showalter's airport because Captain Floyd Showalter started a flying school there. During the war years, the field was known as "Flight B," a training base affiliated with a detachment of Ft. Benjamin Harrison of Indianapolis. It was a part of the 309th Observation Squadron. Afterwards, the promoter Showalter had to give up the lease on the field because he was indebted to the Standard Oil Company. He also lost his J-1 Standard biplane. Paul H. Hobrock, who graduated with the class of 1919 from Fort Wayne High School and subsequently became chief architectural draftsman for the J.M.E. Riedel firm, started taking his flying lessons at Showalter's field and soloed there on July 23, 1923. Hobrock bought Showalter's biplane and leased the field. Hobrock had been one of Art Smith's friends and was an active participant in the campaign for a permanent memorial for the famed aviator.[4]

Hobrock went into partnership with George Sweet in June of 1925, and the field became known as Sweebrock Airport. It quickly became a hub of activity and served as the city's first municipal airport. About that time, the Park Commissioners bought one hundred and fifty-six acres of land north of the city at the cost of $38,000. Later, fifty-six acres of land were added. The land extended from Ludwig Road to Cook Road, west of the New York Central Railroad tracks. The field was named Baer Field to honor Lieutenant Paul Baer, the flying ace during the war for France; however, in the 1930s, it was called the Smith-Baer Airport.[5]

When Fort Wayne built a new airport, city officials wanted to name it for Baer, but the airport on Lima Road carried that name. Not to worry. The modern, new airport was named Baer Field Municipal Airport, and the former Baer Field on the northeast side of the city was renamed to honor Art Smith, "the charismatic pioneer who made international aviation history for his loop-the-loops and skywriting."[6] The first Board of Aviation commissioners was formed in 1929.[7]

In spite of the protests of hundreds of airplane owners, flying enthusiasts, historians, preservationists, and a majority of Northeast Indiana citizens, on the afternoon of June 26, 2002, the International Fort Wayne–Allen County Airport Authority voted four to one, with one abstaining, to close the historic Smith Field.[8] It was Fort Wayne's first airport and one of the first airfields in the state of Indiana. Their decision was vigorously contested.

Public television station WFWA-TV made a documentary that aired in the summer of 2002 about Art Smith and the local and national legends associated with Smith Field. The documentary preserves information about the history of Smith Field as well as the planes— even the large, four-engine planes— that landed there.

In 1937, Art Smith's mother was the guest of honor on the first courtesy flight made by the giant 21-passenger TWA Skysleeper that landed at the Paul Baer Municipal Airport. The Douglas luxury liner that carried Ida Smith was a far cry from the airplane her son flew at Driving Park in 1910, 1911, and 1912. She was, according to all reports, "a gracious, courageous, little lady."[9]

Indeed, Ida Smith was brave. Twice she had been up in the air with Art when his airplane motor choked. In 1925, she was with him when at two thousand feet, he had to volplane to earth. Fortunately neither one was injured. "I looked at Art and touched his shoulder," she said. "When he smiled at me, I knew I was with my boy and I was safe."[10] The other occasion occurred during the World's Fair at San Francisco. She had gone up for a ride with Art and his engine failed. The plane volplaned dizzily to five hundred feet off the ground, went into a nose dive, and landed on its propeller. Art's plane crashed into a fence, and his mother's ankle was sprained.

After that mishap Art liked to tell how his mother kept her head. "Only a slight tightening of the lips," he said, "indicated she was even aware we were in danger."[11]

Fort Wayne became a part of the airmail system four years after Art's death. The first round-trip mail shuttle between Fort Wayne and South Bend was launched the morning of December 8, 1930, from Baer Municipal Airport (later renamed Smith Field). The first of several round-trips made that day was completed in ninety minutes. During one of the trips, the pilot, Lieutenant George Hill, flew over Memorial Park and dropped a wreath near the monument erected in honor of pioneer aviator Art Smith.[12]

On December 8, 1980, Ed Shenk, a pilot, airplane mechanic, and owner of his own airstrip in Garrett, Indiana, along with Roger Myers, a bombardier in World War II, made a fifty-year commemorative flight from Smith Field to South Bend to mark the event.[13] The occasion afforded the media once again to dwell on the accomplishments of Fort Wayne's famous Birdboy.

When in 1956, the autobiography of Art Smith was re-printed in *The News-Sentinel* (Fort Wayne), it awakened memories among people who had known the aviator. In an article dated August 22, 1956, Robert S. Bradley, owner and operator of the National Neon Sign Company and a pastor of the Church of the Nazarene for forty years, said,

> I helped Art Smith build his second plane, the one he used to elope to Hillsdale, Michigan.... Art assembled that plane on the fourth floor of the Charles Batchelor Building at the corner of Clinton and Columbia streets. He had to go through my showrooms (electrical equipment) to get to his shop. When he needed assistance with some part of the work, I went up and helped out. After he had the plane all built, he took it apart, moved it out to the Driving Park, and reassembled it. He asked me to ride in it, but I never did.[14]

It is said that Smith did have a shop at the Batchelor building, so Bradley's recollections may in fact be true. E. Johnson, one of Art's cousins, had a more sardonic recollection:

> There are ... things incorrect in Art's book, but these are of his own making. For instance, he had an uncle that helped him build his first plane from the ground up and was on the road with him for months. This man would assemble the plane ready to fly without any help from Art. Art many times would get to the field just in time to make his flight and would say, "Everything ready to go, Ed?" He would then make his flight and this man would then disassemble the plane and ship it on to the next place he was to fly. This man went home many times in the beginning with no pay or sometimes very little. For some reason, this man never knew why, Art never mentioned his name in his book. This was quite a blow to this man after all he had done for Art, and he never quite got over it. I know this is correct because this man was my father, Edgar E. Johnson, now deceased.[15]

"Wild Bill" Fitzsimmons, who lived south of Auburn, Indiana, recalled a memorial service for Art Smith in 1933, where he used Art's invention of phosphorus skywriting to write Smith's name across the sky. He said,

> Art's invention called for phosphorous. It was kept in a solid state under cold water and liquefied under hot water from the engine. The equipment weighed eight hundred pounds and the whole process was very dangerous. We would work with the phosphorous under water with gloves. When the gloves dried, they burst into flame. Once we set fire to a wheat field and had to pay for the crop.[16]

Fitzsimmons met Art through Al Wertman when Art was flying for the army at McCook Field. Al and Fitzsimmons often visited together at Bryan, Ohio, while Art was night flying for the U.S. Mail Service. Fitzsimmons, who did skywriting for an advertising firm, said that most skywriting planes use ordinary floor oil released under pressure. He said that Art had used his skywriting invention only a few times in experimentation and demonstration before he crashed. "We experimented with it at night and found that the streaks were seen one hundred and fifty miles away. People in Fort Wayne got terribly excited. Many reported seeing a mysterious dirigible and some said they even saw people sitting in it!"[17]

The reputation of Art Smith was sufficient that sixty years later in the 1970s, a national fan club was named in his honor. Members of the Art Smith Aeroplane Society were Billy Parker of Arizona, Bob McComb, an aerobatics pilot for many years, Ralph Bleke, John Fred McComb, George Alford, William Sheets, Harold Kiel, and Paul Hobrock. The men decided to build an authentic replica of Smith's biplane. Theodore Hagerman of the Fort Wayne Air Service provided the working space for the rebuilding project in a shop at Baer Field.[18]

When the OX5 Club of America held its 15th Annual National Convention in Fort Wayne, they dedicated the reunion to Art Smith, "The Birdboy of Fort Wayne." The City of Fort Wayne proclaimed Friday, October 23, 1970, as "Art Smith Memorial Day," and the mayor urged " all school children as well as adults to pay respect to the memory of this great American."[19]

In the convention booklet, an advertisement sought donations of $1.00 or more "to build one 1910 and one 1915 model of Art Smith's first planes, built and flown at Fort Wayne, Indiana. Accompanying the ad was a copy of Will D. (Billy) Parker's lifetime membership card, showing that he was the first to sign as a charter member of the Art Smith Aeroplane Society.[20]

Robert "Bob" McComb, 3rd Vice President of the OX5 Club of America, who wrote the story of Art Smith for the 1970 OX5 Convention, led the Fort Wayne group of flying enthusiasts in the actual building of a faithful re-creation of Art Smith's first successful plane.[21]

The replica was originally planned for the Deihm Museum of Natural History in Fort Wayne, but because the Deihm Museum didn't have enough space for it to be properly showcased, the airplane was placed in the showroom building of the Auburn Automobile Company, now the Auburn Cord Duesenberg Museum. For several reasons it was a logical place. Al Wertman, "the genius behind Smith's plane," had for a time worked for the automobile company; there is a strong parallel between the early auto and aviation industries and Auburn was prominent in both; Art had given exhibitions in Auburn; and it was "Wild Bill" Fitzsimmons, of Auburn, who shared with Art useful suggestions about equipping his mail plane for comfort. Fitzsimmons also worked for the Auburn Automobile Company.[22]

The replica plane took five years to build. It stayed at the Auburn Cord Duesenberg Museum until the mid–1980s, when it was moved to Fort Wayne International Airport, where it hangs in the passenger boarding area. Contrary to the idea of some, it is not a replica of Smith's very *first* airplane experiment. Art's first machine had the tandem bicycle gear, a wheel first and a wheel aft and wing skids, requiring

Taking off. Courtesy: Wertman-Stackhouse.

support alongside both wings in order to get it off the ground. That plane crashed and was destroyed. The replica which hangs in the airport shows the conventional side by side landing gear; consequently, it duplicates the *first successful* machine that Art and Al Wertman constructed and flew.[23]

At any rate, by present day standards, the replica of Art's biplane seems to be made of matchsticks and gossamer. It is a tangible testament to the courage of the early aviator. Its fragile wings and wires offer less than a minimum of protection to its pilot, and it almost brings shivers to anyone who tries to imagine how daring it must have been to fly in such a plane.

People have held on to postcards, letters, and bits of memorabilia as souvenirs. A number of collectors search for Art Smith pins, postcards, and photographs. Some have become "Art Smith buffs," as did Roger K. Myers, founder and curator of the Greater Fort Wayne Aviation Museum. Myers, a Delta manager for forty years, found and bought a copy of the Nagaoka diary in 1982, at the Hugh C. and Susan McCullough auction. (McCullough served on the Art Smith Memorial Committee.)[24] The hardbound book was compiled by the editorial department of the Japanese National Aviation Society and by its president, Lieutenant-General Gaisha Nagaoka. Dated July 20, 1916, the wine-colored cover is embossed with gold letters. A painting in the book depicts the American flag and the Japanese flag connected by a dove of peace and a view of Mount Fuji. Art Smith's airplane is flying in the foreground. The text is written in both Japanese and English, with the first page beginning in the back. There are no page numbers. The book's formal title is *Aeroplane as a Factor in Bringing Japan and the United States Closer in Friendship*; however, it also bears the title of *A Brief History of the Flights of Art Smith in Japan*.[25]

In the preface, General Nagaoka wrote, "I have decided to edit a book entitled *The Brief History of Art Smith's Flights In Japan* to be distributed throughout the county."[26] The book begins with an accounting of the fact that Art landed in March 1916 and was welcomed by two Navy pilots who circled Art's ship in their hydroplanes three times. It lists Art's activities and whereabouts for each day he was on his tour, and states that "Art went to Japan, where aviation was still in comparatively undeveloped stage, in hopes of bringing back to America the good will of the Japanese people." The last day given is July 20, 1916, when Art "left Tokyo for Yokahoma and embarked on the S.S. Empress Russia for the United States."[27]

The Art Smith mystique also extends to people who were closely acquainted with Art: for instance, the letter Al Wertman wrote his little son Herb on May 18, 1938, is of interest: "Well sonny, you may keep this stamped envelope as a sourvenir [*sic*] from the first airmail flight from Auburn. Hoping this letter will in time when you are older bring you good luck, that is, when you are a good munchin [*sic*]."[28] The envelope sports a six-cent stamp stamped with an Art Smith–type biplane.

In the display case at the Greater Fort Wayne Aviation Museum is a model of Art Smith's plane (again, the first successful model) that Louis C. Kintz built in 1914. According to the curator of the Museum, Louis's wife kept the model in her home for thirty years and tried to keep from stepping on it each time she dusted. Finally, because of its size, she donated it to the museum. It is a good model and serves as a fine illustration of just how fragile Art's plane was.[29]

For years a ceremonial Japanese sword hung on Harry and Bernadine Gordon's living room wall. "It was the centerpiece of the wall," Bernadine said. "All I knew was it belonged to Art Smith. It was a family relationship that was mentioned casually when I married Harry. He was a second cousin of Art Smith."[30] Over the years, Bernadine learned more about Art Smith, and she was bothered that more people didn't know about him. In 1989, Bernadine began researching Art Smith's life. Her son, David Cunningham, also was intrigued by the Japanese sword and contacted the Tokyo National Museum requesting information. The curator wrote back saying that the inscriptions, words, and sheath indicate it was a wakizashi sword made by Tsuneie in August 1477 at Osafune in Bishu, the present Okayama.[31]

Convinced that more people, especially young people, should know about Art's accomplishments, Bernadine, in her eighties, took a writer's workshop and began detailing the events surrounding Art's life and flying fame.[32] Other people tucked away special keepsakes of Art Smith. Some were purchased as souvenirs or antiques, others were tenderly wrapped and saved.

21

An Unknown Love — 1995

Art never remarried. Contrary to a rumor that Art was married at the time he died, his mother, speaking over long distance telephone to Fort Wayne's *Journal Gazette* from Cleveland in 1926, said "those reports were without foundation."[1] But legend and history mingle. As people remembered snippets of conversations or recollections about Art Smith, details about his life seemed to become more mysterious. Some old-timers said that Art *was* engaged to a woman in Cleveland at the time of his death, but no one seemed to know for sure.

James Wigner of Fort Wayne happened to read the article in the newspaper that columnist Nancy Vendrely wrote about Bernadine Gordon and the ceremonial Japanese sword. He realized he knew details about Art Smith that no one else knew. He contacted Vendrely. On March 7, 1995, Vendrely published Jim's story, a poignant story Jim learned on the day of his mother's funeral. While at the funeral, his aunt said, "Your mom was going to marry Art Smith."[2]

Florence Straits Woodward was talking to her nephew about her older sister, Garnet Lovonya Straits Wigner. When she and Garnet were young, their family lived on a farm near Flat Rock, Michigan. On October 27, 1922, Art Smith had to make a forced landing in one of their fields. Florence was eight years old and her sister, Garnet, was eighteen. "It was a very big thing for us," Florence recalled.[3]

While Art's engine was being repaired, he stayed with the Straits family. At the time he was living in Dayton, Ohio, but the next year he would move, along with his parents, to Cleveland. While Art was with the Straits, he and Garnet became acquainted. They talked about life and religion. "He was a strong Christian Scientist and enjoyed sharing his beliefs with the sensitive young woman who loved writing poems,"[4] Vendrely wrote in the *Journal Gazette*.

When Art left Flat Rock on November 4, he and Garnet began corresponding.

Garnet Lovonyo Straits. Courtesy: James Wigner.

The following spring, Garnet invited him to return for a visit. His answer was, "God governs the universe, including man. As we are willing to let God direct our paths, we find we are experiencing so much more happiness than when we of ourselves do the outlining…. My desire (prayer) is that I may have the opportunity to see you again soon."[5] From that time on, according to Florence, the two saw each other often, enjoying simple activities such as "going mushrooming and pulling taffy at the kitchen table."[6]

According to Vendrely's article, which was headlined, "Son Never Knew Mom's First Love Was Art Smith," Art was always happy, laughing, and joking. Florence said she didn't remember the exact date, but did remember the day Garnet showed her and her brother a new ring. "My brothers and I were excited about it because it was from Art," she said.[7]

Florence couldn't remember on which day the wedding was scheduled, but according to her recollections, "Garnet's friends from her class at church were giving her a bridal shower the same night Art Smith died — February 12, 1926."[8] The next day the girls' father went to town and came back with a newspaper that carried the headlines that read, "Art Smith Killed."[9]

Right away, Garnet and her older brother went to Cleveland. Garnet stayed with the Smiths, and later she came home, got her things, and moved to Cleveland to be with them. Florence said, "When they moved back to Fort Wayne, she moved with them and lived with them for awhile."[10]

When Jim Wigner learned about his mother's first love, he began sorting through her old letters, photographs, and poetry in order to piece together the story of the

The pearl engagement ring Art gave Garnet. There are two diamonds, one on each side of the 18 karat white gold setting. Courtesy: James Wigner. Photographer Jessica Lukendill.

courtship and impending marriage. According to Wigner, the Smiths gave Garnet many of Art's belongings. "She had a big valise full," he said. "She would sit sometimes and go through it."[11] He said he had always known that Art Smith was special because his mother had a number of photographs and other mementos of him. "There was always a photograph of him hanging in the house." Wigner said, "I still have his altimeter — that came from Art's mother. It's like a pocket watch, but he had it fixed to wear on his wrist. He was wearing it when he crashed."[12]

Top: This is the altimeter Art Smith was wearing at the time of his fiery crash in 1926. The outer scale is calibrated in feet and can be rotated, thus lining up the field elevation with the pointer before taking off. The inner scale is a barometer and measures pressure in pounds per square inch. According to James Wigner, who replaced the broken crystal in the 1950s in order to use it while in the Fort Wayne Air Corps, the calibration is off by 300 feet. The inscription on the face reads "Short & Mason, Ltd. London." The make is "Tycos." The altimeter is marred by scorch marks. *Bottom*: This is the back of the altimeter, which shows where Art soldered a wire in order to wear it on his wrist. The leather strap is original. Courtesy: James Wigner. Photographer Jessica Lukenbill.

Jim recalled that when he was a child, he often went with his mother to visit Art's parents. "Mom used to take me to dinner at their house. I was taught to refer to them as Mom and Dad Smith. We could see the Art Smith monument (in Memorial Park) from where they lived on the south side of Maumee."

Recalling those times, Jim added, "Although there is no way I can prove it, my mother was involved in designing the memorial statue. She said it was she who suggested the idea of a boy going up through the clouds, wearing his helmet, and his arms outstretched."[13] Jim Wigner also he said his mother had a premonition about Art's death. She had a dream in which Art crashed and his plane was on fire. She tried to pull him out. When Garnet told Art about her dream, he had replied that he would want to die while flying.[14]

Jim's mother wrote several poems about Art and his love of flying. In Wigner's album are eight handwritten poems that show they have been folded numerous times. One was dedicated to the searchlight at the Cleveland airmail field after his death and speaks about the night airmail pilots who were guided by its light. The poem concluded as follows:

> *Our eyes are wet, our hearts are heavy*
> *Thou cans't never guide him more*
> *For he saw a brighter vision*
> *Than he ever saw before*
> *And your light to him seemed little*
> *By that Light of Divine Love*
> *So he turned his Mail Plane upward*
> *To that Search Light up above.*[15]

Another, more intimate poem was entitled, "Farewell."

> *Oh Arthur mine, you've gone away*
> *You've left us here alone*
> *That last day when you flew away*
> *You found your heavenly home.*
> *Thine open grave brings forth our tears*
>
> *The flesh is buried nigh*
> *But thy dear spirit Art has flown*
> *It knew no earthly tie.*
> *In solemn grief we stand dear one*
>
> *At thy lone tomb a prison*
> *But truly we who love you say*
> *He is not here but risen.*[16]

Three years later in 1929, Garnet Straits married Warren Wigner, but she remained close to the Smiths until their deaths.

Aimee Cour did remarry. Some accounts say that Aimee continued to express a friendly, supportive attitude toward Art, but most indicate she chose — or attempted — to forget him. Margaret J. Ringenberg, author of *Girls Can't Be Pilots* and who at the age of seventy-nine flew a twelve thousand-mile air race from London to Sydney, knew many of the people connected with Smith Field. She recalled that on one occasion when she talked with Aimee Cour and mentioned Art's name, Aimee remarked, "I don't want to talk about him. That was another chapter in my life."[17] At the time, Aimee was living in Steuben County, Indiana.

The Wigner collection of Art's letters to Garnet Straits begin in 1923. The last letter was written in 1926. Each reveals details about Art's life and the relationship he shared with Garnet.

22

Letters—1923–1926

In the packets of letters James Wigner found in his mother's things, there were none that Garnet wrote to Art, however, his letters reveal a great deal about her. The following excerpts shed light on their relationship, work, interests, and Art's commitment to his Christian Science beliefs (original spellings have been retained).

Selected letters written in 1923

MARCH 7, 1923

Art's first letter to Garnet is postmarked from Dayton and addressed to "Dear Miss Straits." He wrote that he had received the Straits' claim for damages to their field and suggested they send the claim for $29.00 to the Adjutant of McCook Field. He advised them to state that a forced landing was made on their farm on October 27, 1922, by test pilot Art Smith in Airplane P-243, and departure was made on November 4, 1922. Art listed their claim as follows:

> Use of rope, etc.—$2.00
> Use of team, etc.— 2.00
> Damage to field and fences because of
>   Plane and numerous visitors—$25.00.

Art said that he had no doubt the claim for rope and a team would be paid, but the damage to the fields might be contested because the crops had been gathered. "You can put in for it if you feel that it is a just claim and await the action of the government in the settlement of it," he wrote, adding that he would probably be called

Some of the letters art wrote to Garnet Straits during their courtship. Note the one stamped "Air Mail." The cost of a stamp in 1924 was two cents. Courtesy: James Wigner. Photographer Jessica Lukenbill.

upon to verify the claims. "I can only ask that the damage amount be stated with the Golden Rule conscientiously before you."

Art thanked her for her invitation to visit and said, "Maybe I can stop some day if I should be going to Selfridge Field." The letter was signed, "Sincere Regards to All, Art Smith." At the bottom of the page, he added: "Garnet, remembering our short talk about God's willingness to heal all of our diseases, I am sending you under separate cover a Christian Science *Sentinel*. Note the proofs of divine healing as the result of scientific prayer, under the heading of "Testimonies of Healing," page 214, and I can recommend all the other articles also. Thanks very much for the pictures. With sincere good thots Art Smth."[1]

MARCH 16, 1923

"Dear Garnet,

"I rejoice with you, dear friend, in your realization that divine Love is not lost. Mortal material sense is always trying to dim the Christ idea in our consciousness and whenever one is able to give out a truth that reflects divine power that heals and saves, then truly is that one enabled to share in the rejoicing."

He enclosed a Christian Science lecture for her to read and thanked her once
again for her invitation to visit. He said, "In Science we learn to trust God, Divine Mind,
to put us in our right place at the right time. When Mind has need of you and I seeing
each other again, then and there it will occur." He hoped that soon he would have
the opportunity to see her again and signed his letter, "In Truth and Love, Art Smith."[2]

APRIL 16, 1923

Art's ten-page letter was written on Cleveland's Hotel Regent stationery. He
said her letter had been forwarded to him from Dayton. "I have been here since April
1, on a new branch of service. Am now flying Air Mail between here and Chicago. I
like it just fine. So glad to have this new position as I feel that Divine Mind directed
me to it. I only make three round trips each two weeks. Up one day and back the
next. This gives me a lot of time to myself...." He also was glad she had enjoyed the
lecture, and he asked her if he might send her some other literature.

Garnet must have sent him a poem because he also wrote, "I love poetry, Garnet. Often I clip poems from the different Science periodicals." He told her that she
expressed herself well in her poem and added, "But Garnet, it is not true that we
must suffer 'rain' and 'pain,' 'clouds' and 'storms and tears.'" He wrote that he
thought that her "possibilities in writing poetry are unlimited," and he signed his
letter, "With Loving Thots in Truth, Art." At the bottom of the page, he asked, "Did
your folks ever receive their claims against the government?"[3]

APRIL 18, 1923

Obviously Garnet discussed Art's views with a friend because he said, "I was so
glad to hear about your friend with whom you work. Garnet, my friend, I am so glad
to have been of some help to you. That brings me much true joy and happiness...."
He told her he would send her a poem that he had clipped and would mail it in Bryan,
Ohio, "so it will reach you sooner."[4]

MAY 2, 1923

The next letter was written from Cleveland on Chicago hotel stationery. "Yesterday I received the last Christian Science *Sentinel*. While reading it last night, I found
several articles that explain so beautifully the several points I tried to make in my
last letter." He said he would send it to her under separate cover. He signed his letter, "Sincerely."[5]

JUNE 3, 1923

Art suggested that Garnet look up various scriptures and sympathized with her
about "all the bereavements that have befallen you and your family." He enclosed a
little poem he had clipped entitled "Confidence" by Lillian B. Watson, which read:

"Dear Father, Thou alone dost know/The way that I should tread./I only know I am Thy child,/And willing to be led./ E'en though the homeward road be long,/And the path I may not see,/'Tis joy enough for me to know/ That Thou art leading me."[6]

JUNE 24, 1923

Art asked Garnet to reflect about the inspiration that led her to write "The Sunset," a poem she had written and sent to him. He thanked her sincerely for it and told her he had shown the poem to one of his friends in Chicago, "a man that has been for a number of years demonstrating that understanding of the divine principle that Love is healing." Art also consoled her on the loss of two of her friends. "Be not grieved. Friends have not died but passed on to a higher experience."[7]

JULY 1, 1923

In this letter, Art further explained his beliefs about "healing by denying sickness" and quoted Jesus and Mary Baker Eddy. Garnet may have expressed some self-doubt because Art wrote, "The Garnet that God knows really is beautiful, pure, perfect, and that's the only Garnet there really is or ever will be. To know her is to experience a foretaste of the presence and activity of divine Truth."[8]

JULY 15, 1923

By midsummer, Art again was writing from Cleveland. He asked about her dressmaking and said he was sending her "loving thots." He signed his letter "Lovingly, Art," then added that he was sending her another *Sentinel*. He had "enjoyed her poetry so very much. Thanks."[9]

JULY 20, 1923, AND JULY 29, 1923

No doubt Garnet questioned Art about various Christian Science doctrines because his next letter is devoted entirely to the subject of Mary Baker Eddy and the Christian Science *Journal*. He asked if she had received the book he "had purchased for her and had wrapped in Chicago." He sent her some clippings from the *Christian Science Monitor* and "The Poetry of Existence."[10]

Garnet also had discussed her daily activities because Art wrote, "It is indeed a great blessing to be happy in the work we are doing. I know well what it means to me to enjoy work, for I have been so happy in mine. To fly brings songs of gratitude to my life. As I wing my way between here and Chicago, I rejoice all the way." He wrote, "when I am passing south of Toledo, I always think of you and those about you." In closing his letter, he said "Again, Garnet dear, I rejoice with you in your spiritual joy. Lovingly, Art."[11]

AUGUST 7, 1923

In August, Art received a gift from Garnet, and his letter was a thank-you. It was mailed from the Hotel Harrington in Washington, D.C. "I take it that this cake with a candle means that you have been celebrating your birthday. Tho I did not know it in time to have a present there for you on the 28th, I am nevertheless sending you one from here...." He mentioned a few other details about having flown a mail plane to New York and then on Monday having been sent to Washington, D.C., "with another plane to carry pictures of the Harding Funeral to Chicago tomorrow afternoon." He told Garnet that he had a lovely time in both New York and the city and ended his letter saying, "It was loving and sweet of you to remember me with a piece of the celebrating cake. My true appreciation is best shown and made known to you by entertaining true thoughts about you as God's perfect child."[12]

AUGUST 23, 1923

By mid–August, Art was "flying double" on his route. "I have been either to or from Chicago every day except two since Sunday a week ago and the schedule continues each day through next Tuesday." Garnet must have discussed taking a study course because Art wrote, "I think it is a very worthy opportunity to have the correspondence course, and I know you will make the most of it. I took the I.C.S. Architectural course about fifteen years ago, just before I started in the flying game." He signed his letter, "Lovingly, Art," then asked he if she had ordered her copy of *Science and Health*. If not, he said, he would order it for her. "I would enjoy doing so."[13]

Postcard from Art to his mother. Message reads: "Up here this morning, back this afternoon." Courtesy: James Wigner.

SEPTEMBER 9, 1923

Art was "heaps busy" and when not on the mail flight, "was occupied with thoughts and activities connected with my airplane experiments. They are developing nicely and soon I hope to demonstrate some improvements."

He was glad that Garnet's mother had liked the dress Garnet had made for her, and he was glad her friend Verena liked "the copies and clippings of the *Sentinel.*" He ended by saying that "greater even than the joy of being permitted to present you with a copy of the Christian Science textbook is that of having you say you refuse only that you may buy it yourself, which means: You're ready for it." He promised to send her a photograph of himself taken by a Cleveland photographer.[14]

SEPTEMBER 21, 1923

Art wrote from Washington, D.C., and said that besides his mail flights and the experiments that "I am carrying out on my own account, I have had some other outside flying to do, — as per this— enclosed clipping. The speedy transportation of airplanes is being recognized. More and more I look forward to the day when traveling by air will be more common and greater numbers can enjoy the grandeur of flying from place to place."

He sent her a two-verse poem entitled "Apart" written by Anne Campbell and a picture of himself that had appeared in the Pittsburgh *Press.* He mentioned that he liked her poem about children —"expressive of much tender love for them. I know they feel and understand this warm affection. How many beautiful lessons we can get by observing the wholesome and trustful love of the innocent child."

He thanked her for her "sincere desire, unselfish and without envy, for my success in the experiments I am working with. Your prayers will help me I know.... Soon I expect to have my experiments in working order and when they are working, I'll tell you how it went. With loving thots, Art."[15]

OCTOBER 7, 1923

Art's letter indicated he received a letter and three poems from Garnet. He told her he was "so busy flying mail last week that the experiments had to wait. I flew from or to Chicago each day. The other Cleveland pilot was at the races at St. Louis. Will have some time this week though ... and will be scheduled for only one trip."[16]

OCTOBER 28, 1923

Art said that he had experienced something of the meaning of "Love is reflected in love," according to Mrs. Eddy's writings in *Science and Health,* when he "read the verses which you sent me, which you wrote." He continued, "How good that you and your Mother were so beautifully protected during that auto spill." In response to Garnet's queries about his experiments, he wrote, "You want to know more about

This photograph of Art hung in Garnet's home until her death. Courtesy: James Wigner.

the aero experiments. Well, I'll tell you. It is a new system of smoke production to be used in sky writing. Yesterday the installation was completed and I made one test with a small amount of smoke fuel. It was very successful. Even tho the sky was overcast with clouds, the smoke could be seen for some seven or eight minutes from the ground. Under the conditions this is considered very good. I expect to soon get some out against a blue sky when the true value will be fully apparent." He asked her if any of her friends saw the writing of "Lucky Strike" over Detroit during the past summer.[17]

Nearly two months passed before Art wrote again. This time his letter was six pages and postmarked from the Hotel Washington in Chicago.

DECEMBER 10, 1923

"No indeed, Garnet, it is not that I forgot. But I must confess that I am unable to entirely say I am sorry for the tardiness— because a big delight has been mine in receiving such a clever card to remind me that an answer to your letter is past due. Your card is just grand. It is made up very skillfully and expressed much that is beautiful in character...." He told her that besides his regular trips, he had made "several by rail on business, one by plane, and one by auto." With the addition of the activities "of the Air Mail and skywriting, I have been helping my parents get moved from Fort Wayne to Cleveland.... I've carried your letter of November 4th, expecting always the opportunity to answer it, until the address is nearly worn off. And that letter is a delight, too. The verse you quote from Longfellow's 'Building of the Ship' is metaphysical in its deep meaning." He reacted to a poem she sent entitled "A Prayer" and discussed another poem written by Anne Campbell. He quoted Mrs. Eddy that "desire is unceasing prayer," and ended his letter saying, "No distance, however great, can separate us, dear! With loving thoughts in Truth, Art."[18]

DECEMBER 29, 1923

The last letter of that year was written after Christmas and is four pages. He wished Garnet a Happy New Year, and thanked her for the "lovely Christmas present with its more lovely, loving, lovable verse," which reached him before Christmas and "taught me something more about being patient and waiting until the 25th before opening it. Had I known of the contents, I could hardly have done so. And yet I did know that it would contain a bit of your talent at verse."

Art suggested that her writings and her verses could " help a man who makes shoes or a girl who gilded a pretty buckle" and that she should continue to develop her talent. He also thanked her for "a lovely present," which "is just the thing, Garnet. I have been carrying a little package of toilet things in wrapping paper when flying the mail. This little case will be useful and convenient. Thank you."[19]

What began as a casual letter-writing exchange about a damage claim developed into a somewhat lopsided relationship. Art was fourteen years older than Garnet and a divorced man. At first he responded to her letters almost as an older brother or mentor. He loved that she was willing to explore his Christian Science beliefs and accepted it as his duty to answer her questions and instruct her in the Christian Science faith.

In Art, Garnet found a friend and a comforter, a person who recognized her inquisitive mind and her writing abilities. Her letters touch on subjects that would be of a normal interest to any young woman—family, friends, dressmaking, and work, yet Art's determination to explain his beliefs stretched her mind.

It almost seems that Garnet would ask Art questions about Christian Science in order to continue her correspondence with him. He, however, viewed his duty seriously and wrote long involved letters explaining Matter, Truth, Divine Love, and Mrs. Mary Baker Eddy.

The following year they continued their dialogue about Christian Science. Garnet would ask questions, and Art would explain. He seemed pleased to be her tutor. As Art encouraged her, Garnet became more confident. Not only was she intelligent and inquisitive, but Art's letters show she was aware of her feminine charms. Even so, Art remained focused in his task of instructing her about Christian Science. Although Art speaks of love and calls Garnet "dear," he seems cautious. He was charismatic, sophisticated, and well-traveled. He liked to have a good time, but he took his religion seriously. To lead a young girl in her spiritual search was a responsibility he did not take lightly.

Selected letters written in 1924

JANUARY 23, 1924

"Dear Garnet, It has been a long time since you heard from me, — by mail — hasn't it Garnet?" Art thanked her for her New Year's card and suggested she write "verses that would be appropriate for certain holidays." He said there were so many cards on the markets "which are so impoverished of pure thinking. Many desire cards for all sorts of occasions that are uplifting and inspiring. Your Christmas card with your love — that present to me is such a good example. Can you not write a lot of them for many occasions?"

Art said the weather had been bad, "that most people think is very severe for flying. But we are going in comfort. At the first coldness of the season, I put a heating apparatus on my plane. A simple device to retain and direct the heat given off by the exhaust pipe ... with the front end open to receive a volume of air and at the rear, passing along the heated exhaust pipe, a tube directing the heated air into the cockpit of the ship. I have been flying in this zero weather without the fur boots or gloves. And the system has been put on many of the ships between New York and San Francisco."

He said the skywriting business "is progressing very nicely. Expect to make lots of smoke in the early spring, — using several new planes which I will soon be building." He talked about keeping a good mental attitude and said her poem "The New Ledger" is fine.[1]

FEBRUARY 28, 1924

Art began this letter with "My Dear Garnet," and he proceeded to explain that she must think of herself as IS and not what she WILL BECOME. He discussed success, happiness, and completeness, and asked, "What good is the entire world of money and power if one loses his soul in attaining it?"

"Some poetry you sent me this time! 'Pies Versus Poetry' and 'The Air Mail.' I don't just know what to say about them. I know that you have a big laugh when you read the 'Pies and Poetry' one. And yet, why should we not have poetry right along with pies? Both are the expression of art. 'The Air Mail' tells just how we do it."

He went on to say that he had started a little shop in Cleveland and was building two new planes especially for the skywriting business. "Working day and night. Spring and blue skies are coming, and I strive to be ready.... With loving thots of you, Garnet, Art."[2]

MARCH 18, 1924

Art's letter was from Chicago, and he talked about the coming spring. "True, Garnet, spring is coming. As I fly I note so many indications. Already I have met others on the wing, which is the mark of Spring, — geese and ducks, with their heads

Leaving for Chicago on a mail run. Courtesy: James Wigner.

so far out in front. And the fields are beginning to be groomed for spring plantings. Soon the field green will steal over the heavy brown that now shows where the beautiful white was. We birdmen are blessed above other mortals, for so much is spread below us to observe and admire."

Once again Art discussed Garnet's poems. "Oh! But I did like those last two poems which you sent me. They're both so good. The 'Airmail' could be given as our personal creed. And — with a great smile, — I wonder if you have any such thots concerning yourself and 'Pies Versus Poetry.' He asked, "How about it, Garnet, do you bake or do you rhyme — sometimes?"

She must have discussed her sewing because Art talked about the "stack of materials" on her sewing machine. She also must have asked him about an item she saw in the newspaper because he wrote "*The Detroit News* item was for someone else, as our names are alike."[3]

APRIL 19, 1924

"And now, Garnet, what do you think of Spring's arrival? Yesterday while winging my way up here, I got thrill after thrill to look down and see so many of the trees all pink with buds. The snow has gone and most of the fields are dried up so that they could with ease be landed upon, and that's appreciated by we who fly."

He cautioned her to "be not afraid of the unfoldments of divine Truth and Love. Not even a 'wee bit.' Give yourself over entirely to Love's directing and keeping and rejoice that the material sense of limitation is yielding to the spiritual fact that Life and Love are infinite, all power and ever present." He was happy about her spiritual explorations and said, "In my comment on baking and rhyming, I had no thought of the future. I was thinking of the present. What you say about the wish of every true girl's heart is— or ought to be, the wish of every heart — boy or girl." He asked her to "tell Florence that neither Jo nor I need a white flag to tell us where your home is."[4]

May 13, 1924

The entire letter is devoted to Mary Baker Eddy's philosophy about being "at one with Divine Truth." In the last paragraph Art comments about the operative law of divine Love in action and says, "because I am privileged to be the channel through which the law herein operates, I am exceedingly happy. Love in Truth, Art."[5]

June 16, 1924

"Dear Garnet, Again it was thoughtful and kind of you to enclose the violets in your letter to me. They bring delightful memories of cool woodlands and shaded brooks. When I was a little boy and would go 'exploring,' sometimes two miles from home, I remember the delights that were ever unfolding before me and I rejoice now in the same expectancy, having learned somewhat that God's goodness is ever appealing, apart from the beliefs of age and youthful innocence." He looked forward to receiving her poem "Walking in the Meadows" and thought it "perfectly grand that you can give expression to poetry."

He also wrote, "My new airplane has been developing nicely and now that the finished work approaches, I am keyed to added effort. While in Cleveland, I spend the day and part of the night working on it. One of these days it will be ready to mount high into the blue above."

Art must have sent Garnet a book because he said, "I knew you would be delighted to have a copy of *Miscellaneous Writings* by Mrs. Eddy. I am glad I could be the channel to supply it to you. It is the mental work that counts. Therefore, Loving thots that's in Truth, Art."[6]

July 13, 1924

In this two-page letter, Art discussed Garnet's poem "Walking in the Meadows" and pronounced it "good." She also sent one entitled "Hope Thou," which he said he liked.[7]

September 7, 1924

The letter was written on formal business stationery on which was printed: "Art Smith, Aviator, U.S. Air Mail Service." On the left hand side was printed: "Baby Racers" and on the right hand side: "Aeroplanes."

"Last night I dreamed that I was visiting you and that I was asked to explain more fully some of the things written. I remember that I proceeded to do so with enthusiasm. So this morning, I am letting nothing interfere with this joy of writing you." He wanted Garnet to stop by Cleveland on her forthcoming vacation. He also told her that in Christian Science, "Jesus and Christ are not synonymous terms." He suggested she study a certain chapter in *Science and Health.* Toward the end of his letter he said, "Of course you are and can be happy, Garnet. And it is because you *are*, not shall be, or going to be married — as you say. Loving thots in Truth, Art. P.S. Do send the pictures."[8]

OCTOBER 14, 1924

Art discussed the "turmoil in the ranks of Christian Science in Boston" and wondered if Garnet wondered why there was "so much error in the church so soon after Mrs. Eddy's passing on." He told her he had studied the issues "thoroughly" and "was convinced of the thorough rightness of the facts stated and immediately sent my church membership resignation in to Boston. It was accepted and I am glad to be free to follow after the next brightest revelation of divine Principle."

He presented a short discussion about the reality of death and thanked her for her invitation to visit again. "I would greatly love to accept your invitation and to talk about Christian Science." He thanked her for a poem and the pictures. "I am glad to have the one of yourself. I don't remember seeing you look like that [in] the group picture. The other, though, is distinctly you. I just wish the picture was a bit sharper. If you get a nice sharp map some day, I would be glad to have one."[9]

NOVEMBER 17, 1924

Because Garnet must have enjoyed "all those splendid articles in *The Watch-man*, No. 1," Art wrote " I know you will just eat this one up." He suggested she read pages 46–47 by William S. Campbell, and he told her that "He and Mrs. Campbell are very dear friends of mine. I did not know they were coming to the new light until I received my copy of the October *Watchman.*" Art then explained how he met the Campbells. "It was during the War time. I had just returned from Japan and gone to Washington to present ideas to the heads of the Air Service." The city was crowded and there were no vacancies, not even in Baltimore. "It looked as though I would have to sit up all night. Yet I knew that there would be unoccupied beds in that large city that night. God knew where they were and in so much as I reflected MIND, I too knew where they were." Art said that on the trip, he became acquainted with a man named Campbell, and the two found "they were of the same mind." As they conversed, Campbell invited Art to spend the night in his home.[10]

NOVEMBER 26, 1924, AND DECEMBER 24, 1924

In Art's November letter, he sent Garnet some pamphlets and said he was flying "double trips between here and Chicago. There are just four pilots on this section."[11] When he wrote on Christmas Eve, he said he had "made a round trip to Chicago today and when I got home your Christmas greeting card awaited me. It is replete with beautiful thoughts. I like it very much. It is grand." After several other paragraphs,

An aerial photograph of Art's U.S. Air Mail plane. Taken by the Department of Engineering in Dayton, Ohio. Courtesy: James Wigner.

he wrote, "And I too, Garnet, have a package — still in the making for you. I have been making trips and trips on the mail, and I asked Mother to do a bit of purchasing for me. She did, but through a bit of misunderstanding, it will be necessary to make an exchange before I can send it on. In a day or two, it will be on its way to you, Loving thots in truth, Art."[12]

Selected letters written in 1925

Nineteen letters are in the 1925 packet. Many were six and ten pages long. Many had to do with general news about Art's activities, his enjoyment of various Christian Science publications, and his hope that Garnet was learning spiritual truths. In a number of letters, he talked about his flying and his airplane inventions. A few excerpts give insight as to how his life and his career were progressing.

JANUARY 14, 1925

Art visited Mr. and Mrs. Campbell in their home while he was in Washington on business. "It was a grand treat to hear them tell of the progress being made by the church, which is evolving scientifically." He thanked Garnet for her Christmas card with its verses and a poem by Edgar A. Guest which she had sent him. He said he "read them to Dad and Ma. We enjoyed them so much ... heaps and heaps." Art then spoke of his father's eyesight. "He has had to struggle hard for a number of years for courage, such as Guest tells us to have, because of a belief of blindness. (Help in Science has not been sought very much.) For him to be so aroused as these poems did, I feel is a benefit to him."

He wrote that "always, Garnet, I am with you in prayer...."[1]

JANUARY 21, 1925

Art sent Garnet a one-page letter saying he had received two lovely letters from her, which he would answer soon. Meanwhile he was enclosing for Garnet an application card for membership in the Christian Science Parent Church of the New Generation. He said he had gone to Washington the previous Sunday, where "I got the rare opportunity of which the Campbells told me. I met and heard our Leader, Mrs. Bill [Annie C.], twice in the Campbell's home and once at the church services." He said Mrs. Bill's message was "a wonderful one. And the clearness with which it is given lifts one right up on the mountain tops. I'll tell you more about it later."[2]

MARCH 29, 1925

Art wrote that it had been a long time since he had written, but that he "had a reason, a big one. Did I not tell you that I had met Mrs. Bill in Washington at the Campbell's home. That was on January 18th. At that time, I was accepted as a student in Mrs. Bill's next class, which was to be held in Washington, at the Campbell's home, March 8–18, incl. I used my 1924–1925 vacation allotment and attended."

He told Garnet that words "were inadequate to tell of the wonderful time" he had. There were twenty-eight students in the class, and it was the third class held in the United States. He said that during the "years I have lived here and there while following the aviation profession, I have made friends, many of them are Scientists." He detailed changes occurring in the Christian Science church. He said he was "very happy to hear that you have sent in your application for church membership." He closed his letter by recalling when they had talked a few minutes together on her back porch. At the end of the letter, he added a postscript about his flying business.

"The planes I was building are being finished at Bryan, Ohio. In 6–10 days the first will probably be finished. I may test it, and there is a slight possibility that I could fly over Carleton [Garnet's location at the time] way. No promise, but I'll love to do it if possible."[3]

APRIL 18, 1925

"Dear Garnet, Nearly did I get to come up to Carleton. Went to Bryan and found the ship flying just fine. Took a ride over to Fort Wayne — my old hometown —

and had a great time telling a few friends something of the new light that has come in Christian Science. To them I have written many letters. But that is so difficult and slow as compared with several hours of conversation. When I got back to Bryan, we refueled the ship to go to Carleton. Then one of the builders asked to go to Dayton. I had written a number of friends at Dayton but had not received a reply from a single one. So to have a few minutes with them, I agreed."

Art told about his stay in Dayton. He said he spent two nights and also had been busy writing a number of letters. "Have thought of you so often and that I should let you know how it was. I was sent to other parts when I was about to visit you." He thanked her for her Easter card and said he hoped soon they would be able "to converse face to face, therefore can we await the time with joy." He couldn't write anymore because it was time "to go to the Field and then to Chicago. Loving thots Art."[4]

MAY 7, 1925

"Dearest Garnet, I am so happy Garnet that you have membership in the Christian Science Parent Church of the New Generation." He talked of the differences between Mrs. Eddy's leadership and the new church leader. He also thanked Garnet for her poems. "I have several business deals developing in Detroit. Should it be necessary for me to be there personally, I would certainly ask for additional time so that I could stop off and see you. I'm sure we would have a grand time...." He signed his letter, "With sincere loving thoughts, Arthur."[5]

JUNE 3, 1925

In Art's June letter, he talked about Mr. J.V. Dittemore, who had given a lecture on "Old and New Developments in Christian Science" in Cleveland. "I was on two of the committees which made the arrangements."[6]

JUNE 23, 1925

"Dear Garnet," Art wrote. He hoped she would soon visit and told her all-about the new Air Mail Service between New York and Chicago. He was busy because he had been placed on a church committee "to draft a number of needed changes in our by-laws."

Garnet must have talked about a new dress because Art wrote, "from your description, I can well imagine that your new outfit with you in it is quite a pretty combination. I wish I had the opportunity to drive around the corner of the Lake to see you in it, —and to visit the while I was looking."[7]

JULY 23, 1925

"I have been so very slow in writing and telling you it is a happy fact that I rejoice in having your picture. I think it is a remarkably lovely likeness of you, Garnet. That bit of a smile means, to me, irresistible evidence of a well-spring of happiness in your consciousness." His other news was that he had moved from Endora Road to a different house located on Riveredge.

In one of her letters, Garnet must have told him of plans to travel to Columbus, Ohio, because Art asked, "Does the date draw nigh? We are hoping you will be able to stop off in Cleveland for a nice visit on your way home. We are fairly well settled in our new location now and will be so glad to have you and yours with us for a rest period while on your way home. Tho I say rest period, I do not mean that we would not show you around the city a bit." He asked about the property Garnet's father was interested in buying, and said he was waiting for "a chance to be away for a day so I can drive up your way again. Prospects are not bright, tho. Very important church meeting here tonight. Many new Bylaws to be adopted. Best thots of love, Art."[8]

AUGUST 1, 1925

"Dear Garnet, Could you get off for a day about Thursday or Friday?? Another plane is ready for testing at Bryan. I'm expecting to run over and try it out. My Aunt is at present visiting with us. She, Mother, and I will probably make the trip. If you could join us, we would detour at Toledo by way of Carleton and pick you up." Art's plans were to leave during the night and get to Carleton around dawn. "Want to have the entire day at Bryan … let me know." In his postscript, he said he was going to a meeting of church officers that night. "Had election last night. Love, Art."[9]

AUGUST 11, 1925

Art began his letter, "My Dear Garnet," and told her he was sorry to have disappointed her on that trip to Bryan last week. "The boys out there thought sure they would have the ship all ready. They didn't — and as yet have not finished it. Expect to this week, tho." His schedule was changing and he would be flying "Wednesday night west and Thursday night back east." He said "if the ship is ready, I may go out to Bryan Friday or Saturday morning. My Aunt has gone home and Mom says she may not want to make the trip. If she won't go, it rather spoils it for us. If she will go, tho, I will wire you as far ahead of our arrival as possible. Then if you can be away for a day — or two— all fine. If not, we won't mind the little extra ride, via Carleton. Hurriedly, as I must go to the city and look for a Reading Room for Cleveland Branch I."[10]

AUGUST 17, 1925

Art bemoaned the fact that his mother didn't feel like making the trip to Bryan. "Sorry Mother did not want to go along to Bryan and sorry that the machine to be tested did not act right so I could have flown over to Carleton to say hello." He shared

various details of his Bryan trip. He had left Cleveland on Friday evening and arrived
in Bryan about midnight. "Tried the ship out about 2:00 Sat. afternoon. It acted
badly and wound up by stopping upside-down, much splintered." He thought it
might take several weeks to make the repairs necessary on the plane. "When completed, I may try it again. I feel certain we know where the mistake lay. This is being
corrected as the repairs go on. When does that vacation of yours start — and when
can we expect you here in Cleveland?"[11]

AUGUST 28, 1925

"'Visit us on your way going' is the selfish plea, of me; 'while coming back' is
the other. If you can come while on your way maybe we can entice you to stay
longer…. Either coming or going, we want you and Elmer to allot us as much of your
vacation as you can." Art said he had a couple of days off between flights, so he would
have plenty of time to be with her. "We are in the southwest corner of the city.
Riveredge Road runs south from Loraine Avenue…." He wrote detailed directions,
then ended, " Mother calls. As I promised to go uptown with her this afternoon. Come
along as soon as you can, — and Garnet, bring the list of questions and we will try to
get them straightened out. Loving thoughts of you and yours, Art."[12]

SEPTEMBER 8, 1925, AND SEPTEMBER 29, 1925

In the first letter, Art again gave directions to his house. He included a map.
"We'll be so glad to have you and Elmer visit us, — and we'll keep you as long as we
can."[13]

Art's September 29th letter included a letter from his mother [dated September 22nd] in which she said she was "enclosing a handkerchief that was in your
room." In Art's two-page letter he made references to some "great talk about
prophecy, given by a card from a 'dummy witch.'" It seems that while Garnet was
visiting, they may have passed some type of machine that gave out fortune telling
cards, and for fun, Art's mother suggested that Garnet put in a nickel. Out had come
some sort of prediction about an accident because Art wrote that he was sorry Elmer's
car was banged up, and that "she should not permit [belief in] those evils [the card]."
He was glad she had no scar as "a result of your auto experience." He then teased,
"Was the 'witch-card' all hokum? It 'fell from you' after the accident happened."

His said mother sent her love, "and dad does to (I feel sure). With loving thots,
Art."[14]

OCTOBER 12, 1925

"Dearest Garnet, all we Pilots in the Mail are so glad that the search for Ames
is over." Art chronicled details about a desperate search for "the missing Pilot Ames."
Art was "deeply sorry that Ames is no longer here with us but glad that the mystery

This photograph of Art was taken in Dayton, Ohio, in 1925, the year before his death. Courtesy:
Allen County–Fort Wayne Historical Society & Museum.

concerning his experience has been cleared up. It was the hardest flying job I have
ever had. Just round and round over the wooded hills and vallies, looking so hard all
the time." Art said he had stopped by the Air Field to give his mother a tour of the
place "when the phone call came in about the disappearance of Pilot Ames south of
Shippenville, Pennsylvania." A pilot was there from Chicago, and "he and I were dis-
patched to look. We had eight to ten ships in the air the same day — looking — looking — looking." Art wrote that he was glad Garnet was enjoying her stay in Columbus,
Ohio, and said he had to get to the Field because he had 100 hours on his engine and
needed another one.[15]

OCTOBER 23, 1925

"Every time our little church Branch of the New Generation has a business meeting, it means a lot of writing, — minutes and letters, — on the part of the clerk." He
talked about their annual meeting and various Board meetings. "Flying again this
afternoon," he said. He wanted to talk with her and "clear up several little points."
He also wanted to wait and write when he wasn't so distracted. "In the quietness and

freedom from the things of this world is when inspiration comes, dearest, — and then is when I like to write you. Lovingly, Art."[16]

NOVEMBER 11, 1925

Art apologized for not writing earlier, saying he had good intentions but had been busy. He told Garnet he had flown a trip for one of the other pilots, so, on his extra day, "we, my Mother and I, took advantage of it and went on an auto trip to Detroit. We didn't stop by your house as it was very early in the morning. We made the trip at night. While up there, we had some work done on the car, which finally included a new set of pistons." This required slow driving all the way back home. He was sorry about not having the time to stop for a visit. He signed his letter, "Lovingly, Art.[17]

DECEMBER 22, 1925

"Dear Garnet — Christmas greetings to you, Garnet, and all of yours. I have ordered for you a Christmas remembrance, but as yet it has not arrived. I shall tell you what it is and will send it on to you as soon as it reaches me, — a copy of Mrs. Bill's messages." He wrote that "with the Sunday Lessons and this book, you will have with you each Parent church or one of its Branches." He received the *Miracle in Stone* and was glad she had enjoyed reading it. He liked the poem she sent by Anne Campbell, which reminded him "so much of my Dad during the days when he was able to help out the rest." Art said he was looking forward to Garnet's new poem. "Do send it to me. I'm always happy to receive your thoughts. I send mine. The're loving, Art."[18]

One letter written by Art Smith in 1926, and one written by Ida Smith

The following letter is the one Art wrote three weeks before he died.

JANUARY 27, 1926

"My Dear Garnet, Tho it has been long since I wrote you last, still I know that you know I have been thinking of you often. Thoughts which reflect Truth and Love reach their object unimpeded by material appendages. And they are entirely secure from curious mortal mind, ignorant of reality and always ready to misunderstand. What a grand advantage the reflecting of divine Love has over the material, human concept of attraction.

"Your lovely Christmas present arrived several days before the 25th. But I did not notice your 'cross as a bear' notation until after I had read half the poems to dad and mother. I think the most outstanding characteristic of bears is playfulness, — not crossness. Therefore I am going to hope that your threat of crossness will not be evidenced. Honest, I didn't see the warning until way after the package was opened.

"Sometimes before this the *Miracle in Stone* was received. Have loaned it again to an earnest student. Glad you enjoyed reading it. I received a nice Christmas card from our mutual friend J.M. Frederick. The postmark is Hempstead, N. Y. I suppose he is located at Mitchell Field. By the time we may be making another trip to Detroit (none contemplated just now), I suppose you all will be over on your new farm, — far off the 'Telegraph Road.' Even so, you can expect to see us if it is possible to come.

"Enclosed is a notice of classes in Christian Science to be held in Washington. I am sure you will be interested in knowing about them. I do hope I will be able to attend some of them. Have written making inquiries regarding these classes as compared with the one which I attended. I don't remember sending you a copy of Mr. Dittemore's lecture, — am therefore enclosing one of these also. I surely have been busy for the last month or so. Have been finishing one of those babycars which should have been delivered last fall. Saw the purchaser get started for Detroit on Monday with it. Tuesday he phoned from Fremont that he had been in a smashup. He is sending the car back for repairs. Loving thoughts in truth, Art. P.S. Many thanks, Garnet, for the Poems."[1]

The following letter was written to Garnet by Ida Smith after Art's death. It was written in Fort Wayne, Indiana.

MARCH 26, 1926

"Dear Garnet, My dear girl, I have been reading your letters over and would like to answer but I don't feel that I do justes in writing but I will offer this sugestion if you are going to work for your self now. Come to us and get something to do and live with us. I have a nice room to spare. And we can talk it all over and read and study Divine truth together and we will lissen for the still small voice that gives comfort when nothing else can. A boy friend of Arts was here today and he said Art seems so near him 2 or 3 times a week. He just feels he will meet his smiling face. A girl from California rites me she has been coresponding in Science with Art and for the last 2 years she has (when alone) heard a beautifull ringing sound before a letter and the message would come from him and she has heard it a dozen times since he has passed on and with it the assuring that he is safe. Yes he is working rite on for he is more alive than ever before.

"I try to picture him in a spiritual body. I am trying to forget all the material, for I know his spirit is helping me to be brave in Christ, my All. I read in God's word and in Mrs. Bills messages and in *Science and Health* the beautifull truths and in this way I can keep from grieving for I want his spirit to be free happy to do his work over there. He will not come back to me but I will go to him…. I have written this letter without tears. Daddy is standing it all pretty well. I will send you some pictures of the flowers when I get them but let us forget the material and walk with God. Write soon. To my loving girl, Mrs. Smith."

"P.S. We got moved very nicely. My nephew came to Cleveland and drove home with us. Dad and my niece Florence that went home with me and was such a good help. We have bought a home. I felt it was the thing Art would want me to do and then to get settled so Dad would not worry. We are not straitened up yet. I am waiting on the Electritian to set up my range and the man to lay the kitchen lanolium I sold my Dining room table and rug in Cleveland so I will have a rug and table and buffay to buy. So you see, we are having a rough time to get a long now. I am so glad you like your new home. We should like each one better until we reach the final one. The memorial fund is near seven thousand now. Your loving friend."[2]

Although in the Wigner collection of letters Art made no specific reference about his marriage to Garnet — unless the September 1924 letter would qualify — there is evidence Art and Garnet were planning to marry. Garnet had received a pearl ring from Art, which Jim and Lois Wigner have in their possession. Garnet's Sunday School class was giving her a wedding shower the night of Art's crash. After Art's death, Garnet immediately went to Cleveland to be with Art's family. Art's mother and father invited Garnet to live with them, which she did. Such an invitation would not have been extended to a mere casual acquaintance. Even after Garnet married, she stayed close to the Smiths, calling them Mom and Dad Smith. Jim Wigner accompanied his mother on many of those visits. He said, "Dad Smith used to sit and hold in his hand a little metal car that had belonged to Art. He was blind, you know, and I remember he would sit there in his chair and hold that little car and run his hand over and over it while he listened to Mom talk with Mother Smith."[3]

Suddenly the poem tucked in Ida Smith's scrapbook makes sense. It reads:

Mom

A world of words could never tell
My tender love and true
So this is but a poor attempt
To speak my thoughts of you.

And yet I know you'll understand
Just as you always do,
That though I write and write and write
I can say nothing new.
Each sweetly wrinkled smile you give
Means all the world to me
In every little favor done
Your love for me I see.

There is a work for me to do
I'll wipe away your tears,
I can't be Art, dear Mom, I'll be
A daughter through the years.
Your Garnet (1926)[4]

Art and Garnet's letters started as a casual friendship and developed into a personal relationship. From Art's letters and comments, it seems that Garnet might have wished that her intrepid and dashing aviator would be more passionate or speak more directly about their physical relationship, but Art was cautious. Perhaps he didn't write more openly about his feelings for her because he was fourteen years older than she, had been married, and was divorced. In those days divorce was viewed as shameful, and certainly Art would have been aware that many people would consider it scandalous if Garnet were to be seen with, much less were dating, a divorced man. It is also possible that Art used his role as Garnet's spiritual counselor to cement a bond of affection that was more involved. Several times in his letters, he refers to having not talked with Garnet "by mail in some time," which implies that he may have talked with her from time to time by telephone or in person.

Garnet was young, imaginative, and talented. She was interested in poetry, and when Art responded to her poems, she wrote more of them. She was intelligent, a good seamstress, and interested in homemaking. She debated whether to take a certain study course, and she worried about her ability to drive a car, but she was determined to learn. She questioned Art over and over again about his beliefs. He on the other hand was challenged by her mind, her extraordinary loveliness, and her feminine charms.

It would have been an interesting marriage.

23

A Final Word

One year after Art's death, Lucky Lindy caught the nation's—and the area's—fancy, and like Lincoln Beachey, Art Smith was eclipsed by heroes emerging from the war. His memorials and accolades began to slip into legend, and soon Art Smith was lost amidst a new age. On the fiftieth anniversary of his death, there were a few articles published. On the one hundredth anniversary, practically nothing.

"In an era of moon landings and space shuttles, perhaps the exploits of a young man who built and flew his own plane in 1910, seem tame," wrote Vendrely, but "the accomplishments of this aviation and aerobatics pioneer were amazing."[1]

Art's place in aviation history, however, cannot be overlooked. He was one of the first stunt flyers. He invented descending spiral maneuvers, perfected phosphorus smoke skywriting, popularized and glamorized aviation for millions, and represented the spirit of youthful adventure for Americans. His was the first aerial elopement; he was one of America's first aviation spokesmen about military air-preparedness; and his patents and inventions were utilized to improve aviation.

The man who became known as "The Birdboy" was a showman, and his daring spirit and his charismatic personality charmed nations. He was a bona fide hero in Fort Wayne, San Francisco, Japan, and points in between. As a boy wonder, he gave millions the thrill of their lives. On a personal level, he was a most devoted son and a loyal friend. His enthusiasm for flying, even yet, speaks of American entrepreneurship and adventure.[2]

The early 1900s saw the development of two exciting facets of American life: the automobile and the airplane. The technology of one would not have been strange to the other; the risks were similar, and the rewards, likewise. It is no surprise that Art found them both attractive.

Aviation was a grand adventure during the early days of the century. The newness, the unknown, the danger all contributed to the growing love affair America developed for flying. Pilots were the brave pioneers on the aerial frontier. They were the chivalrous heroes with little or no fear of challenging nature itself with their attempts to break free from their earthly confines and venture out upon the heavens themselves.[3]

If readers wonder how a boy who was not well-founded technically could achieve so much, they will better understand Art's success after considering the remark his father made shortly after Art's death. "I knew the kind of boy Art was. I had watched him from the time he was this high (indicating babyhood). When he told me he wanted to build an airplane, I told him I'd put every cent I had into it, and I knew that if he did not have too many obstacles in his way, he would succeed. I was willing to risk everything on him."[4]

Art Smith during his celebrity days. Courtesy: Wertman-Stackhouse.

The letters Art wrote during the last three years of his life reveal a busy but reflective and thoughtful person. They express a much different voice from the exuberant and breezy tone of his autobiography. The grand exhibitions and interviews he gave when he was a fun-loving matinee star and an international celebrity were over, but he never lost his enthusiasm for flying or his excitement about his inventions and his work. He was articulate and had a good vocabulary. A graphologist who looked at Art's handwriting said his penmanship revealed "a person who is restless"; however, "he has an open-mind and loves to travel."[5]

Art was loyal to his family and friends. He was committed to his Christian Scientist beliefs and felt called to spread the word about the doctrines of the church. Although in one of Art's letters there is a reference to Garnet's joining the Christian Science church, Jim Wigner said his mother was not a Christian Scientist. Jim said that as a child, he was brought up attending the Methodist Church and later affiliated with the Lutheran faith.[6]

Art liked to read, he enjoyed poetry, and he was a searcher for wisdom. As he flew his route from Cleveland to Chicago, he said that he would look down on the fields below and become reflective about the beauty of nature and God's creativity. He was a happy man.

He was thankful for the opportunities he enjoyed. He was adventurous and not afraid to take risks. He also was interested in business. He not only gave exhibitions and received good fees for his work, he dealt with managers, foreign dignitaries, and the general public. He started his own company, building planes, and he had ideas about improvements in aviation that he wished to pursue. He was interested in starting an aviation school.

Art liked people, and he liked to talk. He especially liked to talk with them about flying and navigating the open skies. Had he lived, no doubt he would have been involved in some flying or racing adventure because the love of flying was in his heart. When he wrote "Lucky Strike" over Detroit with his skywriting apparatus, it was a far cry from the days when he had scrimped and saved and worked day and night to build a plane using cloth, wood, piano wire and sealing wax.

In his June 23, 1925, letter to Garnet he wrote, "The New Air Mail Service between New York and Chicago at night is to be inaugurated July 1st. The city is planning a big celebration as it will be the opening of their new 1,000-acre flying field. We of the Air Mail will deliver a goodly share of the flying. I myself may make one of my old time fireworks flights...."[7]

Dates blur, memories fade, and newspaper clippings turn to dust, but the Art Smith story becomes more romantic as aviation technology and information progress. As a pioneer aviator, his words about a world where flying would be commonplace to the average person were visionary. In his autobiography, he wrote:

> The world is carried forward by man's great dreams. The greatest dream of all is the conquest of the air. What it will mean to human life we know no more than Watt knew when he watched the lid of the kettle and dreamed of the first steam engine. Aerial navigation will mean, as the steam engine did, more than we can imagine now.
>
> Big men are working on it. Big men will some day conquer all the difficulties which we are fighting.
>
> We are only pioneers, but we are pioneers with a great idea. Some time in future centuries, the whole world will be revolutionized by that idea. Then it will know the value of the hope and the thrill we feel as our airplanes rise from the earth, pass through the clouds, and fly high in the clear upper air.[8]

A century has passed since the birth of aviation, and it is hard to imagine a world without airplanes. Thanks to pioneers such as John J. Montgomery, Orville and Wilbur Wright, Art Smith, Charles Lindbergh, and other daredevil flyers and adventurers, today it is possible for every person at some time or another to soar upward on invisible currents of wind and experience the freedom of space.

Note

James F. Smith died on July 10, 1939. His wife, Ida Krick Smith, died on June 4, 1940. Both are buried near Art in Lindenwood Cemetery, Fort Wayne, Indiana.

Notes

Preface

1. Lane, Rose, ed. *Art Smith's Story, The Autobiography* (San Francisco *Bulletin*, 1915), p. 3.
2. Stackhouse, Hubert L. *A Brief Candle* (Butler, Indiana: Butler Printing Co., 1998), p. 4.
3. *Ibid.*, p. 3.
4. *Ibid.*, p. 2.
5. Internet: www.airmailpioneers.org/pilots.html

Chapter 1

1. "Work of City's First Birdboy Is Perpetuated," *The Journal Gazette* (Fort Wayne), August 16, 1928, p. 1.
2. Lane, pp. 6–7.
3. *Ibid.*, p. 7.
4. *Ibid.*
5. *Ibid.*
6. *Ibid.*, p. 6.
7. *Ibid.*, pp. 6–7.
8. *Ibid.*, p. 8.
9. *Ibid.*
10. *Ibid.*
11. McComb, Robert P. "1970 Reunion Dedicated to Art Smith," *OX 5 Club of American News*, XII, no. 3, p. 1.

12. Lane, p. 8.
13. *Ibid.*
14. *Ibid.*, p. 10.
15. *Ibid.*
16. *Ibid.*
17. *Ibid.*
18. *Ibid.*, p. 11.
19. *Ibid.*
20. *Ibid.*
21. "Birdboy's Parents Married 50 Years," *The News-Sentinel* (Fort Wayne), March 18, 1933.
22. Lane, p. 4.
23. *Ibid.*
24. *Ibid.*
25. *Ibid.*, p. 12.

Chapter 2

1. *The News-Sentinel* (Fort Wayne), March 18, 1933.
2. "Relatives, Friends Add to Art Smith Lore," *The News-Sentinel* (Fort Wayne), August 22, 1956.
3. Stackhouse, p. 22.
4. *Ibid.*
5. Lane, p. 28.
6. *Ibid.*
7. *Ibid.*, p. 12.
8. *Ibid.*, p. 13.

9. *Ibid.*
10. *Ibid.*
11. *Ibid.*
12. *Ibid.*
13. *Ibid.*, p. 14.
14. *Ibid.*
15. Hobrock, Paul. "Paul Hobrock's Own Account of Early Fort Wayne Aviation," *15th OX 5 Club of America Annual National Convention Program*, 1970, October 22–24, p. 9.
16. Lane, p. 14.
17. *Ibid.*
18. *Ibid.*
19. *Ibid.*, p. 15.
20. *Ibid.*
21. *Ibid.*, p. 16.
22. *Ibid.*
23. *Ibid.*
24. *Ibid.*
25. *Ibid.*, pp. 16–17.
26. *Ibid.*, p. 17.
27. *Ibid.*, p. 18.
28. *Ibid.*
29. *Ibid.*, p. 19.
30. *Ibid.*
31. *Ibid.*
32. *Ibid.*
33. *Ibid.*, pp. 19–20.
34. *Ibid.*, p. 20.
35. *Ibid.*
36. *Ibid.*
37. *Ibid.*, p. 21.
38. *Ibid.*, p. 22.
39. *Ibid.*, p. 23.
40. *Ibid.*
41. *Ibid.*
42. *Ibid.*
43. *Ibid.*, p. 24.
44. *Ibid.*
45. *Ibid.*
46. *Ibid.*
47. *Ibid.*, p. 25.
48. *Ibid.*

Chapter 3

1. Lane, p. 26.
2. *Ibid.*
3. *Ibid.*
4. *Ibid.*
5. *Ibid.*, p. 27.
6. *Ibid.*, p. 28.
7. *Ibid.*, p. 29.

8. *Ibid.*
9. *Ibid.*, pp. 29–30.
10. *Ibid.*
22. *Ibid.*, p. 30.
12. *Ibid.*
13. *Ibid.*, p. 31.
14. *Ibid.*, p. 33.
15. *Ibid.*, p. 34.
16. *Ibid.*, p. 35.
17. *Ibid.*, p. 36.
18. *Ibid.*
19. *Ibid.*
21. *Ibid.*, p. 37.
22. *Ibid.*, pp. 37–38.
23. *Ibid.*, p. 39.

Chapter 4

1. Lane, p. 40.
2. *Ibid.*
3. *Ibid.*, p. 41.
4. *Ibid.*
5. *Ibid.*, p. 42.
6. *Ibid.*, p. 43.
7. *Ibid.*
8. *Ibid.*
9. *Ibid.*, p. 44.
10. *Ibid.*
11. *Ibid.*
12. *Ibid.*
13. *Ibid.* p. 45.
14. *Ibid.*, p. 46.
15. *Ibid.*, p. 47.
16. *Ibid.*, p. 46.
17. *Ibid.*, p. 47.
18. *Ibid.*
19. *Ibid*
20. *Ibid.*

Chapter 5

1. Lane, p. 48.
2. *Ibid.*
3. *Ibid.*, p. 49.
4. *Ibid.*
5. *Ibid.*
6. *Ibid.*
7. *Ibid.*, p. 50.
8. *Ibid.*
9. *Ibid.*
10. *Ibid.*, p. 51.

11. *Ibid.*
12. *Ibid.*, p. 52.
13. *Ibid.*
14. *Ibid.*
15. *Ibid.*, p. 53.
16. *Ibid.*
17. *Ibid.*
18. *Ibid.*
19. *Ibid.*
20. *Ibid.*
21. *Ibid.*, p. 55.
22. *Ibid.*
23. *Ibid.*
24. *Ibid.*
25. *Ibid.*
26. *Ibid.*, pp. 56–57.
27. *Ibid.*, p. 57.
28. *Ibid.*
29. *Ibid.*
30. *Ibid.*

Chapter 6

1. Lane, p. 58.
2. *Ibid.*
3. *Ibid.*, p. 59
4. *Ibid.*
5. *Ibid.*
6. *Ibid.*, p. 60.
7. *Ibid.*
8. *Ibid.*
9. *Ibid.*
10. *Ibid.*, p. 61.
11. *Ibid.*
12. *Ibid.*
13. *Ibid.*, p. 62.
14. *Ibid.*, pp. 62–63.
15. *Ibid.*, p. 63.
16. *Ibid.*
17. *Ibid.*
18. *Ibid.*, p. 64.
19. *Ibid.*
20. *Ibid.*
21. *Ibid.*
22. *Ibid.*, p. 65.
23. *Ibid.*
24. *Ibid.*
25. *Ibid.*
26. *Ibid.*
27. *Ibid.*, p. 66.
28. *Ibid.*
29. *Ibid.*
30. *Ibid.*, p. 67.

31. *Ibid.*, p. 68.
32. *Ibid.*
33. *Ibid.*
34. *Ibid.*, p. 69.
35. *Ibid.*, p. 68.
36. *Ibid.*, p. 69.
37. *Ibid.*
38. *Ibid.*
39. *Ibid.*

Chapter 7

1. Lane, p. 70.
2. *Ibid.*
3. *Ibid.*, p. 71.
4. *Ibid.*
5. *Ibid.*
6. *Ibid.*
7. Stackhouse, p. 29.
8. *Ibid.*, p. 13.
9. Stackhouse, Hubert L. "Art Smith Lands in Auburn," *Auburn Reflections* (Hicksville, Ohio: Hicksville Press, 1993), p. 31.
10. Lane, p. 71.
11. *Ibid.*, p. 72.
12. *Ibid.*
13. *Ibid.*
14. *Ibid.*
15. *Ibid.*, p. 73.
16. *Ibid.*, pp. 73–74.
17. *Ibid.*
18. *Ibid.*
19. *Ibid.*, p. 75.
20. *Ibid.*
21. *Ibid.*
22. *Ibid.*
23. *Ibid.*
24. *Ibid.*, p. 77.
25. *Ibid.*
26. *Ibid.*, p. 78.

Chapter 8

1. Lane, p. 77.
2. *Ibid.*, p. 78.
3. *Ibid.*
4. *Ibid.*
5. *Ibid.*
6. *Ibid.*
7. "Aeroplane Elopers Pass Over Auburn," *The Auburn Courier* (Auburn, Indiana), October 31, 1912, p. 1, c. 1.

8. Massie, Larry. "Nuptial Flight Ends Abruptly in Farm Field," *Kalamazoo Gazette* (Kalamazoo, Michigan), July 23, 1989, F-1.

9. Lane., p. 79.

10. *Ibid.*

11. *Ibid.*, pp. 79–80.

12. *Ibid.*, p. 80.

13. *Ibid.*

14. *Ibid.*

15. *Ibid.*

16. *Ibid.*

17. Stackhouse, *A Brief Candle*, p. 14.

18. Lane, p. 81.

19. *Ibid.*

20. Massie, F-1.

21. Lane, p. 81.

22. *The Auburn Courier*, October 31, 1912, p. 1, c. 1.

23. Lane, p. 81.

24. *Ibid.*, p. 82.

25. *Ibid.*

26. Stackhouse, *A Brief Candle*, p. 14.

27. *The Auburn Courier*, October 31, 1912, p. 1, c. 1.

28. Massie, F-1.

29. *The Auburn Courier*, October 31, 1912, p. 1.

30. Lane, p. 83.

31. *The Auburn Courier*, October 31, 1912, p. 1.

32. *Ibid.*

33. Massie, F-1.

34. *Ibid.*

35. Lane, p. 83.

36. *Ibid.*

37. *Ibid.*

38. *Ibid.*

39. Stackhouse, personal interview.

40. Massie, F-2.

41. Lane, p. 84.

Chapter 9

1. Lane, p. 84.

2. *Ibid.*

3. *Ibid.*, p. 86.

4. *Ibid.*

5. *Ibid.*

6. *Ibid.*, p. 87.

7. *Ibid.*

8. *Ibid.*

9. *Ibid.*

10. *Ibid.*

11. *Ibid.*, p. 88.

12. *Ibid.*

13. *Ibid.*

14. *Ibid.*

15. *Ibid.*, pp. 4–5.

16. *Ibid.*, p. 87.

17. *Ibid.*

18. "Post Visited Parents of Art Smith," *The Journal Gazette* (Fort Wayne), September 13, 1933, in the Greater Fort Wayne Aviation Museum Scrapbook, No. 2, hereafter referred to as F. W. Scrapbook.

19. "Wiley Post," *The World Book Encyclopedia*, 1950 Edition, XVIII, p. 6522.

20. Stackhouse, *A Brief Candle*, p. 11.

21. Lane., pp. 89–90.

22. McComb, p. 1.

Chapter 10

1. "U.S. Aviators Should Learn Loop-the-Loop," San Diego, California, *Union*, August 11, 1915, Wertman Scrapbook.

2. Lane., p. 3.

3. Postcard. Wertman Collection.

4. *Ibid.*

5. *Ibid.*

6. "Fort Wayne Aviator May Fly to Auburn," *The Auburn Courier*, October 12, 1911, p. 1, c. 5.

7. "Contract for Art Smith Is Signed," *The Auburn Courier*, October 5, 1914, p. 4.

8. *Ibid.*

9. "Birdman — Special Day," *The Auburn Courier*, October 8, 1914, p. 2.

10. "Birdman at Angola Had Narrow Escape," *The Auburn Courier*, October 12, 1914, p. 5.

11. "Flying Exhibition Must Be Postponed," *The Auburn Courier*, October 12, 1914, p. 1, c. 4.

12. Announcement — "Special Inducements," *The Auburn Courier*, October 15, 1914, p. 3, c. 3.

13. "Only Two Days Until 'Art Smith' Day," *The Auburn Courier*, October 15, 1914, p. 3, c. 3.

14. "Motor Breaks; Smith Forced to Descend," *The Auburn Courier*, October 19, 1914, p. 3, c. 5.

15. "Smith Desirous of Flying Here Again," *The Auburn Courier*, October 22, 1914, p. 1, c. 6.

16. "Aviator Says He Will Redeem Himself," *The Auburn Courier*, October 22, 1914, p. 3, c. 7.

17. *Ibid.*

18. *Ibid.*

19. *Ibid.*

20. "Only Two Days Until 'Art Smith' Day," *The Auburn Courier*, October 15, 1914, p. 3, c. 3.

21. "Smith's Flying Wins Many New Admirers," *The Auburn Courier*, October 26, 1914, p. 3, c. 4.

22. *Ibid.*

23. *Ibid.*

24. *Ibid.*

25. *Ibid.*

26. *Ibid.*

Chapter 11

1. Internet: www.sanfranciscomemories.com/ppie/panamapacific.html

2. Internet: www. amacord.com/fillmore/museum/beachey2.html

3. *Ibid.*

4. "World's Greatest Aviator Will Fly at South Dakota State Fair," Bruce(S.D.) *Herald*, August 18, 1915, Wertman Scrapbook.

5. "'Art' Smith Says U.S. Should Buy Flying Machine," *Clarinda Journal*, August 26, 1915, Wertman Scrapbook.

6. "Art Smith at the Fair," *Clarinda Demo*, August 19, 1915, Wertman Scrapbook.

7. "Great Story of Art Smith Selling Fast," San Francisco *Bulletin*, August 13, 1915, Wertman Scrapbook.

8. *Ibid.*

9. Lane, p. 94.

10. *Ibid.*, p. 90.

11. *Ibid.*, p. 91.

12. *Ibid.*

13. *Ibid.*

14. *Ibid.*

15. *Ibid.*

16. *Ibid.*, p. 93.

17. *Ibid.*

18. *Ibid.*

19. *Ibid.*, p. 4.

20. *Ibid.*

21. *Ibid.*, p. 4.

22. *Ibid.*, pp. 4–5.

23. *Ibid.*, p. 5.

24. *Ibid.*

25. *Ibid.*

26. *Ibid.*

27. *Ibid.*

28. *Ibid.*, p. 89.

29. *Ibid.*

30. *Ibid.*

31. *Ibid.*, p. 90.

32. Internet: www.sanfrancisicomemories.com/ppie/panamapacific.html

33. Lane, p. 3.

Chapter 12

1. "World's Aviator Will Fly at South Dakota State Fair," Chester (S.D.) *Journal*, August 5, 1915, Wertman Scrapbook.

2. "Art Smith Crazy! That Word Doesn't Express It," *San Diego Union*, August 12, 1915, Wertman Scrapbook.

3. "Art Smith, The Fearless Air Navigator," Mystic (Iowa) *Register*, August 26, 1915, Wertman Scrapbook.

4. "Coming from Frisco to Hamline," Shaloppe (Minn.) *Tribune*, August 6, 1915, Wertman Scrapbook.

5. Pinkerton, F.E., "Art Smith Has Closed Contract," Monmouth (Ill.) *Atlas*, August 3, 1915, Wertman Scrapbook.

6. "'Art Smith' Day at Fair," *The News-Sentinel* (Fort Wayne), August 11, 1915, Wertman Scrapbook.

7. Telegram sent to Al and Lucille Wertman on May 23, 1915, Stackhouse Collection.

8. "Tot Watching Smith Fly Falls to Death," *San Francisco Chronicle*, August 9, 1915, Wertman Scrapbook.

9. "Pride of Fort Wayne," *The News-Sentinel*, August 11, 1915, Wertman Scrapbook.

10. "Programme Today at the Exposition," *San Francisco Chronicle*, August 3, 1915, Wertman Scrapbook.

11. "Remarkable Night Picture of Aviator Art Smith, *Oakland Inquirer*, July 30, 1915, Wertman Scrapbook.

12. *Ibid.*

13. "Art Smith Is Back; Gives New Thrills," *The San Francisco Examiner* [no date], Stackhouse Collection.

14. *Ibid.*

15. *Ibid.*

16. *Ibid.*

17. McComb, p. 1.

18. *Ibid.*, pp. 1, 6.

19. "Art Smith Is Back" [no date], Stackhouse Collection.

20. "Art Smith Helped...Blind Boy," *Berkeley Cal. Gazette*, December 17, 1915, Greater Fort Wayne Aviation Museum Scrapbook, No. 1.

21. "Art Smith...Will be Seen at... Olympia Club," International Film Service Photo [no date], F.W. Scrapbook, No. 1.

22. Clipping. July 21, 1915, F.W. Scrapbook, No. 1.

23. "Art Drops Wreath to Memory of Lincoln Beachey," *Popular Mechanics*, August 1915; F.W. Scrapbook, No. 1.

24. "She'll Help 'Little Dipper's' Stunts," San Francisco *Bulletin*, November 13, 1915, F.W. Scrapbook, No. 1.

25. "Birdman as Santa Claus Role," San Francisco *Bulletin*, December 23, 1915, F. W. Scrapbook, No. 1.

26. Photograph in Greater Fort Wayne Aviation Museum Scrapbook, No. 2.

27. *Ibid.*

28. "Does Mrs. Aviator Get Excited...," Dallas, 1915, F.W. Scrapbook, No. 2.

29. "Art Smith Is Back," *The San Francisco Examiner* [no date], Stackhouse Collection.

30. Clipping: *Clear Lake* (Iowa) *Mirror*, August 26, 1915, Wertman Scrapbook.

31. "Boy Aviator Saves His Mother's Perilous Dip," *New Orleans States*, August 15, 1915, Wertman Scrapbook.

32. "Friends Plan Tribune for 'Art' Smith," *Orville (Calif.) Mercury*, July 31, 1915, Wertman Scrapbook.

33. "He's a-Leaving Us," San Francisco *Bulletin*, August 4, 1915, Wertman Scrapbook.

34. "Friends Plan Tribute," Wertman Scrapbook.

35. *Ibid.*

36. "Throngs Cheer 'Art Smith' at Farewell Fete," San Francisco *Bulletin*, August 9, 1915, Wertman Scrapbook.

37. *Ibid.*

38. "Sunday Will Be 'Art' Smith Day," San Francisco *Bulletin*, August 5, 1915, Wertman Scrapbook.

39. "'Kissel Komet' for Aviator Art Smith, *San Francisco Chronicle*, August 7, 1915, Wertman Scrapbook.

40. "'Goodby' Writes Art Smith in Air," *San Francisco Chronicle*, August 9, 1915, Wertman Scrapbook.

41. "22 Loops Made by 'Art Smith,'" *San Francisco Examiner*, August 9, 1915, Wertman Scrapbook.

42. *Ibid.*

43. *Ibid.*

44. *Ibid.*

45. "So Long, Art," San Francisco *Bulletin*, August 4, 1915, Wertman Scrapbook.

46. Lane, p. 3.

47. *Ibid.*, p. 85.

48. *Ibid.*

49. *Ibid.*

Chapter 13

1. Numerous clippings in the Wertman Scrapbook.

2. "Daring Flier Signed by Fair," San Diego *Union*, August 1, 1915, Wertman Scrapbook.

3. "We Are Still Inclined to Believe the Marvelous," San Diego *Union*, July 25, 1915, Wertman Scrapbook.

4. *Ibid.*

5. *Ibid.*

6. *Ibid.*

7. "Greatest Aeroplane Act in the World," Henning (Minn.) *Advocate*, August 5, 1915, Wertman Scrapbook.

8. "Art Smith Will Arrive Tonight," San Diego *Sun*, August 10, 1915, Wertman Scrapbook.

9. *Ibid.*

10. *Ibid.*

11. "Birdboy Pays Big Price for Policy," San Diego *Union*, August 8, 1915, Wertman Scrapbook.

12. *Ibid.*

13. "Daring Flier Signed," San Diego *Union*, August 1, 1915, Wertman Scrapbook.

14. "Sensational Boy Aviator," Pasadena *Star*, August 10, 1915, Wertman Scrapbook.

15. *Ibid.*

16. *Ibid.*

17. *Ibid.*

18. *Ibid.*

19. *Ibid.*

20. *Ibid.*

21. *Ibid.*

22. "Aviator Chooses Dodge Car for Pleasure," *Omaha Bee*, August 15, 1915, Wertman Scrapbook.

23. *Ibid.*

24. *Ibid.*

25. *Ibid.*

26. "San Diego Management," Osakis (Minn.) *Review*, August 12, 1915, Wertman Scrapbook.

27. "Aviator Takes 11 Loops," *Los Angeles Examiner*, August 12, 1915, Wertman Scrapbook.

28. Stackhouse, p. 17.

29. Clipping [no date] in the Greater F. W. Aviation Museum Scrapbook, No. 1.

30. *Portland Telegram*, March 2, 1916, F. W. Aviation Museum Scrapbook, No. 1.

31. Postcards and Photographs. Stackhouse Collection.

32. "Birdboy Thrills Thousands at Exposition," San Diego *Union*, August 12, 1915, Wertman Scrapbook.

33. Stackhouse, *A Brief Candle,* pp. 17, 24.

34. "Art Smith's Wrecked Machine," Des Moines *Capital*, August 25, 1915, Wertman Scrapbook.

35. "Art Smith Is Very Sensational," Lovelock (Nev.) *Review*, July 30, 1915, Wertman Scrapbook.

36. "Friend of Motors," Des Moines *Register*, August 29, 1915, Scrapbook, No. 1.

37. "Smith Is Aero Reserve," San Jose *Mercury*, August 8, 1915, Wertman Scrapbook.

38. "Art Smith Decorates His Flying Machine," Mason City (Iowa) *Times*, July 24, 1915, Wertman Scrapbook.

39. "Art Smith Comes Eastward," Clarinda *Journal*, August 19, 1915, F.W. Scrapbook, No. 1.

40. *Ibid.*

41. "Aviation History Made Last Night," New Orleans *Picayune*, February [no date], F. W. Scrapbook, No. 1.

42. "World's Greatest Aviator Will Fly at Fair," Springfield *Times*, July 24, 1915, Wertman Scrapbook.

43. Clipping [no date] in the F.W. Scrapbook, No. 1.

44. "Art Smith in Dare-Devil Act," Villisca (Iowa) *Review*, July 28, 1915, Wertman Scrapbook.

45. "World's Greatest Aviator to Fly," Hurley (Iowa) *Herald*, July 29, 1915, Wertman Scrapbook.

46. "World's Greatest Aviator to Fly at State," Alpena (S.D.) *Journal*, July 30, 1915, Wertman Scrapbook.

47. "Smith Is a Friend of Motors," Des Moines *Register*, August 29, 1915, Wertman Scrapbook.

48. "Unique Good Luck Charm Accompanies," San Diego *Union*, August 25, 1915, Wertman Scrapbook.

49. *Ibid.*

50. Ray, Rex, "Brunet Wants Trip in Clouds," Des Moines *News*, August 23, 1915, Wertman Scrapbook.

51. Poem on loose paper in the F. W. Scrapbook, No. 1.

52. Dallas Clipping [no date] in the F.W. Scrapbook, No. 1.

Chapter 14

1. "Mikado's Flag Will Fly with Art Smith," San Francisco *Bulletin*, November 9, 1915, F.W. Scrapbook, No. 1.

2. Stackhouse, *A Brief Candle*, p. 41.

3. *Ibid.*, pp. 17–18.

4. "Aimee C. Left Here," *Portland Telegraph*, March 2, 1916, F.W. Scrapbook, No. 1.

5. "On Eve of Departure," Kendallville (Ind.) *News-Sun*, March 3, 1916, F.W. Scrapbook, No. 1.

6. "Art Smith Asks for Divorce," *Pasadena News*, March 4, 1916, F.W. Scrapbook, No. 1.

7. "Files," Santa Rosa *Press-Democrat*, March 3, 1916, F.W. Scrapbook, No. 1.

8. "Relatives, Friends Add to Art Smith Lore," *The News-Sentinel* (Fort Wayne), August 22, 1956, p. 23.

9. Stackhouse Collection.

10. *Ibid.*

11. "The First Night Flight in Japan," *The Japanese Times*, June 3, 1916, Stackhouse Collection.

12. *Ibid.*

13. *Ibid.*

14. *Ibid.*

15. *Ibid.*

16. *Ibid.*

17. *Ibid.*

18. *Ibid.*

19. *Ibid.*

20. *Ibid.*

21. *Ibid.*

22. "Fort Wayne's Birdboy Is Making a Hit with Japanese," *The News-Sentinel* (Fort Wayne), June 3, 1916, p. 1.

23. "Medals Given Him Here Mean More to Aviator Than Money," *The Japan Advertiser*, June 2, 1916, Stackhouse Collection.

24. *Ibid.*

25. "Fort Wayne's Birdboy...," *The News-Sentinel* (Fort Wayne), June 3, 1916, p. 1.

26. *Ibid.*

27. *Ibid.*

28. "Their Majesties See American Aviator Fly," Clipping [no date, no place], p. 10, Wertman Scrapbook.

29. *Ibid.*

30. *Ibid.*

31. Stackhouse, *A Brief Candle*, p. 41.

32. "Fort Wayne's Birdboy...," *The News-Sentinel* (Fort Wayne), June 3, 1916.

33. "The Aerial Wonder," *The Japan Times*, June 7, 1916, p. 8, Stackhouse Collection.

34. "Tokyo's Leading Men at Art Smith Dinner," *The Japan Advertiser*, June 3, 1916.

35. "Fort Wayne's Birdboy...," *The News-Sentinel* (Fort Wayne), June 3, 1916.

36. *Ibid.*

37. Bill of sale. Stackhouse Collection.

38. Losh, Bernard J. "When the World Lost Its Greatest 'Stunt' Flyer," *The Dayton News*, included in *Art Smith, His Own Story of His Thrilling Career*, reprinted by *The News-Sentinel* (Fort Wayne), 1956, p. 95.

39. *Ibid.*

40. "Medals Given Him Here...," *The Japan Advertiser*, June 2, 1916.

41. "Art Smith's Views on Subject of Vice," *The Japan Advertiser*, June 6, 1916, p. 1, Wertman Scrapbook.

42. Losh, p. 91.

43. "Smith Wouldn't Risk Injuring Spectators," *The Japan Advertiser*, June 18, 1916, Stackhouse Collection.

44. *Ibid.*

45. Gaisha, Nagaoka. *Aeroplane as a Factor in Bringing Japanese and United States Closer in Friendship* (Japan: National Aviation Society of Japan), 1916.

Chapter 15

1. "Art Smith Suing Wife," Waco *Morning News*, March 3, 1916, F.W. Scrapbook, No. 1.

2. "Aviator's Wife Fights Case," Portland *Telegram*, March 2, 1916, F.W. Scrapbook, No. 1.

3. "Sues His Airship Bride," Preston (Iowa) *Gazette*, March 3, 1916, F.W. Scrapbook, No. 1.

4. "Birdboy Thrills Thousands," August 12, 1915, Wertman Scrapbook.

5. "Aviator's Wife Says Too Much Swelled Head Caused Discord," Portland *News*, March 3, 1916, F.W. Scrapbook, No. 1.

6. San Francisco *Bulletin*, March 3, 1916, F.W. Scrapbook, No. 1.

7. "Aviator's Wife Says," March 3, 1916.

8. Nagaoka, *Aeroplane as a Factor*.

9. Various clippings in the F.W. Scrapbook, No. 1.

10. "Aviator's Wife Fights," Portland *News*, September 2, 1916. F.W. Scrapbook, No. 1.

11. "Excerpts from 'Love Notes' in Smith Divorce," Oakland *Tribune*, March 3, 1916, F.W. Scrapbook, No. l.

12. "Wife Busy on Earth While the Young Husband Goes Up in the Air," Carson City *News*, March 5, 1916, F.W. Scrapbook, No. 1.

13. *Ibid.*

14. "Caples to Declare Intention to Name Aviator in Complaint," Los Angeles *Tribune*, March 11, 1916, F.W. Scrapbook, No. 1.

15. "Mother of Art Smith's Wife Prostrated," San Francisco *Bulletin*, March 2, 1916, F.W. Scrapbook, No. 1.

16. "Caples Fails to Name Art Smith," San Francisco *Bulletin*, March 17, 1916, F.W. Scrapbook, No. 1.

17. "Aviator's Wife Says," March 3, 1916.

18. *Ibid.*

19. "I Don't Love Art Smith, Declares Mrs. Wm. J. Caples," San Francisco *Chronicle*, March 9, 1916, F.W. Scrapbook, No. 1.

20. *Ibid.*

21. "Paul Cooley," San Francisco *Examiner*, March 2, 1916, F.W. Scrapbook, No. 1.

22. "Absolutely New Cause," San Diego *Union*, April 9, 1916, F.W. Scrapbook, No. 1.

23. *Ibid.*

24. "Art Smith Files New Divorce Suit," Los Angeles *Record*, May 9, 1916, F.W. Scrapbook, No. 1.

25. "Aviator's Wife Demands Cash," Los Angeles *Herald*, March 21, 1916, F.W. Scrapbook, No. 1.

26. "Japanese Purse Must Go for Ali-

mony," San Bernardino *Index*, March 27, 1916, F.W. Scrapbook, No. 1.

27. "Art Smith Granted Divorce Today," San Francisco *Bulletin*, Feb. 2, 1917, F.W. Scrapbook, No. 1.

28. Nagaoka, *Aeroplane as a Factor.*

29. "Fell in Japan," Sacramento *Union*, July 19, 1917, F.W. Scrapbook, No. 1.

30. "Surgeon's Death Is Blow to Art Smith," San Francisco *Bulletin*, August 12, 1916, F.W. Scrapbook, No. 1.

31. *Ibid.*

32. "Yankee Airman Who Was Badly Injured in Japan," Spokane *Review*, August 20, 1916, F.W. Scrapbook, No. 1.

33. "'Art Smith' in Fight for Air Millions," San Francisco *Examiner*, March 24, 1917, F.W. Scrapbook, No. 1.

34. "Art Smith Starts Aviation School," Los Angeles, *Record*, April [no day], 1917, F.W. Scrapbook, No. 1.

35. "'Art' Smith in Fight for Air Millions," San Francisco *Examiner*, F.W. Scrapbook, No. 1.

36. "Intrepid Exposition Flyer Takes Stand for Montgomery," Sacramento *Bee*, March 30, 1917, F.W. Scrapbook, No. 1.

37. "'Art' Smith in Fight For," F.W. Scrapbook, No. 1.

38. "Art Smith Starts Aviation School," F.W. Scrapbook, No. 1.

39. "Exposition Aviators All Dead But Smith," Sacramento *Union*, November 4, 1916, F.W. Scrapbook, No. 1.

40. "Art Smith Expects to Build Biplanes," Omega *Report*, January 30, 1917, F.W. Scrapbook, No. 1.

41. *Ibid.*

42. "Art Smith Returns to Fill His Contracts," *The Japan Advertiser*, April 2, 1917, p. 1.

43. "Art Smith Granted Divorce Today," San Francisco *Bulletin*, Feb. 2, 1917, F.W. Scrapbook, No. 1.

Chapter 16

1. "Art Smith Is Back," *The Japan Advertiser* [no date], Stackhouse Collection.

2. *Ibid.*

3. Photographs. Wertman Collection.

4. "Art Smith Thrills Big Aoyama Crowd," *The Japan Advertiser*, April 26, 1917.

5. "Art Smith Flies Again," *The Japan Advertiser*, April 26, 1917.

6. "Art Smith Thrills Big…," *The Japan Advertiser*, April 26, 1917.

7. *Ibid.*

8. *Ibid.*

9. *Ibid.*

10. *Ibid.*

11. "Art Smith Receives Ovation at Aoyama," *The Japan Advertiser*, April 26, 1917.

12. *Ibid.*

13. *Ibid.*

14. *Ibid.*

15. *Ibid.*

16. *Ibid.*

17. *Ibid.*

18. "Medals Given Him Here…," *The Japan Advertiser*, July 2, 1916.

19. "Art Smith Returns to Fill His Contracts," *The Japan Advertiser*, April 22, 1917.

20. "Medals Given Him Here…," *The Japan Advertiser*, July 2, 1916.

21. *Ibid.*

22. *Ibid.*

23. *Ibid.*

24. Photographs. The Greater Fort Wayne Aviation Museum, Scrapbook, No. 2.

25. "Learned Here Flyer on Important Trip," San Jose *News*, April 9, 1917, F.W. Scrapbook, No. 1.

26. "Art Smith Returns to Fill His Contracts," *The Japan Advertiser*, April 22, 1917.

27. Photograph. Wertman Collection.

28. "Most Daring Youngster in America," *The Japan Advertiser* [no date], 1916.

29. Stackhouse Collection.

30. *Ibid.*

31. "News Item," *The Auburn Courier*, September 18, 1917.

32. Photograph. Wertman Collection.

Chapter 17

1. "Most Daring Youngster in America," Stackhouse Collection.

2. Lane, p. 84.

3. *Ibid.*

4. "Most Daring Youngster in America," Stackhouse Collection.

5. Lane, p. 84.

6. "Smith Memorial Fund Hits $1,500,"

The Journal Gazette (Fort Wayne), February 21, 1926, p. 1.

7. *Ibid.*, p.8.

8. "Sorrowing Mother of Art Smith Fears Future Without Her Son," *The Journal Gazette* (Fort Wayne), February 14, 1926, pp. 1, 6.

9. Lane, p. 84.

10. Losh, p. 97.

11. Benson, Mae Biddison, "World's Most Spectacular Flier, Art Smith of Stunt Fame Sent to Carruthers," Fort Worth *Star-Telegram* [no date], p. 12, Stackhouse Collection.

12. *Ibid.*

13. *Ibid.*

14. *Ibid.*

15. *Ibid.*

16. "Art Smith Is Ready to Teach Aviation," Riverside (Calif.) *Press*, January 17, 1916, F.W. Scrapbook, No. 1.

17. "Military Preparedness," *The Journal Gazette* (Fort Wayne) [no date], F.W. Scrapbook, No. 1.

18. *Ibid.*

19. *Ibid.*

20. *Ibid.*

21. *Ibid.*

22. Benson, Fort Worth *Star-Telegram*, p. 12, Stackhouse Collection.

23. *Ibid.*

24. *Ibid.*

25. *Ibid.*

26. *Ibid.*

27. "Art Smith Baby Cars for Sale," San Francisco *Examiner*, March 4, 1917, F.W. Scrapbook, No. 1.

28. Benson, p. 12, Stackhouse Collection.

29. *Ibid.*

30. "'Art' Smith Says U.S. Should Buy Flying Machines," Clarinda *Herald*, August 25, 1915, Wertman Scrapbook.

31. *Ibid.*

32. "Art Says," Des Moines *News*, August 3, 1915, Wertman Scrapbook.

33. "Lack of Military Training," Sacramento *Bee*, July 23, 1915, Wertman Scrapbook.

34. "U.S. Aviators Should Learn the Loop-the-Loop," San Diego *Union*, August 11, 1915, Wertman Scrapbook.

35. *Ibid.*

36. *Ibid.*

37. *Ibid.*

38. "Roosevelt and Aviator Are Photographed," Sacramento *Bee*, July 23, 1915, F.W. Scrapbook, No. 1.

39. *Ibid.*

40. "U.S. Aviators Should Learn the Loop-the-Loop," Wertman Scrapbook.

Chapter 18

1. McComb, p. 14.

2. "Art Smith's Air Mail Chief Praises His Record," *The Journal Gazette* (Fort Wayne), August 6, 1927, p. 2.

3. Internet: www.airmailpioneers.org/pilots.html

4. McComb, p. 14.

5. *Ibid.*

6. *Ibid.*

7. *Ibid*

8. *Ibid*

9. *Ibid.*

10. Membership Card. Stackhouse Collection.

11. "Art Smith, Flyer Killed," *The Journal Gazette* (Fort Wayne), February 13, 1926, p. 1.

12. McComb, p. 14.

13. "Art Smith's Air Mail Chief Praises," p. 2.

14. *Ibid.*

15. "Art Smith, Flyer Killed," p. 1.

16. "Elaborate Service Banned By Mother," *The Journal Gazette* (Fort Wayne), February 14, 1926, p. 6.

17. *Ibid.*

18. "Sorrowing Mother of Art Smith Fears Future Without Her Son," *The Journal Gazette* (Fort Wayne), February 14, 1926, p. 1.

19. *Ibid.*

20. "Public Service for Art Smith," *The Journal Gazette* (Fort Wayne), February 16, 1926, p. 1.

21. *Ibid.*

Chapter 19

1. "Mother Consents to Allow Friends Pay Final Tribute," *The Journal Gazette* (Fort Wayne), February 16, 1926, p. 1.

2. *Ibid.*

3. *Ibid.*, p. 6.

4. *Ibid.*

5. "Sorrowing Mother of Art Smith," *The Journal Gazette* (Fort Wayne), February 14, 1926, p. 1.

6. "Smith Flyer Killed," *The Journal Gazette* (Fort Wayne), February 13, 1926, p. 1.

7. "Move to Create Smith Memorial," *The Journal Gazette* (Fort Wayne), February 14, 1926, p. 1.

8. "Smith Memorial Is Taking Shape," *The Journal Gazette* (Fort Wayne), February 17, 1926, p. 1.

9. "Art Smith Buried with Simple Rites," *The Journal Gazette* (Fort Wayne), February 17, 1926, p. 2.

10. *Ibid.*

11. *Ibid.*, p. 1.

12. *Ibid.*

13. "Government Flyers from McCook Field, Dayton," *The Journal Gazette* (Fort Wayne), February 17, 1926, p. 1.

14. *Ibid.*

15. Losh, Bernard J., "When the World Lost Its Greatest 'Stunt' Flyer," *The Dayton News.*

16. "Art Smith Buried with Simple Rites," pp. 1–2.

17. *Ibid.*

18. "Smith Project Endorsed," *The Journal Gazette* (Fort Wayne), February 22, 1926.

19. *Ibid.*

20. "Art Smith's Parents Here in Memory of Dead Flyer," *The Journal Gazette* (Fort Wayne), February 18, 1926, p. 1.

21. *Ibid.*

22. "Contributions Already Received for Art Smith Memorial," *The Journal Gazette* (Fort Wayne), February 19, 1926, p. 1.

23. "Smith Fund Total Near $2,000 Mark," *The Journal Gazette* (Fort Wayne), February 23, 1926, p. 1.

24. *Ibid.*, pp. 1–2.

25. "Smith Memorial Campaign Opened," *The Journal Gazette* (Fort Wayne), February 18, 1926, p.2.

26. "Propose Benefit Basketball Tilt to Aid Art Smith Memorial Fund," *The Journal Gazette* (Fort Wayne), February 25, 1926, p. 1.

27. *Ibid.*

28. "Decatur Man Boosts Art Smith Memorial," *The Journal Gazette* (Fort Wayne), February 28, 1926, p. 1.

29. "Contest Suggested for Smith Memorial," *The Journal Gazette* (Fort Wayne), February 27, 1926, p. 1.

30. *Ibid.*

31. "Fame of Art Smith Committed to Bronze and Granite," *The Journal Gazette* (Fort Wayne), August 7, 1928, p. 1.

32. Fort Wayne Greater Aviation Museum Scrapbooks.

33. "Lindbergh Honors Fort Wayne by Air," *The Journal Gazette* (Fort Wayne), August 11, 1928, p. 1.

34. "Mother to Unveil Tribute to Flyer," *The Journal Gazette* (Fort Wayne), August 14, 1928, p. 1.

35. "Homage Paid to Art Smith," *The Journal Gazette* (Fort Wayne), August 16, 1928, p. 1.

36. *Ibid.*

37. "Decatur Man Boosts Art Smith Memorial," p. 1

38. "Homage Paid to Art Smith," p. 1.

39. *Ibid.*

40. "Fame of Art Smith Committed to Bronze and Granite," p. 1.

41. "Homage Paid to Art Smith," p. 1.

42. "Work of City's First Birdboy Perpetuated," *The Journal Gazette* (Fort Wayne), August 16, 1928, p.2.

43. *Ibid.*

44. *Ibid.*

45. *Ibid.*

46. "Art Smith's Air Mail Chief Praises His Record as Flyer," *The Journal Gazette* (Fort Wayne), August 16, 1928, p. 2.

47. Internet: www.airmailpioneers.org

48. "Homage Paid to Art Smith," p. 1.

49. "Birdboy's Record Reads Like Magic," *The Journal Gazette* (Fort Wayne), August 16, 1928, p. 2.

50. "Smith Memorial Is Taking Shape," *The Journal Gazette* (Fort Wayne), February 17, 1926, p. 1.

Chapter 20

1. Internet: www. fwairport.com/baer. html

2. Photo [1926] *The News-Sentinel* (Fort Wayne), Stackhouse Collection.

3. Hobrock, Paul. "Paul Hobrock's Own Account of Early Fort Wayne Aviation," 15th *Annual National Convention Program*, October 22–24, 1970, p. 9.

4. *Ibid.*

5. Thumma, William. *Early Aviation in Indiana* (Elwood, Indiana: Elwood Printing, 1989), p. 39.

6. Ankenbruck, John. *Twentieth Century History of Fort Wayne*, Fort Wayne, Indiana: Twentieth Century Historical Fort Wayne, Inc., 1975, p. 219.

7. *Ibid.*

8. Gamill, Andy. "Board Votes 4–1 to Close Smith Field," *The Journal Gazette* (Fort Wayne), June 27, 2002, p. 1.

9. "Mother of 'Birdboy' TWA Guest," *The News-Sentinel* (Fort Wayne), August 16, 1957.

10. "Sorrowing Mother of Art Smith Fears Future Without Son," *The Journal Gazette* (Fort Wayne), February 14, 1926, p. 6.

11. *Ibid.*

12. Ankenbruck, p. 220.

13. Myers, Roger K. Personal Interview.

14. "Relatives, Friends Add to Art Smith Lore," *The News-Sentinel* (Fort Wayne), August 22, 1956.

15. *Ibid.*

16. *Ibid.*

17. *Ibid.*

18. Ankenbruck, p. 219.

19. "Art Smith Memorial Day," *OX5 15th Annual National Convention*, p. 1.

20. *Ibid.*, inside front cover.

21. Stackhouse, "Art Smith: The Birdboy at 100," *The Accelerator*, XVIII, no. 1, April 1991, p. 15.

22. *Ibid.*

23. *Ibid.*

24. Myers, Roger K. Personal Interview.

25. Nagaoka, *Aeroplane as a Factor.*

26. *Ibid.*

27. *Ibid.*

28. Al Wertman letter to his son Herb Wertman. Stackhouse Collection.

29. Myers, Roger K. Personal Interview.

30. Vendrely, Nancy. "'Birdboy' Once Famous from Here to Japan," *The Journal Gazette, Yesterday* (People/Southwest), January 31, 1995, p. 8.

31. *Ibid.*

32. *Ibid.*

Chapter 21

1. "Sorrowing Mother of Art Smith Fears Future Without Her Son," *The Journal Gazette* (Fort Wayne), February 14, 1926, p. 6.

2. Vendrely, Nancy, "Son Never Knew Mom's First Love Was Art Smith," *The Journal Gazette Yesterday* (People/Northeast), March 7, 1995, p. 2.

3. *Ibid.*

4. *Ibid.*

5. *Ibid.*

6. *Ibid.*

7. *Ibid.*

8. *Ibid.*

9. *Ibid.*

10. *Ibid.*

11. Wigner, James. Personal Interview.

12. *Ibid.*

13. *Ibid.*

14. Vendrely, p. 2.

15. *Ibid.*

16. *Ibid.*

17. Telephone Conversation.

Chapter 22

Selected letters written by Art Smith to Garnet Straits in 1923:

1. March 7 — Flying Section, McCook Field, Dayton.

2. March 16 — 734 North Main St., Dayton.

3. April 16 — # 511, Hotel Regent, Euclid Ave., Cleveland.

4. April 18 — *Ibid.*

5. May 2 — 2042 E. 102, Cleveland.

6. June 3 — *Ibid.*

7. June 24 — *Ibid.*

8. July 1 — *Ibid.*

9. July 15 — Cleveland.

10. July 20 — *Ibid.*

11. July 29 — *Ibid.*

12. August 7 — Hotel Harrington, Eleventh and E. Streets, N.W., Washington, D.C.

13. August 23 — 2042 E. 102, Cleveland.

14. September 9 — *Ibid.*

15. September 21 — Hotel Washington, Washington Street Between LaSalle and North Wells Streets, Chicago.

16. October 7 — Cleveland.

17. October 28 — Cleveland.

18. December 10 — Hotel Washington, Washington Street Between LaSalle and North Wells Streets, Chicago.

19. December 29 — 16902 Endora Rd., Cleveland.

Selected letters written by Art Smith to Garnet Straits in 1924:

1. January 23 — Hotel Washington; mailed in Chicago.

2. February 28 — Hotel Washington; mailed in Bryan, Ohio.

3. March 18 —*Ibid.*

4. April 19 — Hotel Washington; mailed in Chicago.

5. May 13 — Hotel Washington; mailed in Bryan, Ohio.

6. June 16 —*Ibid.*

7. July 13 — 16902 Endora Rd., Cleveland.

8. September 7 —*Ibid.*

9. October 14 —*Ibid.*

10. November 17 —*Ibid.*

11. November 26 —*Ibid.*

12. December 24 —*Ibid.*

Selected letters written by Art Smith to Garnet Straits in 1925:

1. January 14 — Cleveland.

2. January 21—*Ibid.*

3. March 29 —*Ibid.*

4. April 18 —*Ibid.*

5. May 7 —*Ibid.*

6. June 3 —*Ibid.*

7. June 23 — 16902 Endora Road, Cleveland.

8. July 23 — 4013 Riveredge Road, Cleveland.

9. August 1—*Ibid.*

10. August 11—*Ibid.*

11. August 17 —*Ibid.*

12. August 28 —*Ibid.*

13. September 8 —*Ibid.*

14. September 29 —*Ibid.*

15. October 12 —*Ibid.*

16. October 23 —*Ibid.*

17. November 11—*Ibid.*

18. December 22 —*Ibid.*

1926 letters:

1. January 27 —from Cleveland.

2. March 26 —from 1611 Spring Street, Fort Wayne, Indiana.

3. Wigner, Personal Interview, October 21, 2002.

4. Poem, "Mom." Loose in the Greater Fort Wayne Aviation Museum Scrapbook, No. 2.

Chapter 23

1. Vendrely, "'Birdboy' Once Famous from Here to Japan," *The Journal Gazette Yesterday* (People/Southwest), January 31, 1995.

2. Stackhouse, *A Brief Candle*, p. 3.

3. Wegner, Jeremy, "The Death of an American Romance," *The Triangle* (Angola, Indiana: Tri-State University), April 6, 1995.

4. "Smith's Parents Live in Memory of Dead Flyer," *The Journal Gazette* (Fort Wayne), February 18, 1926, p. 6, c. 2.

5. Wintrode, Ann P., Personal Interview.

6. Smith, Art. Letter to Garnet Straits: June 23, 1925.

7. Wigner, James. Personal Interview.

8. Lane, p. 94.

Selected Bibliography

Books

Ankenbruck, John. *Twentieth Century History of Fort Wayne.* Fort Wayne, Indiana: Twentieth Century Historical Fort Wayne, Inc., 1975.

Gaisha, Nagaoka. *Aeroplane as a Factor in Bringing Japanese and United States Closer in Friendship.* Japan: National Aviation Society of Japan, 1916.

Lane, Rose, ed. *Art Smith's Story, The Autobiography.* San Francisco *Bulletin*, 1915.

Ringenberg, Margaret J. *Girls Can't Be Pilots.* Fort Wayne, Indiana: Daedalus Press, 1998.

Shenk, Ed. *Comes to Mind.* Goshen, Kentucky: KLS Enterprises, 1998.

Smith, John Martin. *DeKalb County.* Vol. 1. Auburn, Indiana: DeKalb Sesquicentennial, Inc., 1990.

Stackhouse, Hubert L. *A Brief Candle.* Butler, Indiana: Butler Printing Co., 1998.

_____. *Auburn Reflections.* Bryan, Ohio: Hicksville Printing, 1993.

Thumma, William. *Early Aviation in Indiana.* Elwood, Indiana: Elwood Printing, 1989.

Articles, Program Booklets, etc.

Hobrock, Paul, "Paul Hobrock's Own Account of Early Fort Wayne Aviation." *OX5 Annual National Convention Program Booklet.* 1970.

McComb, Robert P. "The Birdboy of Fort The Art Smith Story." *OX5 Club of America News* XII, no. 3.

_____. "1970 Reunion Dedicated to Art Smith." *OX5 Annual National Convention Program Booklet.* 1970.

Stackhouse, Hubert L. "Art Smith — The Bird Boy at 100." *The Accelerator.* Auburn, Indiana: Auburn Cord Duesenberg Museum XVII, no. 1, April 1991.

Wegner, Jeremy. "A Student Essay: 'The Death of an American Romance.'" *The Triangle.* Angola, Indiana: Tri-State University, 6 April 1995.

"Wiley Post." *World Book Encyclopedia.* 1950 Edition.

Newspapers

The Auburn Courier (Auburn, Ind.): 1911— October 12; 1912 — October 5, 8, 12, 15, 22, 26, 31; and various years on microfilm.

The Evening Star (Auburn, Ind.): 1976— January 24

The Journal Gazette (Fort Wayne, IN): 1926 — February 13, 14, 16, 17, 18, 19, 22, 23, 25, 27, 28; 1927 — August 6; 1928 — August 7, 11, 14, 16; 1933 — August 22, September 13; 1995 — January 31, March 5; 2002 — June 26; and various years on microfilm.

The Kalamazoo Gazette (Kalamazoo, Mich.): 1989 — July 23.

The News-Sentinel (Fort Wayne, Ind.): 1933 — March 8; 1956 — August 22; and various years on microfilm.

Electronic Data

"Buildings and Image Gallery." San Francisco Memories. 1915. www. sanfranciscomemories. com/ppie/panamapacific.

Calisch, Woolner. "Richmond Air Show 1909." Richmond *Times Dispatch*. 23 April 1939. www.thenandnow.bravepages.com

Gray, Carroll F. "All about Pre–WWI Pioneer Aviators." The Early Birds of Aviation. 18 Nov. 2002. www.earlybirds.org

_____._____. "Frequently Asked Questions about Pioneer Aviators." The Pioneer Aviators. 18 Nov. 2002. www.pioneeraviators.com.

"John Joseph Montgomery." The Pioneer Aviation Group. 11 Nov. 2002. www.flyingmachines. org

_____. "Lincoln Beachey, A Brief Biography." The Pioneer Aviators. 19 Nov. 2002. www.pioneer aviators.com

"Lt. Paul Baer." Fort Wayne International Airport [n.d.]. www.fwairport.com/baer.htm

McCarthy, Ken. "Lincoln Beachey." Fillmore Museum. 2001. amacord.com/fillmore/museum/ beachey2.htm

Wright, Nancy Allison. "U.S. Air Mail Fatalities in the Line of Duty." 1 Dec. 2002. Airmail Pioneers. www. airmailpioneers.org

Other

Letters, Art Smith to Garnet Straits. 1923–1926. James Wigner Collection.

_____, Ida Smith to Garnet Straits, 1925, 1926. James Wigner Collection.

Greater Fort Wayne Aviation Museum Scrapbooks, No. 1 and No. 2.

Interview, Myers, Roger K. 10 Oct. 2002.

_____, Ringenberg, Margaret R. 1 Nov. 2001.

_____, Stackhouse, Hubert L. 21 Aug. 2002.

_____, Wigner, James. 21 Oct. 2002.

_____, Wintrode, Ann P. 16 Oct. 2002.

Postcards, Photographs, and Clippings. Stackhouse Collection.

Wertman Scrapbook of Art Smith Newspaper Clippings. 1915–1917.

Index

Numbers in *italics* refer to pages with photographs.

Nishimura, S. (dealer in
embroideries) 116
Novelli, James 150, 151–152

Oakland Inquirer 87
Oechtering, Rt. Rev. Msgr.
J.H. 150
Okuda, Dr. (mayor of Tokyo)
115
Okuma, Count Shigenobu 116
"Old and New Developments
in Christian Science" (lec-
ture) 180
Oliver, S.A. 151
Olympia Club Minstrel Show
90
Omaha *Bee* 99
Oriental Hotel 105
Osaka Ashuri Newspaper
Company 113
OX5 Clubs of America 158
OX5 News 89

Pal's Club 122
Panama Canal-Pacific Ocean
Exposition 77, 87, 91–93
Park Commissioners (Fort
Wayne) 155
Parker, Billy 89, 158
Patch, J. W. 39
Peddicord, James S. 145, 147,
149
Pegoud, Aldolphe 63, 65, 139
Peters, Will 15–16, 56, 60
Pettirossi, Silvio (Argentine
aviator) 123–124
Phelan, Sen. James D. 91
Phi Beta Psi Sorority 150
photograph (historic first) 87,
142
Pi Kappa Alpha 87
"Pies versus Poetry" (poem by
Garnet Straits) 175
Pitcairn mail wing 142
Pittsburgh *Press* 171
Plymouth Congregational
Church 152
"Poetry of Existence" 169
Pond, Rear-Adm. Clark F. 91
Post, Augustine 91
Post, Wiley 67–68
Post Office Department 147
Practical Aeronatics (book by
Haywood) 8
Pratt & Whitney Motors 151
"Prayer" (poem by Anne
Campbell) 173
presentation at memorial cer-
emony 153

Press Club 135
Preston, Harold 152
Prince Atsu & Prince Taka-
matsu 110
"Punk" (kitten) 25–26

Reese, Lt. L. P. R . 148
Rieke, Glen 142
Rieke, Irv 142
Ringenberg, Margaret 165
Rolph, James, Jr. (mayor of
San Francisco) 91, 93
Roosevelt, Theodore 93–94,
139–140
Rotary Club 87, 103, 135
Rub-No-More Company 148
Ryan, Judge Charles J. 146–
147

Sacramento, California 123
Sacramento *Bee* 123
St. Francis Hotel (San Fran-
cisco) 91
San Diego *Union* 95–97, 104,
137
San Francisco *Bulletin* 78, 93,
123
San Francisco *Chronicle* 91
San Franciso Examiner 88, 90,
93, 123
San Francisco Panama-Pacific
Exposition 77–78, 86–87,
89, 91
Sapporo Agricultural School
117
Sawyer, W. H. (Dr.) 60
Schaaf, Albert 147
Schebler prize 9
Schloss, Adolf J. 73
Schnorr, W. H. 151
Science and Health 148, 170,
185
Scientific American prize 9,
24, 25
Sefridge Field (Michigan) 167,
170
Seiyoken Hotel (Japan) 127
Shaver, Howard B. 144
Sheets, William 158
Shenk, Ed 156
Showalter, Capt. Floyd 155
Shrine Auditorium 150
Shriners 86
Shubawasa, Baron Eiichi 110,
115
Siberia Maru 125
Sloan, Tod 104
Smith, Aimee (wife) *see*
Cour, Aimee

Smith, Art: altimeter 142, 163;
application and pilot for
U.S. Mail Service 144; audi-
tion for San Francisco
Panama-Pacific Exposition
79–81; autobiography (*Story
of Art Smith*) 78; baseball
fan (Santa Clara) 89; best
friend *see* Wertman, Al;
birth date 10; boyhood
activities and interests 7–8,
133; building first model
airplane 9–10; burial site
154; car rental 99–100;
celebrity and success 42, 90,
97–98; Chicago trip 23–24;
Christian Science Church
member 133, 161, 165, 168–
169 171, 173, 178–179, 181,
185–186 189; companies and
products advertised 100–101,
150; control designs for
instructing pilots 136;
dippy-twist 88; divorce 106,
120–124; engagement, 51;
elopement 55–57, 59–60,
64–65, 98, 157; exhibitions
and flights: (Aberdeen,
South Dakota 101; Adrian,
Michigan 43–44; Angola,
Indiana 73; Aoyama, Japan
110, 125; Aoyama-Itchome,
Japan 109, 111; Asakusa,
Japan 111; Auburn, Indiana
49, 50, 72, 75; Bay City,
Texas 30–33; Beauregard,
Montana 49; Beresford,
South Dakota 36–38, 40,
42, 66, 101; Bryan, Texas 30,
32–33; Butte, Montana 101;
Carthage, Illinois 65;
Chicago, Illinois 103;
Cincinnati, Ohio 73, 75;
Clarinda, Iowa 88, 101;
Clifton, Montana 49; Clin-
ton, Montana 49; Corning,
Iowa 50–51, 103; Dallas,
Texas 103, 105; Daylors,
California 170; Deadwood,
South Dakota 44–47, 51;
Des Moines, Iowa 100–101;
Durant, Oklahoma 65;
Elkhart, Indiana 41–42; Fort
Wayne, Indiana 29, 39,
52–54; Hamlin, Iowa
100–101; Havelock,
Nebraska 49; Hillsdale,
Michigan 43, 56–60, 62, 74;
Huron, North Dakota 101,